I0031571

THE
ALIGNED
WORKPLACE

THE
ALIGNED
WORKPLACE

MORE PRODUCTIVITY! LESS STRESS!

Unlock Potential, Boost Employee Performance and Increase Success

ALLEN E. FISHMAN
WALL STREET JOURNAL BESTSELLING AUTHOR

The Aligned Workplace

Published by Direct Communication Service, Inc.

Copyright © 2016 by Allen E. Fishman

All rights reserved. No part of this book may be reproduced or transmitted in any form or by any means, electronic or mechanical, including photocopying and recording, or by any information storage and retrieval system, without permission in writing from the publisher.

Direct Communication Service, Inc

11031 Sheridan Blvd.

Westminster, Colorado USA 800250

Printed in the United States of America.

2016 – First Edition

Book cover design: 99designs.com

Interior layout and design by: AuthorSupport.com

For further information about AlignUp training – please visit www.AlignUptraining.com

To Deev, Zick, and Monkey,
with my firm belief that each of you
will find your path to careers you love.

Acknowledgments

One of the things that made writing this book an enjoyable and enlightening experience was the willingness of so many talented people to contribute to it. I would like to thank Dana Besbris, Julie Preble who helped with proofing and editing the book.

I would also like to thank Jodie Shaw who came up with the title, but managed the project from beginning to end. Without her involvement, you would not be holding a copy of my book today.

I would like to thank the talented designers at 99designs.com who designed the cover and Jerry Dorris from AuthorSupport.com who did a wonderful job with the interior layout of the book.

And last but not least, a big thank you to my entire family for your love and support.

CONTENTS

COMMITMENT

COMMUNICATION

CULTURE

COLLABORATION

COMMITMENT

INTRODUCTION

One of the most critical prerequisites to the success of my own organizations and those with whom I have advised is great organizational Alignment. This book will share an easy-to-use alignment system that I started developing while I was co-owner of an organization, which became so successful that it became a publicly owned organization. The alignment methods shared in this book are based upon the principles of my AlignUp™ training program. Organizational Alignment is a side-by-side working relationship among employees, from the top to the bottom level of the organization, which makes great results a daily reality for an organization.

I refer to great organizational Alignment by the name: The Aligned Workplace™. The Aligned Workplace is essential for the type of transformative dynamics that drives growth in virtually every organization. It is also the key to survival for many others.

If an organization has an Aligned Workplace, it has the engine to power the achievement of truly great results within the organization, no matter what challenges and obstacles the organization may be facing. Great Alignment also brings about higher levels of performance and extraordinary results for the individuals in the organization.

It is the Aligned Workplace relationships that create great organizations— by creating higher-producing members of the organization with significantly increased effectiveness.

Lack of an Aligned Workplace results in high levels of frustration and stress. When workplace Alignment is not present, the result is frustration, stress and wasted effort; not to mention wasted money.

These unpleasant outcomes are, unfortunately, quite common experiences for everyone working in an organization in which there is poor alignment. What we may not always realize is that the stress and other frustrations we face when there is poor Alignment have much more to do with the dynamics within our own organization than with external circumstances.

The kind of stress I'm talking about plays out in cycles that intensify over time—hurting the effectiveness of every employee from the Key Decision Maker or KDM to the lowest level employee. This stress may express itself in you with chronic feelings of uneasiness about the decisions awaiting you at work or the feeling that someone who you work with just does not know how to work with you. It may express itself in problems in your home life, such as keeping you from getting a good night's sleep.

Ignoring the warning signs of a lack of workplace Alignment only makes the problem worse. The good news is this lack of Alignment does not have to be a way of life for you or the organization. If your organization does not have a highly Aligned Workplace, the problem can be fixed by a commitment to follow the program shared in this book. The commitment starts with getting a high level of Alignment between the KDM of an organization and those who report directly to the KDM.

An Aligned Workplace is a side-by-side working relationship that makes great results a daily reality for your organization, which will in turn power your organization's journey to greater success. An Aligned Workplace will impact every single component of your organization.

An Aligned Workplace has benefited many types of organizations, from privately owned organizations, to publicly owned organizations, subsidiaries and divisions of publicly owned organizations, government divisions, and even non-profit organizations. It is a tested and proven alignment process that has helped many organizations' leaders around the world achieve greater success and increase the value of their organizations.

An Aligned Workplace results in less diversion and fragmentation of the time and efforts of your organization's leaders, and other employee who report to them, into areas that are not critical to the success of your organization. It will empower your organization to make the timely strategic decisions and "knee-jerk" reactions and "seat-of-the-pants" decisions will stop happening

GET ALL ROWING THEIR OARS IN SAME DIRECTION

Having an Aligned Workplace is one of the most important steps to reaching your organization's full potential. In this book, I share with you everything you need to know for getting your employees, from the top to the lowest level, to be "rowing all their oars" in the same direction. This is essential for your organization to achieve the results desired for the organization.

If your organization is already successful, bringing about a more Aligned Workplace will help your organization to achieve its full potential. If your organization is experiencing a lack of satisfactory results, bringing about an Aligned Workplace will move your organization to achieve greater success.

By creating an Aligned Workplace, you will gain a collective focus from all your employees on satisfying what is critical to the success of your organization long term vision as well as its shorter term goals, strategies and action plans.

In an Aligned Workplace, your employees will share the same easy-to-understand picture of the strategic direction desired for your organization and the actions needed to get there. Having an Aligned Workplace helps your managers and other employees make the right decisions in regards to resources, time allocation, and efforts for themselves and their subordinates.

Also, lower-priority issues will be clearly understood to be such. There will be an increased level of accountability along with a disciplined follow-up mechanism to insure that action-plan results are reviewed against projected results and modified as needed to maximize outcomes.

You will find that the methods shared in this book will works effectively for your organization, regardless of the type or size of your organization. The process has been designed so that when implementing the elements needed for an Aligned Workplace, it is easy to customize your organization, regardless of your type or size of organization. In a small size organization, for example, your regularly scheduled top management meetings may need to be scheduled to take place semi bi weekly or monthly while these meetings should be scheduled weekly with larger organizations.

COMPOSITE ORGANIZATIONS USED AS EXAMPLES

In this book I have used examples of organizations to illustrate points for how the methods can be applied. Because of my desire to keep confidentiality for the specific organizations referred to, the names of the actual organizations and the organizations' leaders, and even their industries, have been changed. Also, some of these organizations are actually composites of more than one organization, rather than specific organizations.

IT STARTS AT THE TOP

Workplace Alignment starts with the top leaders of the organization. Great organizational Alignment requires both a high level of Aligned engagement between the key decision maker (Key Decision Maker or KDM), and those who report directly to the KDM (Direct Reports or DRs). It also requires a high level of Aligned engagement among the DRs.

Let there be no mistake about it, an Aligned Workplace will not take place without commitment to workplace Alignment from those in top management who are responsible for leading their organizations. Consequently, this book shares a holistic approach for Aligning the KDMs and DRs in an organization and, in turn, for them to push down Alignment to employees at every level in an organization.

When you first start implementing what you learn in this book, there will be some diversion of top management time from working on day-to-day responsibilities to focusing some time on achieving Alignment. But, it doesn't take long for an Aligned Workplace to reduce wasted time, because it enables your management and non-management employees to focus on activities Aligned with the goals of the organization.

It doesn't take long for one result of an Aligned Workplace to be the creating — rather than absorbing — of KDM, DRs and other management and non-management time. This happens by bringing about more focus on those things for which time should be focused. The natural effect from this is increased efficiencies and greatly reducing wasted time by all levels in your organization.

In an organization with an Aligned Workplace, the KDM and DRs are committed to the same organization goals and ways for achieving the goals. Organizations with an Aligned Workplace have a harmonious organization relationship among the top leaders even when the parties need to work out their differences. Maintaining Alignment is a mutual, ongoing responsibility that makes both KDMs and DRs more effective.

If your organization's leaders are not Aligned, their subordinates are also not operating in an Aligned manner. So if your organization does not have great Alignment at the top level of your organization, you will not have an Aligned Workplace.

To achieve an Aligned Workplace, a highly Aligned relationship must first be brought about between KDMs and their DRs. With practice and persistence, this can be achieved. This book will focus on bringing about this Alignment between the KDMs and their DRs, but every method you learn must then be pushed down to the subordinates who report to the DRs and any employees who report to the subordinates. Pushing it down is essential to achieving The Aligned Workplace

A trusting, respectful, mutually committed relationship among employees, starting with the top level leaders of an organization, is essential for any organization that wants to achieve the highest possible level of success.

Consequently, my focus in this book is to show the KDM and the DRs in each organization what they need to do to bring about an Aligned Workplace. Each chapter shows what DRs need to do and how to do it. There is also a homework assignment at the end of each chapter to be completed before moving on to the next chapter in the book.

Because my experience has shown that many KDMs of organizations do not complete the homework assignments, I have provided at the beginning of most of the chapters, a brief summary that the KDM must understand and be committed to making part of the organization's DNA.

ENJOY THE JOURNEY

My goal is for my book to show you how to develop an Aligned Workplace that will move your organization along a road that leads to a higher level of success with a lower level of stress for you and all the others working for the organization.

Each chapter in this book shows a different way to support and sustain the needed trusting, respectful relationship to take your organization and your career to the next level. Implementing what I share with you in this book will have an amazingly synergistic impact on your organization's ability to work together to reach greater levels of success. Each of the twelve chapters represents a factor of alignment, which is listed below:

1. **Identify Misalignment and Commit to Eliminate It**— There will never be outstanding workplace Alignment without a commitment to invest time and effort in it.

2. **Align to PAVE Your Way to Success**— Learn how to bring about the kinds of results that will allow you to experience the most personal fulfillment—and deliver the most "bang for the buck" to the organization.

3. **Align on Plans and Priorities**— Learn how to take advantage of one-on-one meetings between the KDM and each DR, so each side know exactly how much time, effort and energy will be focused.

4. **Align on Weekly Strategic Leadership Team Meetings**— Learn how to bring about the most effective type of regularly scheduled team meetings among KDMs and their DRs, so that each participant knows exactly how time, effort, and energy should be focused.

5. **Align on Annual Strategic Team Meetings**— Learn how to improve Alignment between the KDM and the DRs with annual Strategic Leadership Team meetings. At these meetings, team members can pull back from the day-to-day work of "putting out fires" and focus on leading the organization in an Aligned manner.

6. **Align on Working Dynamics**—As I mentioned earlier, the KDM and the DR do not have to like each other, but they do have to respect each other if they expect to deliver positive results for the organization. Learn what the two of you can do to bring about a mutually respectful relationship.

7. **Align on the Organization's Values and Working Environment**— Learn how to Align on critical cultural values you and your KDM should be modeling for the rest of the organization. What kind of daily working environment should you create?

8. **Align on the Organization's Vision**— Learn how to identify and understand all the elements of the KDM's vision.

9. **Align on Roles and Responsibilities**—Learn how the DR can make life easier for the KDM, starting right now. Understand how this factor

of Alignment can bring about major gains for the organization in both the short and long terms.

10. **Align on Critical Success Factors**—Learn how to identify the objectives so critical to the organization that its success depends on achieving them. Then learn to prioritize so that the organization's resources are focused on the most vital objectives.

11. **Align on Strategic Direction Initiatives**—Identify the organization's strategic direction, and ensure that the efforts of every member of the executive team are consistent with that strategic direction.

12. **Alignment is Evergreen**—Learn how to monitor Alignment after you have finished this book ... and maintain the organization's commitment to Alignment over time.

As with any journey, there will be rough spots and your organization will need to make some unexpected detours. But, when you have an Aligned Workplace, you will find that it will power your organization's journey to achieving its optimal future.

Enjoy the journey!

IMPORTANT NOTE FOR KDMs: Your DRs cannot bring about an Aligned Workplace, using what I share in this book, without your help and guidance. This requires that you invest the time needed for a one-on-one meeting with each of your DRs to discuss the actions and ideas shared in each chapter of this book. At these meetings you will need to also discuss the results from the homework assignments completed by each of your DRs for each chapter in this book.

IMPORTANT NOTE FOR DRs: Just a few hours a month invested by a DR in implementing the twelve factors of Alignment covered in this book typically results in greater financial rewards and greater career advancement for the DR.

CHAPTER 1

Identify Misalignment and Commit to Eliminate It

For your organization to get the greatest amount of benefit from this book, it requires a commitment to the entire Aligned Workplace process. Reaching and keeping an Aligned Workplace must be totally embraced by the organization's management team and then throughout the entire workplace, to get maximum benefits. Once an Aligned Workplace is part of your organization management belief structure, Aligned Workplace thinking will trickle down through your entire organization.

The commitment must be ongoing, so that all employees understand and follow the protocols required in The Aligned Workplace so they work at their most effective level for your organization. To make this happen, the Aligned Workplace process must be ingrained into your organization's culture.

My aim in shining a spotlight on Commitment and the rest of The Aligned Workplace factors is simply to help KDMs and DRs reach the shared destination of greater productivity and lower stress. I want to do this by sharing the most effective and rigorously field-tested system I have developed.

Let me emphasize: None of what I will be sharing with you is experimental or theoretical. All of it is pragmatic and based on experience. And all of it is proven to work.

On a personal level, I must say I have experienced a deep level of fulfillment from seeing the outstanding results that can come about from organizations using my system to bring about an Aligned Workplace.

I can't expect you to make this commitment without some understanding of the twelve factors or interlocking links in the Alignment process you will be learning in this book. The twelve factors are the most critical factors for creating and supporting Alignment. These are the factors that, once implemented, will make your work experience more effective with an increased likelihood of success. The implementation of these factors makes it easier to work with lower frustration levels.

All twelve of these factors of Alignment work together! All twelve require constant effort and reinforcement!

WHERE IS YOUR ORGANIZATION OUT OF ALIGNMENT?

Now that you have an overview of how we will be attacking poor workplace alignment, you are ready to identify the current status of where your organization is out of Alignment. To identify how your organization is out of Alignment, your organization's KDM should complete the quick simple Alignment Check questionnaire below. At the same time, all the KDM's DRs need to answer the same questions ... but SEPARATELY from the KDM or any other DR, without discussing the answers to the questions.

When all of the organization's leaders have completed the questionnaires, meet to compare the answers. This meeting should show you where your organization is out of Alignment.

Alignment Check Questionnaire

- Do I believe there is an ongoing effort toward continuous improvement of Alignment in this workplace? (YES/NO)
- Do I feel that my subordinates are in Alignment and are focusing their energies on the factors critical to the success of the organization? (YES/NO)

- Are ideas from DRs elicited, encouraged, discussed, and—where relevant and appropriate—implemented? (YES/NO)
- Are there weekly ONE-ON-ONE meetings between the organization's leader and EACH manager who reports to him or her? (YES/NO)
- Are DRs updating their To-Do lists and project plans for which they're responsible prior to attending a one-on-one weekly meeting with the organization's leader? (YES/NO)
- In this workplace, do we have and keep mutually understood, mutually acceptable agreements with regard to respectful communication? (YES/NO)
- Is there a clearly identified Strategic Leadership Team composed of the organization's leader and the managers who report directly to him or her?
- Are Strategic Leadership Team Meetings taking place every week? (YES/NO)
- Are Annual Strategic Leadership Team Meetings held once a year, in a locale different from the normal work environment? (YES/NO)
- Is our stated or desired working culture USUALLY the same as our actual daily working culture? (YES/NO)
- Does my organization have a culture of working together in an aligned fashion? (YES/NO)
- Do all my subordinates clearly understand my long term vision for the organization? (YES/NO)
- Do all members of the Strategic Leadership Team understand and support the Organization's Vision well enough to focus on fulfilling it? (YES/NO)
- Is the organization's leader consciously avoiding going into "hands on" mode? Note: "Hands on mode" = doing something that one or more DRs can do and should be doing. (YES/NO)
- Do I personally have a clear sense of what my own Competitive Edge Strengths are ... and use those strengths MOST of the time during the typical working day? (YES/NO)
- Can I identify the organization's Critical Success Factors—the factors that, if left unattained, will prevent the organization from attaining its vision? (YES/NO)
- Is there at least one complete, written Strategic Plan? (YES/NO—answer NO if you don't know.)

If there is a single "NO" answer, then you can be sure that your organization is out of Alignment!

Common Excuses

The following are two of the most common excuses that have kept organizations from implementing what is needed to reach an Aligned Workplace:

1. **I Don't Have The Time And Resources For This**

    A lot of organizational leaders have given me the excuse that, "We're just too busy to spend a few hours a week working on something like this." Of course, I realize that in a small or midsize organization, there's a great deal for every manager to do, resources are limited, and it's easy for a KDM to conclude that the to-do list is already more than long enough. But the reality is that the principles in this program have been proven, over and over again and in every major industry, to save both DRs and KDMs an enormous amount of time, typically within a month of beginning the process. And time, as we all know, is money. Alignment also brings about more efficient use of the time you have available.

    One KDM told me: "The two to three weekly hours that my key manager spent on this material created many, many more new working hours each week—both for me and for him—than those hours he invested learning the principles."

    A great deal of time is wasted in un-Aligned organizations. Why? Because people are working on the wrong priorities, wasting time on things that are not essential to the success of the organization, or duplicating tasks that other people are already working on. It's a downward performance cycle. *That cycle only turns around when you make a commitment to Alignment.*

    The complaint that your organization "does not have time" for Alignment is proof you need to invest time for this. If you find yourself pushing back on that idea, ask yourself: Would you like to be able to do more each week, using the same number of working hours? Would you like the whole management team to be able to do that? How many times have you found people in your organization working on something they weren't supposed to be? Or working on something somebody else was already working on? How much longer do you want that pattern to continue?

2. **I Don't Know If The Aligned Work Place System Is Right For Our Organization Because We Operate In A Unique Industry/Market**

    The principles, strategies and tools you will find in this book have helped to build and sustain Alignment in **thousands of organizations** around the world in virtually every industry you can imagine. The hurdles you will learn how to overcome here—lack of clarity about the owner's vision, rivalry and infighting among the members of the management team, or a habit of focusing on low-priority or no-priority projects—are not industry-specific, or organization-specific, or product-specific, or service-specific. They are relevant to every growing organization.

    At the end of the day, your organization really falls into one of two very clear categories—it is either moving closer to Alignment with the KDM's vision, or moving away from Alignment. **If your organization is moving away from Alignment, it may not be around for long.**

SELF-ASSESSMENTS FOR BOTH KDMS AND DRS

Organizations that do not have Alignment between their KDM and their DRs are destined to underperform and are often not able to survive. So, it is essential that KDMs and their DRs look at themselves objectively as to how they contribute to or keep the organization from having great Alignment.

The following questions are important self-assessments for both KDMs and DRs. Please consider them closely. Take the time right now to create clear answers to each question, in whatever format that feels most comfortable to you.

- **How would you describe the value you bring to the organization?**
- **Right now, would you say you are satisfied with the impact you have on your organization?**
- **Are you using your abilities to the maximum potential on behalf of your organization?**
- **Would you say that, on a typical day, there is complete clarity about critical work priorities?**
- **Please identify any of the ways you are not satisfied with the way your organization is operating as an Aligned Workplace.**
- **Give an example of a time that you weren't in sync with your KDM or those reporting to you were not in sync with you.**
- **Do you find that important "balls" are being dropped in the organization and if so why?**
- **How effective are your team meetings in sharing communications so that there is no duplicating of efforts and working at cross-purposes?**

Usually, when we ask DRs these questions, in private, they answer with some uncertainty and hesitation to the first one, and with a "NO" to each one after that. They offer a general sense of the value they bring to the organization, but they wish they could bring greater value. They are not satisfied with the impact they currently have, wishing they could have a bigger one than they do. They do not feel they are using their abilities to the absolute fullest.

Now please take the time to write down your answer to these questions. If you are not yet satisfied with the impact you have on your organization, this is very likely because there are still unresolved Alignment challenges.

The last part of this self-assessment is to answer a question about the quality of your relationships with your DRs or KDM. This question has two variants:

1. **If You Are The KDM: How would you describe the quality of your relationship with each of your DRs?**

2. If You Are The DR: How would you describe the quality of your relationship with your KDM?

Before you answer this question, reflect on the following:

- Would you say the relationship is mutually respectful? If you DON'T respect the other person, then the relationship is NOT mutually respectful. (You don't have to like someone in order to respect him or her!)
- Do you look forward to interactions with this person, or do you tend to avoid them? By the way, this is an excellent way to run a reality check on whatever your initial answer was to the question about the quality of the relationship. If you are avoiding interactions with someone, then that definitely means there is something about the relationship that isn't supporting you!
- Is the relationship free of any smoldering resentments? You know, the kind of resentment you never quite resolve; the kind that gets worse over time?
- Are the two of you focused on the same major goals, and the same strategies for achieving those goals? In other words, do you feel like you're "on the same page" with this person most days, at least when it comes to big, important goals and the strategies for achieving them?
- Is the relationship with this person reasonably stress-free, most of the time? What I mean here is: would you say the uncomfortable stress that shows up in your relationship with this person is an occasional exception, or would you say it is something that happens on a regular basis and is actually part of the job?

It's common for DRs to be experiencing some kind of problem in the relationship with their KDMs. It could be a small problem. It could be a big problem. Very often, it is a problem that seems big to the DR, but small or nonexistent to the KDM. It's interesting how often KDMs are quite likely to report, with some pride, that there are "no problems at all" in the relationship in those organizations in which the DRs report some kind of problem.

When DRs who say they are experiencing challenges with their KDM, are asked whether they've ever tried to address the problems in the relationship, they typically respond by saying something like: "Sure—I've tried. But nothing happened. What are you going to do? He/she isn't going to change."

Well I can tell you that if this is part of your situation, don't be so sure that your KDM can't change. One of the common results of these exercises is greater awareness by the KDM of their perceived relationships with their DRs and steps to work on the problems.

You can learn to tactfully, assertively engage in a way that changes the dynamic and benefits both sides. You can change the relationship for the better. You can work together to create a higher-impact role for you in the organization. And you can enjoy much bigger rewards as a result.

CHANGING YOUR PATTERNS OF INTERACTION

Whether you are a KDM or a DR, you will achieve your highest level of organization and career success only when you accept the importance of understanding the other person. Once each of you become aware of the personal effect you have on each other and use this knowledge to improve things, truly great Alignment is possible.

The secret to addressing these Alignment issues constructively lies in recognizing that you cannot solve these challenges on your own. You can only create Alignment in a relationship when you understand how the other person thinks about his or her world. That means understanding how the other person reacts to challenges, what his or her motivational values are, and what are his or her natural behavioral and communication styles.

The desired highest level of success can only happen when both of you make a conscious effort to *change your patterns of interaction in a way that maximizes* Alignment with each other. This does not come easily. It is a matter of commitment to constant practice and continuous working on the relationship—like the continual work required for sustaining a good marriage.

In order to achieve the full potential from the relationship, each of you must look honestly at whom the other person is and how he or she feels—even when this is hard to do. Each of you must learn to be empathetic with the other. This means understanding and sharing what the other person is feeling. This can be done without necessarily agreeing with the specific point the other person is making.

For instance, if you are a DR, the KDM might say to you, "I'm disappointed in the way you've let the project get completely out of control." You can empathize with the disappointment without agreeing the project is out of control! This kind of empathetic response needs to become second nature.

Another significant benefit, you will enjoy work more along with a significantly lower level of stress—thanks to Aligned co-existence in your working environment.

You do not have a monopoly on defining reality. You will have to control your emotional responses and learn to deal constructively with those in your organization who have different motivations and different ways of seeing the world than you do.

TRUSTING ENVIRONMENT OF MUTUAL RESPECT

When my twelve-part Alignment process is followed, it improves solid working relationships—and transforms even a destructive or dysfunctional working dynamic—by creating a trusting environment of mutual respect. This environment supports much greater productivity for both people.

This kind of trusting, respectful relationship is absolutely essential to

Alignment. It is the exact opposite of the common "us vs. them" mentality DRs often adopt as a group—a mentality that can threaten the organization's ability to deliver positive results and, in some cases, its very existence.

> **Commitment to Alignment on the individual level means commitment to growth, adaptation, and innovation on the organizational level.**

Making a commitment to build and expand this trust and respect is important for the emotional and physical health of KDMs, and for the fiscal health of the organization! The Aligned Workplace™ shows you exactly how to build and sustain such a trusting, respectful relationship, step by step, interlocking link by link.

POTENTIAL OBSTACLES TO ALIGNMENT

> *We are the music-makers, And we are the dreamers of dreams.* —Arthur William Edgar O'Shaughnessy

There are many potential obstacles to Alignment, which we will be described and examined in depth in this book. What is important to understand here is that these obstacles are likely to be perceived and described in very different ways by the KDM and the DRs. It is not uncommon to have dramatically different ways two people can have of looking at the same situation.

These differences do not mean there is a lack of commitment to Alignment. All it means is that there are different perspectives as to what is the commitment. So to increase the level of Alignment in a working relationship, it is essential both parties commit to understanding the other person's viewpoint.

COMMITMENT TO IMPROVING ALIGNMENT

The first of the twelve factors or interlocking links of Alignment is commitment by all the leaders in your organization to achieving an Aligned Workplace. To improve your organization's Alignment, a commitment to the Aligned Workplace process is needed from the top-level of your organization. This is absolutely essential.

An organization's commitment to an Aligned Workplace requires the organization's KDM and DRs willingness and ability to tactfully, assertively engage for constructive change needed to integrate the process presented in this book. This includes following my tips about how and when to begin these conversations about improving Alignment.

COMMITMENT TO AN ALIGNED WORKPLACE

Note that COMMITMENT, the first factor or link of Alignment, begins the process—but it also must be an "**Evergreen**" presence in the ongoing effort to improve Alignment. Commitment supports and encompasses all the other factors of Alignment.

This much I can promise from personal experience: the principles outlined in The Aligned Workplace™, when adopted by both the KDM and the DRs in an organization, will spread throughout the organization and will bring about measurably better organization results. Also, the workplace experience will be considerably more enjoyable for all employees from the top to the bottom of the organization.

> **The ability to challenge the "status quo" and make constructive, mutually acceptable changes is a central requirement to attaining Alignment.**

The tactics and processes I am sharing here work but you must make the needed commitment to make them work. Alignment is more than a way of working with someone. It is a way of life. Once you commit to that way of life, you are likely to experience a *higher level of organization success that is attributable to you personally.*

Doing what is needed to create and keep an Aligned Workplace is a process that never ends. It starts with completing this chapter's Homework and attending a meeting between the KDM and DRs of your organization, before you move on to the next chapter.

Alignment is not something you do once and then check off a list. Don't stop with this chapter. Keep going until every interlocking link of The Aligned Workplace process chain is integrated into your organization!

> **Optimal Alignment can only become a daily reality for an organization if the KDM and all DRs have an ongoing commitment to improve Alignment.**

HOMEWORK

Complete the **Alignment Check** survey that appears in this chapter. Be sure the KDM and the DR fill out the survey separately, without discussing the answers with each other as they do so. Then, when the written surveys are complete, compare and discuss the results. Do not change the written answers. HOLD ON TO ALL COMPLETED SURVEYS. You will need them later on.

CHAPTER 2

Align to PAVE Your
Way to Success

EXECUTIVE SUMMARY FOR THE KEY DECISION MAKER

In this chapter, your **Direct Report (DR)*** will do some personal evaluation exercises that will help him or her to become, not just somewhat more motivated, efficient, and productive in areas that directly affect the success of your organization but exponentially more so. Once your DR has completed these exercises, please take the time necessary to review the results carefully. Consider revisions to his or her workload that reflect the strengths, motivations, and attitudes the exercises have uncovered.

One of the most important behaviors of the contributors I call "**High Impact DRs**" is their ability to realize and act first on what is essential to the success of the organization.

High Impact DRs know how to separate the wheat from the chaff. They know how to set priorities in writing their to-do list, so as to generate results that have a measurably positive impact. By doing so, they are paving their own road to success—the road to a role of greater importance within the organization.

Can you do that? Absolutely, and sooner than you think. The secret is to ensure there is little or no gap between who you are and the work you do. To do this, you first need to know who you are. In this chapter, you will learn to look in the mirror as you never have before, and conduct the kind of self-examination that will help you attain the most important goals for your organization, your KDM, and yourself.

11

Who Are You?

In Plato's Apology, written nearly twenty-four centuries ago, Socrates says, "The unexamined life is not worth living." That sounds extreme, but it is certainly true that life must be examined carefully and reflected upon by those who expect true happiness and success. That definitely includes your Key Decision Maker (KDM) and it also includes you, the DR.

LOOK IN THE MIRROR

Before undertaking any major life-goal, you should first have a basic understanding and acceptance of who you are as a person.

> **High Impact DRs understand and accept both their strengths and weaknesses.**

By following the four-step process outlined in this chapter, you can achieve a measure of genuine self-knowledge. This means taking a clear look at both your strengths and your weaknesses.

The kind of self-knowledge I'm talking about will allow you to determine whether what you desire for your future is, in fact, attainable. It will also show you where you are most in need of help. What you uncover in this self-analysis will likely result in the modification, or perhaps even the elimination, of some parts of your plan for success.

Your Starting Point

Beginning from the premise that you are a good and worthy individual is extremely important. This "pre-step" sounds elemental to some people, and sounds quite difficult to others. Whatever it sounds like to you, it is the starting point for all healthy self-assessment.

> *Wanting to be someone else is a waste*
> *of the person you are.* —Marilyn Monroe

Who Wants What?

Another essential "pre-step" is the ability to know what you really want in life. Specifically, you must also be able to distinguish between your own desires and the expectations of others. These are two very different things.

This is an especially important point for any DR who has experienced any kind of positive career visibility. Whenever other people start to regard you as "successful," it is often quite difficult not to want to deliver the reality they describe and praise. It is natural to want to please those who watch and admire your life. You, however, are the one who must live your life. It takes real courage to separate yourself from the expectations of others, to see yourself for who you really are, and to identify what you actually want to do with your talents during what is, after all, a very limited time here on earth.

> *Your time is limited, so don't waste it living someone else's life. Don't be trapped by dogma—which is living with the results of other people's thinking. Don't let the noise of other's opinions drown out your own inner voice. And most important, have the courage to follow your heart and intuition. They somehow already know what you truly want to become. Everything else is secondary.* —Steve Jobs

Your Competitive Edge Strengths

With those two "pre-steps" taken care of, you are ready to pave your way to success and remove any bumps in the road. How will you do that? By accessing not just any strengths, but those strengths that stand out as your **Competitive Edge Strengths.** These strengths are the engine that will propel you to greater success.

> **Make sure your plan is built around what YOU want, NOT what someone else wants.**

Not every strength is a Competitive Edge Strength. For instance, you may be an excellent typist, but that does not necessarily mean you should build your entire plan for success around your ability to type. The acronym PAVE represents four important criteria for identifying your true competitive edge strengths.

P: Do you have a strong **Passion** for doing this?
A: Do you have a strong **Aptitude** for doing this?
V: Does doing this support your "big picture" **Vision** for where you want to go next in your life?
E: Can you do this while maintaining an **Empathetic** Personality?

I should go into more depth about the last element of the PAVE acronym, which tends to be the only one that people don't understand the first time they see this formula. What I mean by saying, "maintaining an Empathetic personality" is to pose this question: Does doing this type of work match with your own image of yourself? In other words, does doing this feel like a natural extension of who you are, rather than something forced and unnatural? Does it make you feel as though you are identifying and empathizing with your own "best self"?

Let's look at how to identify each of the four criteria needed to form your Competitive Edge Strengths. We'll start with P, which stands for the first (and probably easiest to remember) element: Passion.

Passion

Without a driving **Passion,** you might have the ability to excel in specific organization-related activities, but be unlikely to give it your best effort in the long run. This driving Passion creates great focus and ensures you end up with results that simply cannot happen without that level of focus. Every great piece of work you have ever been truly inspired by was almost certainly the result of a driving Passion: the Sistine Chapel, Disneyland, Facebook, you name it.

Driving Passion is what gets things done at a high level of excellence. As a result, identifying the organization areas for which you have a true and driving Passion is the first and perhaps most important step when it comes to identifying your **Personal Organization Strengths.** If you don't truly love doing something, you are not very likely to do it well!

When you focus on workplace strengths that incorporate your driving Passion, you are much more likely to become obsessively focused on excelling in that activity (in a healthy way, of course!). Driving Passion is the reason most successful organizations' leaders have great success.

Generally speaking, people only feel passionate about doing activities that match an element that some refer to as the natural personality. Others refer to this same element as their natural behavioral style. Whatever you call this element, understanding it is essentially a willingness to be who you are without apology. There are many resources that can inexpensively provide an accurate analysis of your personality/behavior style; most of these take only minutes of answering questions in survey form. One such system is the DISC test, which I would strongly recommend you and your organization invest in. You can learn more about DISC at www.thediscpersonalitytest.com.

To illustrate this first part of the PAVE self-examination process, let me share some examples of my own driving Passions in the workplace. Most of the time I enjoy and feel passion about creating processes with protocols that help our team deliver greater value to our customers. Often, I get ideas that result in me being pulled away from other things I am doing. I spend much of my typical day focused on creating or refining these processes—thank goodness! My driving Passion for these activities urges me to focus on them relentlessly and with great enthusiasm, therefore, I spend a large amount of time refining and perfecting them. I have this driving Passion because it fits who I am.

If you feel Passion for something you do at work, it's likely the work-related activities you are engaged in when you feel that Passion are suited to your natural personality/behavioral style. The classic clue: You don't have to adapt or force yourself to do these activities. No one has to "motivate" you to undertake these activities!

On the other hand, if the required work activity goes contrary to your natural personality/behavioral style, you will undoubtedly create stress in your life. It's likely you can identify these activities fairly easily, too.

The bottom line is this: If the organization activities you choose are in strong enough harmony with your basic personality/behavioral style to elicit Passion, you will enjoy the experience. If they aren't, you won't.

Bridget, a DR at an ergonomic office furniture manufacturing organization, identified the activities in which she has driving Passion. All of them involved interacting with key prospects to get more sales for her organization. Bridget, as it turns out, is strongly socially driven and loves using her ample selling skills to open new major accounts. This is an area she has great Passion for that also has significant Big-Picture Potential **(more about that later). Bridget described her personal organization strength as follows:**

- Creates, develops, and maintains strong relationships with key account customers

Her personal plan for success involved finding and leveraging ways to increase her work time allocation on selling big accounts. In other words, she found lots of ways to play to her Passion!

Aptitude

It is a very rare individual, indeed, who is outstanding in all areas of organization. To me, these people who manage to excel at everything are like Bigfoot—some may claim to have seen such a creature, but I never have. The vast majority of us go into the game with identifiable strengths and weaknesses. There are some things we're just plain better at compared to others.

Sometimes **Aptitude**—by which I mean something you do better than most other people—is obvious. In other situations, people struggle to identify their own premier abilities—analytical, verbal, or otherwise—in comparison to the abilities of others.

I have a passion for creating systems and processes for which I feel driving Passion. Fortunately, I also have an Aptitude for doing these things. What do I mean by that? I mean, if you asked 100 people who have worked with me whether I am better at creating systems and processes than the average person, I believe at least 95 out of 100 of those people would instantly say yes. I don't offer this example in order to brag, but rather to give you a clear sense of what an Aptitude is (and isn't). If you asked those same 100 people about my golf game, you would see a very different consensus emerge!

If you do not have Aptitude in a particular organization activity, it almost goes without saying that you won't excel in it over the long term, no matter how passionately you may feel about the activity. You can love doing something but never be good at it. So having driving Passion without Aptitude is not going to be enough to put an activity among your Personal Organization Strengths!

There are many excellent free and low-cost aptitude tests to choose from online. Search on "aptitude test" and see what comes up. A good test will measure a broad spectrum of abilities in order to positively determine your best

Aptitudes. Alternatively, you can ask the people around you—the people who know you best, such as family, friends or peers—for honest feedback on what they consider your greatest abilities.

Vision

Now ask yourself what activities you have Passion for and have an Aptitude for doing that also have the potential to make a major positive impact on the organization you work for. We are talking here about activities that bring the organization closer to the KDM's vision for the organization—or, as I call them, "Big Picture Potential" activities (recall that Bridget's ability to close sales and create new relationships fell into this category).

The fact you are passionate about doing certain things, and better than the average person at doing them, doesn't mean that any of those things should be major workplace time investments. Your Personal Organization Strengths must have Big Picture Potential, in addition to Passion and Aptitude.

Now, if you're an entrepreneur (or if you work for one) and your organization is still in an initial growth stage, you will probably have to come to terms with a challenging reality: the smaller the organization, the more likely it is that you may have to spend a lot of your time doing things you don't enjoy and that may not have Big Picture Potential. You don't even have to be better than average at doing these things. You just have to make sure they get done to a certain level of competence. As an example, picture the entrepreneur who manages his or her own payroll and pays the organization's bill during the first year of operation. It's likely this person doesn't exactly have a passion for balancing the checkbook and comparing checks to purchase orders, and may not even be capable of doing it at an above-average level. These activities, which typically have low Big Picture Potential, are among the first to be delegated to a DR.

This can be a problem. If there are activities on which you spend a lot of time that do not have Big Picture Potential, you should engage directly and discuss with your KDM how you can transition your efforts to focusing less of your time on those activities.

One final note is in order here. In many organizations, both KDMs and DRs spend too much time on the mundane. The evaluation process I have just described will help re-balance things, so the mundane activities are delegated into the organization, and senior executives can spend more of their time on Big Picture Potential activities.

Empathetic Personality Match

Within each of us is a set of characteristics—ways of thinking, feeling, and acting—that mark us as individuals. Sometimes we have to dig around a little, ask a few pointed questions and commit to some level of research in order to better define and understand what it is that makes us unique.

To identify their own competitive-edge strengths, effective DRs and KDMs must be willing to ask a question with a seemingly obvious answer: is this who I really am?

Suppose you are a computer programmer. You are quite good at what you do, and programming is important to the software government department for which you work. Yet you feel conflicted, because you feel you are interacting all day with a machine and not with other people. Instead, your empathy may be drawing you to spend more time with customers, perhaps in a consultative role where you help customers envision software solutions that will improve the organizations and help deliver better solutions to their customers.

You are who you are. That means you must take the necessary strategic steps to begin the process of closing the gap between "who I am" and "what I do": first for yourself, then for your partner in the KDM/DR relationship, and ultimately for everyone in your organization.

As the final part of the PAVE self-analysis process, I'd like to challenge you to identify what workplace tasks or responsibilities you "feel funny" about doing, do not enjoy doing, or even dread doing in your organization because they go against your own sense of who you are. Each of us will have our own answer to this question. Common examples of this, mentioned to me, by both KDMs and DRs, include: handling employee conflict; firing employees; conducting employee reviews; selling your organization products or services; and developing operational protocols.

> **The bottom line is: you need to "do what you are" in order to give your best efforts and deliver the strongest results over the long term.**

Putting It All Together

So let's look at how this plays out. Creating and sustaining financial security is one of those goals we all face, yet the pursuit of money is only one factor that motivates us to get up every day and go to work. For many people, the driver that propels us towards work is an integral facet of self, known as Passion.

We may need money, but we want passion; we want to feel vibrantly alive and engaged in our lives. In the workplace, the passion for passion, the passion to do what we were "meant to do" can and should be stronger than even the need for financial security. That's why you hear so many stories about people who walk away from high-paying jobs in order to realize their dreams. Money really can't buy happiness.

If you've ever seen someone shuffling mindlessly through work, merely going through the motions, you've seen a situation where no one is winning. Customers or clients certainly aren't getting the service they want and deserve and the organization is getting shoddy performance. The employee is certainly not winning. A paycheck may seem like a reward for doing nothing, but is that miserable employee really getting away with something? I hope you would not be willing to trade a satisfying working life for one you hate just for the security of paying your bills.

> **If there's no joy, ever, in one's work, the financial reward is irrelevant because it is not enough to inspire our happiness, let alone the desire to do a good job.**

Sure, we all have to perform work tasks we'd love to delegate, but what if the stuff you hate to do was ALL you ever got to do? That would be a situation where no one is winning—certainly not you!

On the flip-side of this coin are the people who gladly go above and beyond the call of duty for reasons that surpass financial incentive. These are the ones who make customers feel extra special, who take on a client's seemingly impossible demands with a smile, and who, when they spot a threat to organization wellness, not only tell the boss about it, but also offer good ideas on how to correct the situation. These are employees with passion to burn, because they have learned how to spend most of their time doing the thing they love, are good at, and were born to do.

These people generally don't mind taking on a few unpleasant tasks along the way, because, overall, they love what they do and are well suited to it. These are the kinds of people that top KDMs want to inspire and lead, specifically including the DR. If you are the DR, then you must start that process by inspiring the employee you see in the mirror each and every morning: YOURSELF.

Your day must be built mostly around doing what you love doing, you do well, and were born to do. It is your job to ensure it becomes your daily reality. Engage assertively with your KDM to make sure this happens. But you can't do that unless you identify exactly WHAT IT IS that you love doing and can do well!

DAISY'S TWO PAVE EVALUATIONS

Daisy, who spent fifteen percent of her week working on market research for her KDM, conducted the following self-evaluation and started looking for new assignments that drew more effectively on her PAVE strengths and aptitudes. The KDM gave her more copywriting responsibility and delegated the market research work to another team member.

P: Do I have a strong **Passion** for conducting market research? NO
A: Do I have a strong **Aptitude** for doing this? YES
V: Does doing this support my "big picture" **Vision** for where I want to go next in my life? NO
E: Can I do this while maintaining an **Empathetic** Personality? **NO**

P: Do I have a strong **Passion** for revising, refining, and improving the written word? YES

A: Do I have a strong **Aptitude** for doing this? YES

V: Does doing this support my "big picture" **Vision** for where you want to go next in my life? YES

E: Can I do this while maintaining an **Empathetic** Personality? **YES**

EXPERIMENT WITH PAVE

Keith, a DR at a software government department, has a positive Passion for social interaction and a knack for making people want to work with him. Known as the class clown in school, Keith continues to crave being the center of attention. I'm sure he'd be just as successful as an actor or comedian as he is in the role of Director of Sales for a hot Silicon Valley enterprise.

Obviously, deploying his people skills is something Keith enjoys, and his stellar sales record proves he's good at it. He genuinely loves networking. However, Keith wonders whether focusing on tasks that utilize his people skills are really the best use of his time. After all, he also enjoys developing department plans and making projections. It's just not what people have come to expect from him. Should he expand his list of PAVE Competitive Edge strengths to include his planning skills? Is that what he should be spending more of his day doing?

Where Do Strengths Come From?

Finding the answer to a question like Keith's takes a little experimentation and careful self-analysis. We all have numerous strengths, and we come about them in all sorts of ways. Some strengths are the result of our upbringing and/or our day-to-day experiences and interests. For instance, if you like music, you may feel a desire to take up the guitar and, in time, you might get quite good at playing it. Whether your skill stems from natural talent, early influence (maybe both your parents are musicians), or the result of lots of practice, what started out as an interest can eventually become a strength. Similarly, when you choose a course of study in college, that decision dictates the skills with which you will graduate.

Strengths can also be thrust upon you. When this happens, it is usually the result of an encounter with an outside force interested in meeting a want or need that you don't necessarily share—for instance, a job that requires you to learn JavaScript, a spouse who asks you with some intensity when you plan on getting around to fixing the leaky sink in the bathroom, or (going back to when you were quite young) a parent who constantly reminds you to sit up straight and be polite. These are all scenarios that might result in new strengths you might never have sought out if left to your own devices.

Close-Up on Competitive Edge Strengths

To identify your Competitive Edge Strengths, start by writing down those major activities on which you spend a lot of your organization time right now. Ask yourself whether these are areas in which you have talent. Would most people say that you are better than average at completing these organization tasks?

Let's go back to Keith's example. It's obvious Keith genuinely loves interacting with people. These social skills also happen to be a requirement of his job in sales. Notice, though, that no one is forcing Keith to get out there and network. His desire to do so comes from a place of personal **Passion**.

In addition, his success record proves he has great ability and **Aptitude** for the work. What's more, he's regularly gaining new clients and making continual success for the government department; something that, in his case, certainly has overall Big Picture potential to fulfill the **Vision** of Keith's top KDM.

Finally, he's well suited to sales work. It matches up with his sense of who he is. There's an **Empathetic** personality match: there are no gaps between who Keith is and the work he does.

So far, the PAVE criteria all apply!

Now let's look the other Strength Keith identified: developing plans. Just as he enjoys sales, he enjoys this kind of work. But that's where the similarities end. The fact is, the time Keith spends on plans detracts from the time he has for sales. As a result, when he's crunching the numbers in plan-making mode (something several of his peers are actually more qualified to do than he is) his sales numbers decrease dramatically. Keith is adequate as a planner and analyst; he has a strong Aptitude when it comes to selling. The problem is that he might come to believe he has an Aptitude for planning, analyzing, and crunching numbers—without amassing any evidence to support his belief. In fact, if you asked Keith whether he was better than average in this department, he would say, "Yes." But if you asked 100 people who know him well and work with him whether he was above-average in the area of planning, analyzing, and crunching numbers, and if you guaranteed those people anonymity, none of them would say he is above-average in this area.

In fact, if Keith really thought about it, he would realize he actually feels a bit stressed out when his focus is primarily directed to developing new plans and analyzing numbers. Yes, he's got a sales quota to meet, but it's more than that. Person-to-person sales work is just better suited to who he is than planning. What's more, the results of his sales work deliver a much bigger "bang for the buck" in terms of his own personal happiness and his department's well-being, not to mention his personal income.

Remember, a Competitive Edge Strength will always meet all four of the PAVE criteria. This is not to say you won't have other, non-competitive edge strengths. You may be able to balance a budget like nobody's business. But unless you love doing it, are great at it, can deploy it in such a way that it brings a "big bang" to your own and your organization's success, and you know it creates no gaps between who you are and what you do, it's not a Strength that deserves the best use of your time and talents.

Work that you recognize as subpar is a clear indication of a lack of passion. Clear away the tasks that definitely don't inspire passion. When you're done, you should have a clear list of the things for which you do feel passion.

Take some time now to examine what you do over the course of a single day at work. Grab a new notebook specifically for this task. Break your day up into fifteen-minute increments. Place a star by all those tasks for which you feel Passion. Once you do this you'll have the first element that defines a Competitive Edge Strength.

> **Regardless of how great you may be at something, if you don't enjoy doing it, you will not put your heart into it and the results will not be your best.**

I have never met someone who suffered from burnout as the result of following his/her true passion. This is because in addition to doing things they love, these leaders appropriately delegate those functions they abhor. This creates a balance that eliminates negative factors that lead to undue stress and burnout.

Spending Your Time On Your Competitive Edge Strengths

Most of the people I work with in a coaching setting spend less than twenty-five percent of their time on organization activities involving their Competitive Edge Strengths! The most successful KDMs and DRs, by contrast, typically spend at least seventy-five percent of their time in organization pursuits that make use of their Competitive Edge Strengths.

If you focus seventy-five percent of your time working in areas that use your Competitive Edge, and keep all other activities to twenty-five percent or less, both you and your organization will make great strides forward; and you will get more satisfaction from your involvement in the organization.

Engage assertively! As a DR, you have a responsibility to request, lobby persistently for, or, where appropriate, simply take on those assignments best suited to your passions and abilities. The consistent failure to do this means many problems—notably job dissatisfaction, burnout, and a lack of career growth—will result from your failure to tactfully educate the KDM about your strong suits. Advocate for the right assignments.

Of course, both parties—KDM and DR—have a duty to identify what they want to be doing most and what will satisfy their needs. This should result in more time spent doing work that is personally rewarding and at the same time important to the organization.

If you and your KDM are in disagreement about what you should be doing,

I would suggest you each take time to closely evaluate your DISC results then discuss the issue again.

Pick Something That Excites You!

Consider the following true story then ask yourself whether anything similar has ever happened to you.

Many years ago my father told me, "People who dread going to work usually fail, so pick a profession or organization that makes you excited to get up every day and get at it." I was especially glad to have this advice when, as an undergraduate, I found myself facing a heady dilemma.

While working in a local accounting firm I had been recognized by the partners for what they termed my "outstanding aptitude" for the work. I was offered an early partnership if I agreed to go with the firm after graduation. It was an appealing offer, especially for a young guy just starting out in life.

The only problem was that I hated doing accounting work. I was good at it, but I had no passion for the work. Every day that I went to work, I felt nothing but dread for what I was doing. The idea of a lifetime doing accounting work made me feel tired and defeated before I'd even begun. I took my Dad's advice and turned down the offer. I knew I would never be truly happy unless I was doing work that brought me joy. And if I wasn't happy, I wouldn't be really living.

As an aside, to this day I still take little to no pleasure in doing accounting-related work. I have, however, over the years, found many other kinds of work that fill me with joy and contentment, work that, not coincidentally, has also brought me a desired level of success. Whenever I take stock of the many positives in my professional and personal life today, I'm sure glad I held out for passion way back when.

Have you completed the process I've shared with you in this chapter? If so, please continue. If not, take some time now to finish the PAVE exercise.

Your Competitive Edge Strengths Statement

As a result of applying the PAVE criteria to your strengths, you should now be able to identify your Competitive Edge Strengths. Record these findings in a short, written statement of not more than 100 words.

I can't stress enough the importance of putting your Competitive Edge Strengths into a brief written document. The human brain is an amazing bit of hardware, but it can't retain everything. The act of writing this information down solidifies and secures your thoughts and will help you catch any inconsistencies or errors, and take action on what you learn about yourself.

Sample Competitive Edge Strengths

- High energy level
- Creative problem solver
- Ability to speak before trade associations that include potential customers

- Maintains and develops strong relationships with key account customers
- Communicates effectively with employees
- Maintains a sense of humor when under pressure

Double-check It! Competitive Edge Strengths Checklist

Review each Competitive Strength you list in your notebook, and ask yourself the following:

- Do I feel **Passion** for this strength?
- Do my greatest **Aptitudes** play a role in this strength?
- Does this strength have Big Picture **Vision** potential?
- Is there an **Empathetic** personality match between my natural behavior and this strength?

If you answer "no" to any of these questions, the strength being reviewed is not a Competitive Edge Strength and must be removed from the list. Revise your statement!

WHAT'S A SWOT?

Your look in the mirror must also help you determine your **strengths, weaknesses, opportunities**, and **threats**. This process is referred to as your "SWOT analysis." The results of your SWOT analysis will help you clearly identify—in writing—exactly who you are and what the "real" world in which you exist is actually like. You will need a notebook for this exercise.

While most KDMs and DRs I have coached have felt quite comfortable doing their SWOT analysis, there have been those who have felt resistance to getting to know their true self. Part of this has to do with the difficult task of identifying weaknesses. Few of us are eager to explore our flaws. However, we have to realize that self-awareness, brought on by the SWOT analysis, brings with it an opportunity to manage (rather than deny or ignore) those problematic personal characteristics.

Only when you are aware of the traits that have the potential to thwart your success can you implement the necessary actions to neutralize or overcome them.

The Revolving Mirror

Conducting a meaningful SWOT analysis is like looking long and hard into a constantly revolving mirror. It is not like taking a quick glance at a mirror just to make sure everything on the surface looks okay. This kind of look in the mirror takes time and attention.

You must look inside and out, emotionally, mentally, and physically: you must look at both the personal and the professional aspects of your life. You must record your findings in a written statement of all that is essentially you.

Your SWOT analysis takes a little work, but it is invaluable. Once you determine your strengths, weaknesses, opportunities, and threats, you'll know, in writing, exactly who you are, what it takes to make you happy, and what you need to be the best possible you.

I've included some stories in this chapter that give real-life examples that will help you learn to conduct your own SWOT. Once you do this, you will have the increased insight and efficiency necessary to better:

- Monitor and track your own performance.
- Identify training programs that get you where you need to go AND WHERE YOU WANT TO GO next in your career.
- Improve productivity.
- Eliminate any gaps you may have between factors like personality, experience, knowledge, and background.
- Build and retain a stronger team (by sharing the SWOT process with those who report to you).
- Stay focused on "Big Picture" goals.

LOOK IN THE MIRROR STEP ONE: STRENGTHS

You've already done all the hard work on this one. The Competitive Edge Strengths Statement you just identified should be the main focus of your Strength Statement for your SWOT. Of course, you may have other Strengths you would like to list, but resist the temptation to include them. Mention only your Competitive Edge Strengths. Remember to keep your statement to one hundred words or less.

LOOK IN THE MIRROR STEP TWO: WEAKNESSES

We've all got Weaknesses. The Weaknesses portion of your SWOT analysis will help you identify the ones that most limit your chances of success. This exercise sometimes appears scary. Once you get rolling, you'll find it's not that bad. Weaknesses can be some pretty tough things to look at, but this is still an important part of your SWOT. Don't skip it!

Without a Weaknesses inventory, you're working blind. There's no way to see the factors that might topple you, and you operate at a high risk for failure. Successful people aggressively meet this challenge by studying their Weaknesses with total commitment. That's what allows them to dodge the "bullets" that quickly take down others.

Find Your Best Critics

One way to identify your own Weaknesses is by seeking critical feedback from sources who know you well. Usually the best critics are those who don't have a lot to lose from telling you the truth. Spouses and employees may have valuable feedback, but there's also a good chance they will stop short of delivering the entire truth in order to sidestep an uncomfortable and potentially dangerous situation—such as divorce or termination! That's why you should also find someone else to talk to.

If you hear the same Weakness mentioned by more than one person, take heed. If multiple people see and mention something in this category, you may be looking at an important issue. Don't be afraid or ashamed of what you hear. And don't waste time falling back on denial or excuses. Take a calm and open-minded approach to your evaluation. If you discover something that really is a Weakness, stay in the moment and own it—without emotion. Then write about it in your SWOT notebook.

One DR, whom I'll call Tom, absolutely detests writing reports. Unfortunately his job requires him to submit frequent reports to the organization's CEO, including daily status reports. During one coaching session, he told me the hatred he feels for this work is so strong that it's robbing him of time, energy, and efficiency. He's procrastinating, which is not like him. His overall work is starting to suffer because of this.

Tom gets the reports done, though always under the gun. He knows what he wants to say, but he just isn't any good at writing it down. He's a great oral communicator, but he stumbles terribly when it comes to the written word. No one has complained about the quality of his work, but this brings Tom no comfort. "I hate the feeling that I have to produce something I'm no good at doing," Tom says.

Trying to change the innate essence of who you are (or who anyone else is) is unrealistic. Tom is who he is, just as you are who you are. Getting bound up in work that is a poor match with his personality is keeping him from being effective.

We should all learn to notice those kinds of trends. We shouldn't try to change the basic patterns of who we are. Instead, we should identify and accept our Weaknesses and take immediate action to eradicate or neutralize them.

In this case, one solution would be for Tom to delegate the task of writing reports to a member of his team who is a skilled writer. Perhaps Tom could meet with this person and deliver a verbal recap of what he wants to say. He can review and even add final touches to the copy before sending it, to make sure the report accurately represents the facts. But he'll be off the hook for doing work that goes against the grain of who he is.

> **Your Weakness analysis is a great opportunity to identify any clear, consistently appearing gaps between who you are and what you do.**

By the way, this Weakness, which stood in the way of Tom's success, was very easily countered when he took the approach I outlined above!

Potential Weakness Areas

The following are some questions that will help you, as a DR, identify potential areas of Weakness.

- Is any functional area of the organization too dependent on you? i.e. "All our knowledge of IT systems is in my head."
- Do you have an "I" mentality versus a "We" mentality? i.e. "I do not give my fellow DRs and my subordinates as much credit for their ideas as I should."
- Do you have trouble getting your work done because you take on more than you can handle? i.e. "I take on whatever I see that needs help to get done because I believe that it will not get done properly unless I do it myself."
- Do you have difficulty with self-accountability? i.e. "I let things slide because I get busy putting out day-to-day "fires.""
- Do you have difficulty keeping workplace relationships separate from your personal life? Have you created a personal/social relationship with an employee that is causing resentment from other employees? Are these relationships related to morale or organization culture problems? i.e. "I am too friendly with a certain employee(s) who report to me."
- Do you have knowledge deficiencies in areas where specialized knowledge is needed for you to do your job? i.e. "I don't understand how to manage salespeople."

Chip, a DR at a manufacturing firm, worked with his KDM to create a Personal Organization Weakness Statement that showed he has a lack of self-accountability and is weak at strategic leadership, financing, marketing, and sales. This helped Chip complete his SWOT analysis.

Close-Up: Identifying Weaknesses

Remember, just like Competitive Edge Strengths, Weaknesses can exist in both your work and non-work lives.

Here is a sample Personal Organization Weakness Statement:

- Involved in too many political and/or social activities, which takes away time from my organization.
- Lack of self-accountability.
- Weak at strategic leadership, financing, marketing, and sales.

Have you completed the first two steps? If so, congratulations! You've now completed the first half of your SWOT analysis. You've identified the Competitive Edge Strengths that are your greatest ally in creating success, and you've looked your Weaknesses square in the eye. Now it's time to look at your Opportunities.

LOOK IN THE MIRROR STEP THREE: OPPORTUNITIES

Next, you must look for the opportunities that will, if exploited, make you a higher-impact contributor to the organization.

Take a close look in the mirror and recognize your deficiencies—too many DMs are inclined to blame all their problems on their leader.

Take the time needed to identify the full scope of the Opportunities available to you. Only after this should you begin to analyze and choose the Opportunities that are right for you. You might start by asking:

What educational and coaching programs are available to me for improving my skill base?

Naturally, you will want to consider opportunities that relate to such goals as expanding your organization, supporting your career progress, and dominating current and prospective markets. These will vary by industry and change constantly. Indeed, there are so many organization-related opportunities to consider, and they shift so rapidly, that performing a SWOT analysis on at least a quarterly basis is highly recommended.

There are also Opportunities of a more personal nature to consider. One woman I know gave up a challenging and high-paid executive position to do freelance work from home until all her children were attending grade school. While this provided an opportunity to spend more quality time focusing on her children, it also involved a sacrifice of income and a major setback to her career. She eventually discovered, though, that the change in her life circumstances also opened up Opportunities for new ventures that she might have missed had she remained in her previous career.

One DR, Jill, the Head of the Sales Department, concluded through her Opportunity analysis that she was spending most of her time personally selling rather than managing and training her sales staff. She felt if she didn't have to spend so much time selling, she could do a lot more to help her salespeople expand their department sales. Jill and her KDM developed a strategy based on this Opportunity: "To reduce department dependence upon me personally selling department products, and to sell additional services to our current clients."

Regardless of the kind of opportunity you are considering, it should tap into your Passions. I find that helping to bring about something for which I feel strong passion brings with it an incredible emotional euphoria. Those are the kinds of Opportunities I can't wait to pursue! Ask yourself if the opportunity you are considering getting involved in will provide you with an emotional reward that is worthwhile in relation to the time and effort you will have to devote.

Opportunities Checklist

Before we move on to identifying your threats, let's review the following important questions, which will help you develop your written Opportunities Statement. Remember that Opportunities can exist in both your work and non-work life.

- Is there an Opportunity for you to more effectively use your time focusing on your Competitive Edge Strengths?
- Do you have any Weaknesses that could be turned into Opportunities?
- Is there an Opportunity to take a breather and recharge?
- Is there an Opportunity to spend more quality time with family?
- Is there an Opportunity to become active in civic or political causes?
- Is there an Opportunity to partake in hobbies or other fun activities?
- Are there religious or spiritual Opportunities that are important to you?

One DR's Opportunity Statement included these items:

- I have sources of potential investors who could provide funds for expansion.
- I have relationships with importers that could lead to a new distribution channel.

LOOK IN THE MIRROR STEP FOUR: THREATS

Threats are external factors that can negatively impact an organization and, by extension, an individual. Like Weaknesses, these are not all that much fun to consider. You have no real control over a threat, but once something is identified ahead of time as a potential Threat, you can at least develop ways to react to it, should it occur. Creating a Threats Statement helps you identify the most important Threats for which you need to be prepared. It's important to remember that within any crisis there is both danger and the Opportunity for constructive action. Perhaps we can even turn a Threat into an Opportunity!

Let's look at some of the most common Threats identified by the KDMs and DRs I have worked with over the years. Consider these closely, and take them into consideration as possible elements to include when writing your own written Threats Statement.

Potential Threat: If You Become Incapacitated or Die

Consider whether there is someone trained to take over your areas of organization responsibilities if you become incapacitated or die. Should the organization have Key Person Insurance that will protect the organization and pay for the hiring of someone to do what you do for the organization?

Of course, a DR has a lot of other things to consider from this Threat of incapacitation or death, such as the impact it would have on his/her family.

Potential Threats: Market-related and Competitive Challenges

You will also want to list Threats to the viability of the organization you work for. Typically, these are Threats that arise from changes in market trends, new competitive forces, shifts in technology, and regulatory changes. Here, the landscape of possible change is so vast as to require frequent revision to your list—but that doesn't mean you shouldn't make an effort. Create the best list you can right now. You can always update it later.

Potential Threat: Family Difficulties

This is a particularly important category to consider in the situation where you are a DR working in a family organization —but it is certainly not limited to that situation. There are plenty of other family difficulties to consider.

As children in any family enter their adolescent years, for instance, it is common for there to be clashes that create potential threats to parental happiness. Anyone who has children should not be surprised that such problems exist in the relationship between parents and their children. You may not be able to stop relationship clashes, but you can mentally prepare for certain types of adolescent action to take place, and you can create plans that will allow you to navigate the changes gracefully and get though this difficult stage in your children's lives. As odd as it may seem, these plans are actually relevant to the family organization, because relationship clashes are potential Threats to the enterprise.

The potential Threats that shadow the well-being of those you love always carry heavy impact. No matter how much love we feel for a parent, for instance, the inevitable fact is that caring for our parents in their old age can create changes in the life we are accustomed to living. One KDM I know had a mother who survived a series of strokes. Even though she was doing well, it was foreseeable there would soon come a time when she would be incapable of taking care of herself. The identification of this Threat resulted not only in a plan for dealing with the obvious financial considerations, but also in plans to address a related Threat: it would take a great deal of time away from his work activities to tend to his mother's well-being if another stroke should occur.

Marriage problems, too, can profoundly affect your happiness and your ability to fulfill your vision. Identify possible Threats on that front, as well.

A Final Note on Threats

Recognize it is a waste of time and energy worrying about Threats. Just do what you can to be ready if a Threat should turn into reality.

Key Point Review: Your Threats Checklist

Let's review the following important factors regarding your written Threats Statement. Remember, Threats can exist in both your work and non-work lives.

- Do you face significant threats from competitors, market forces, technological changes, or regulatory responsibilities?
- Are there potential problems within your marriage that could impact on your happiness and success?
- Are there potential problems with your children that could impact on your happiness and success?
- Are there potential care issues with your parents or in-laws that could impact on your happiness and success?

One DR wrote the following Threats Statement

- Marriage unsteady
- Husband believes I should be stay-at-home mom
- Husband's job may one day involve his relocation

YOUR HOMEWORK: MAKE IT HAPPEN!

If you have not already done so, complete your PAVE exercise and your personal SWOT analysis. Then discuss your results with your KDM in a one-on-one meeting.

Discuss developing a Plan that will make greater use of your Strengths within the organization, neutralize your Weaknesses, act on new Opportunities, and address certain personal Threats. Be sure to discuss any Personal Organization Weaknesses that could be turned into Big Picture Potential Opportunities for the organization if neutralized.

For instance, delegating the accounting department to another DR, instead of having it continue to report to him, freed up twenty percent of Jim's work time. He used that time to take over the Innovation responsibility, which has Big Picture Potential areas for the organization.

Ted, a CFO DR, mentioned during one training session that his organization would soon need a different type of financing than the organization it was now using. He was not a financing expert and identified this as a Personal Weakness. Ted decided on a plan, for which he received the backing of his KDM: he would enroll in graduate-level college courses to learn enough about organization financing to enable him to understand the financing alternatives available for growing the organization.

One DR expressed his concern about a family member of the organization entering the professional service nonprofit organization. Others at his Alignment training session suggested that he turn this into a Personal Opportunity to help the family member become of greater value to the organization. This turned out to be a win-win situation for everyone.

A sales director DR, in one organization, had responsibility for a technical department he felt took away needed time from his sales department. He saw Opportunity for greater sales results if he could have the technical department taken out of his responsibility. As a result of their discussions, the KDM agreed to hire a highly qualified engineering manager to whom he could delegate many of his technical responsibilities. Soon after the hiring, the organization began a period of much higher rates of sales growth!

Typically these SWOT analysis meetings result in a DR modifying his/her approach to some aspects of the organization based on what he/she has learned during the processes of self-discovery described in this chapter. But don't assume you got everything right! After hearing feedback from your KDM about whether or not he or she agrees with your Personal SWOT assessment, you may wish to go back to modify or eliminate some of the factors in your Personal SWOT analysis.

CHAPTER 3

Align on Plans and Priorities

EXECUTIVE SUMMARY FOR THE KEY DECISION MAKER

Do you have a GPS in your car or on your phone that you use when making a long trip? Many people do.

The great thing about these systems is that, when they are working properly, they tell us the exact moment we go even slightly off-track. Unfortunately, most Key Decision Makers (KDMs) don't have a similar system in place for their organization.

In this chapter your Direct Report (DR) will begin setting up such a guidance system; a system built on the principle of personal accountability— accountability that will be confirmed and reinforced during a special one-on-one meeting with you. This system, which requires weekly reinforcement to become automatic, employs two powerful guidance tools—the Project Plan and the Priority To-Do List. Using both tools, your DR will set up and follow a system that tells you exactly what kind of progress is being made on your journey. It will also alert both of you the instant you've gone off track.

GET WHAT YOU BOTH NEED

> *Things which matter most must never be at the mercy of things which matter least.* —Johann Wolfgang von Goethe

The principles shared in this chapter may not be familiar—at first. They are worth becoming familiar with, however, because they have the advantage of giving both KDMs and DRs exactly what they need.

What do KDMs need? In a word, they need control. Entrepreneurs, after all, can often be "control freaks." The processes you will read about here allow the KDM to feel in control without spending endless hours looking over the DR's shoulder.

What do DRs need? Typically, they want the freedom to reach their full potential. The DRs who have used the ideas you're about to read have told us they felt liberated for having done so. They were able to get the guidance they needed and escape from the feeling of someone looking over their shoulder all the time. After a few weeks, they even found they could make a mistake once in a while without feeling like it was the end of the world.

The concepts in this chapter make for a far more productive and prosperous long-term working environment. Study them. Implement them!

CLARITY COUNTS!

We spend a lot of time debriefing with graduates of the AlignUp training program. Not long ago, I asked Mike, a vice president of operations, what the main take-away from his recently completed AlignUp training had been. He answered instantly: "Clarity."

I asked him what that meant, and he said, "My plans, my priorities, and my time allocations are now crystal clear, both to me and to my boss."

"I'll give you an example. After my first Plan and Priority Review with my boss, I was amazed. I realized many of the day-to-day tasks I thought only I could take care of could successfully be delegated to my subordinates. That was the result of better clarity during my one-on-one meetings with my CEO on what I personally had to be doing—and what I didn't have to do and could delegate to someone else. I was surprised at how quickly that clarity emerged. I was grateful for it, too."

I could not help noticing the big smile Mike directed at his fellow AlignUp trainees, all of whom had also recently completed the training.

Mike finished by saying, "Since starting my one-on-one weekly Alignment meetings with my CEO, I have had far more time to focus on things that have major impact on growing the organization." His time at work had become more focused on his "Big Picture" projects, which have a direct impact on increased organizational growth and success. These results would not have occurred without his assigning authority and resources for certain responsibilities that his KDM felt should not be the priority use of his time. Clarity on expectations regarding his priorities led Mike to focus more of his time at work on bringing about a greater positive impact on his organization.

HOW TO GET THERE

Perhaps you're wondering: how can you get to where Mike is?

The answer is simple: By changing the dynamic. By volunteering for account-ability. By holding yourself to a higher standard than your KDM ever could ... and by asking your KDM for insights and advice as to how you can consistently hit that high standard.

In this chapter, you'll learn how to do just that by means of a special, weekly one-on-one meeting with your KDM called a Plan and Priority Review. This regular meeting serves as a kind of GPS for you and your KDM: it shows both of you how much progress is being made toward your destination and alerts both of you to those instances where you head off-course, so you can get back on track quickly.

I have already shared the key to turning on that GPS. Mike mentioned it: a weekly Plan and Priority Review meeting with your KDM.

THIS IS YOUR RESPONSIBILITY!

To lay the groundwork for this meeting, you, not your KDM, will take the ini-tiative in two critical areas: confirming the plan (and its associated Tactics) and drafting a list of Priorities for the coming week. Some DRs make the mistake of believing that this responsibility is someone else's. They are wrong. High-Performing Direct Reports assume this weekly task is their responsibility.

It's essential there is full Alignment between you and the KDM on your Project Plans and Priorities. The key to bringing this about is a regularly sched-uled, one-on-one meeting each week between you and the KDM (such one-on-one meetings should eventually involve each of the KDM's DRs, but we will start with you). To be truly effective, these meetings should always include two key steps. The steps are:

- Step One: Review the Project Plans for which you are responsible
- Step Two: Reprioritize Your "To Do" list

When these meetings cover both steps (each step will be examined closely in this chapter), the result is greater Alignment between you and your KDM on the vitally important subject of **how your time should best be used**.

This Alignment usually leads to dramatically improved results from the projects and assignments within your areas of responsibility.

These Meetings Take Time Commitment.

The one-on-one KDM/DR meetings are not happenstance affairs. They should be scheduled for up to an hour each, although you may find they end up being concluded in as little as thirty minutes, or even less once you have estab-lished familiarity with the meeting structure. It is not uncommon for DRs to end up spending only ten or fifteen minutes a week with the KDM reviewing the agenda points you are about to learn. This is the likely timeframe for the meeting in which both parties are satisfied that everything is "on track", but it will take you a little while to ramp up to that point. Regardless of how long these meetings take, they should be recurring elements of you and your KDM's weekly schedule.

These weekly meetings should never be cancelled, except in the case of illness or if one of the two parties is on vacation. If one of the parties is out of town on business, it is easy to meet with Skype-type video calls.

WIN AND DEFEND YOUR SPOT ON THE KDM'S CALENDAR

It is your job to tactfully but assertively advocate for your spot on the KDM's weekly calendar.

During an AlignUp training session Liz, a DR, shared that she was supposed to have a one-on-one meeting every week with Mary, her KDM. She told us that most of these meetings, however, were not taking place. They were cancelled because Mary was out of town and "unavailable," or were cancelled because Mary was "too busy" to have the meeting.

Liz was given a homework assignment: to discuss the need of meeting each week with her KDM, face to face, using a list she created that showed why these meetings benefited her and the organization. Mary's response during the very first of these exchanges was one of appreciation that Liv saw such value. From that point forward Mary kept the majority of her one-on-one weekly meetings with Liz.

DEVELOPMENT OF AN ORGANIZATION'S STRATEGIC PLAN

Let's look at the two steps you will take now, before approaching your KDM—the steps that will make this important weekly meeting possible.

STEP ONE: REVIEW OF PROJECT PLANS FOR WHICH YOU ARE RESPONSIBLE

The Driving Critical Success Factor is the most important Critical Success Factor—the one most needed for your organization to excel and, in some cases, to survive.

One of your objectives for your weekly one-on-one meetings is to review your progress on high- impact Project Plans being driven by you. In this step, you will create a uniform Project Plan Template that is relevant to your working environment. This is a particularly important priority if your project has a disproportionately high impact on the attainment of the Driving Critical Success Factor (DCSF).

It is often the case that one department has a greater share of direct responsibility than other departments in fulfilling a Strategic Goal. Aligned collaboration across multiple departments to attain the DCSF is, however, an indirect responsibility that affects everyone.

In most small and midsize organizations, important Strategic Goals connect to a single department's Project Plan; something that is the sole responsibility of the DR in charge of the department. That would be you. The question is: how will you keep track of your Project Plans?

The Driving Critical Success Factor is the most important Critical Success Factor – the one most needed for your organization to excel and, in some cases, to survive.

I recommend the following simple and easy to use Project Plan template, modeled after one used by a technology organization. The example below shows a Project Plan created for this organization strategy: "To make our training program for our software users one that rates high in satisfaction with those who undertake the program."

Here are some excerpts from the Project Plan that syncs up with this organization strategy. Note that the column on the left lists the specific Tactics that should, when undertaken and completed, fulfill the strategic objective that connects to this Plan.

The reason there are two "percentage complete" columns (on the far right) is simply to show progress on the project that has taken place between the last meeting and the current meeting, which might otherwise be difficult for the KDM to keep track of. The KDM can drill down into the tasks that have made progress since the last meeting, and may also want to look more closely at important tasks where the expected progress is not being made.

Strategy: To make our training program for our software users highly rated for satisfaction level by those who go though the training.

PROJECT PLAN TACTICS	RESPON- SIBLE PERSON	TARGET DATE	PRIORITY	STATUS	% COM- PLETE LAST MEETING	% COM- PLETE THIS MEETIN
Develop PowerPoint and other materials for all training sessions (**Project #1**)						
Create short videos and other visu- als to be embedded in Power- Point	DK	Sept 6	Medium	In prog- ress	25%	50%
Create survey questions or online modules	DK	Sept 16	Low	Not started	0%	0%
Produce Live training session (**Project #2**)						
Practice training support session before using with a training class.	CG	May 7	High	In prog- ress	30%	30%
Create Slides, handouts and role- play ac- tivities to build and strengthen facilita- tion and coaching skills	CG	May 7	High	In prog- ress	50%	75%

One of the subjects you will want to address with your KDM during your first in-depth meeting is the importance of limiting the total number of Project Plans for which you are responsible. A DR should be responsible for no more than five Project Plans, and in most cases it is preferable to be responsible for between one and three.

PREPARE

Prior to attending any of these weekly meetings you will need to prepare and/or update each Project Plan for which you are responsible, so that responsibilities and action items are crystal-clear. This is an important part of helping your KDM see the benefit of the process, and it may require a level of "prep time" for the meeting that you have not yet invested. Invest the time. Remember, the goal is to hold yourself to a higher standard than the KDM could possibly hold you to.

Let me repeat; You must be prepared to do all the up-front work necessary to make this meeting as efficient as possible. Ask yourself: "What does my KDM need to know, and what do I need to be ready to discuss so we don't waste everyone's time?"

Expect your KDM to ask for explanations about why expected results have not yet been achieved, and what, specifically, will be done to address any obstacles you have encountered.

FIND THE ANSWERS BEFORE HEARING THE QUESTION

As the DR responsible for the results of the Tactics in your plan, you should be prepared to answer questions like these for each of the tactical commitments in your Project Plan:

- What are the measured results of the Project Plan or Tactic compared to projected results?
- Are the projected results on track? (Yes or no?)
- If the projected results of the Project Plan are not on track, which Tactics are not being completed on schedule?
- What caused the below-expectation results? (These reasons need to be understood before you try to overcome the roadblocks that stand in the way of success).
- If the project is not on track, what is needed to get it back on track?
- If the project can't get back on track, what is the new track, and what is needed to hit and stay on this track?

Your Project Plans should break down what may seem to be an overwhelming task into small, manageable units. If this is not the case, consider what you can recommend during the meeting with your KDM to make this happen.

DISCUSS REAL-WORLD MILESTONES

If you do not use the Plan and Priority Review meeting with your KDM to discuss real-world milestones that actually measure forward progress on the project, then you will be wasting everybody's time.

Angie, a DR, was responsible for a major design project for a customized fabrication that was to be completed by the beginning of June. The Project Plan had milestone dates for partial completion to take place by the previous March, April and May, which was committed to by the manager who was the responsible party. Literally, each week this DR said the project was right on target. However, the DR responsible for the project never discussed the status of the milestones, which would show her KDM the specific progress on the Plan. Months before the entire project was to be completed, the DR for the Project Plan fired an employee who was working on the Project Plan. The fired employee then contacted the KDM, out of a sense of personal responsibility, to let her know there was absolutely no way the project was going to be even partially complete by the due date!

When the KDM then asked the DR to give her a demonstration of the completed milestone, the manager couldn't do so because, just as Angie had said, the project was in fact greatly behind schedule.

Don't let this happen to you. Be prepared to show your KDM the achieved milestones to show whether they are tracking within the projected framework. If they are not tracking on target, be prepared to explain why and what should be done about it.

USE MEASUREMENT DASHBOARDS

It is not enough to make progress on your plan. You must also be able to convey such progress in a visually arresting, instantly understandable way! This is where dashboards come in handy. Dashboards provide a summary of the state of your Plans on one page. Spending a very small amount of time to put in place this easily accessible technology will save you many hours and enable you to lead the discussion in an objective way, based upon measurements.

If you are not yet familiar with dashboards, it is time to become familiar with them. As technology becomes more and more capable of measuring and displaying the outcomes that connect to virtually any human endeavor, it becomes easier and less expensive to create status graphics that take the form of computer-generated measurement dashboards that compare projected results versus actual results.

Jacqueline, a DR, used an Excel spreadsheet to color-code the actual-versus-predicted results as follows: red if she had missed predicted results, yellow if she was close, and green if the actual results met or exceeded the prediction (also known as a "traffic light" system). At the weekly meetings, she made a point of focusing her KDM's attention on those items in which predicted results for those priorities were not achieved—the "red zone." Addressing such items directly, on your own initiative, is a big part of holding yourself to a higher standard than the KDM would.

This one change in approach transformed the entire dynamic of the relationship Jacqueline had with her KDM.

VOLUNTEER TO DISCUSS TIMELINES

During the Project Review portion of your weekly one-on-one meetings with your KDM, you will volunteer to discuss the status and results of timeline commitments for each objective in the Project Plan for which you have responsibility. The discussion should center on predicted results versus actual results.

Be prepared to demonstrate to your KDM, in a memorable way, the tangible progress that has been made toward fulfilling key aspects of the Project Plan over the course of the previous week. This is very different than just "reporting on the status." If each week's "status report" is that the project is two weeks behind schedule, and you issue that same "status report" for five straight weeks, the information you are offering is essentially meaningless.

Alignment cannot exist if there is lack of confidence in the quality of the information you are sharing with your KDM.

It may seem obvious, but it is important to make sure you are giving updates on actual, measurable results, not "projections," so you do not lose credibility when a deeper review comparing actual to predicted results takes place.

> To be highly efficient at these meetings, you need to focus on removing any and all obstacles standing in the way of Alignment between you and your KDM in relation to your Project Plans.

USE THE SMART CRITERIA

Your Project Plan should meet all the classic SMART criteria. These require that the Project Plan be Specific, Measurable and Achievable, that it have specific, designated people who are Responsible for results, and that it includes a clear Timeframe. Let's take a look in a little more detail at all five of the SMART criteria.

Specific: Spell out exactly what needs to be done, major step by major step.

Measurable: Knowing upfront how results from your Project Plans will be measured is the only way to confirm whether or not you are on target. There are going to be different methods for measuring results. Choose the right ones—carefully. These measurements must be clear, objective, and easy to confirm (for example: gross sales income increasing by a certain percentage).

Achievable: Your Project Plan must have a realistic chance of success, otherwise the Plan will be demoralizing to you and others working on the project. Your Project Plan should address resource issues such as funding, staffing, and equipment needs in a way that confirms the Goal is in fact achievable. Of course, you will need the support of your KDM on these important issues.

Responsible Party: There must clearly be one person, not two or more people, designated as the Responsible Party who has committed to implement a specific Project Plan. You must be that person. As the Responsible Party, you must have both the authority and the responsibility to see it through to success.

> Take time to think about realistic and attainable timeframes, rather than estimating or arbitrarily designating dates, as this will improve your Alignment with the KDM, because you will increase the likelihood of actually hitting those benchmark timeframes.

It's not enough to state that you will "do what it takes" to see a Project Plan through. Project Plan accountability must be designated as yours, and everyone you work with must know that you are solely accountable for managing the Project Plan process.

Time Frame: Establish a realistic Time Frame for how and when the Project Plan is expected to be completed. For example, is accomplishing the Project Plan expected to take six months? If a benchmark along the way isn't accomplished on time, the lack of success in hitting that benchmark should trigger responses for making it happen. Always include an *outside* date for each benchmark of your Project Plan to be completed. Benchmarks with closely tracked deadlines are the monitors that will tell you whether things are going as planned or not.

A SMART PROJECT PLAN MAKES THE REVIEW MEETING EASY

To support his organization's goal to "increase organization sales by twenty percent within two years," Ryan, a DR, was asked to create a Project Plan to fulfill this strategy: "to add salespeople as needed." The following list is an example of questions he needed to answer to create a Project Plan that met the SMART Criteria:

- How many new salespeople will need to be hired this year to achieve the sales goal?
- Have adequate funds been budgeted to train the salespeople and compensate them before they generate sales?
- What tools (such as behavioral surveys and credit checks) should be used during the interviewing process for new sales employees in order to identify those likely to become better-performing salespeople?
- Who will manage the salespeople, and how often will sales results be reviewed?
- How will the sales growth of the organization be financed?

Within each Project Plan, there are typically many Tactics that need to be implemented by you and your subordinate employees for the Project Plan to succeed.

Tactics are the commitments you and your subordinates will follow to bring about a successful Project Plan. Tactics are both specific and measurable; they pinpoint the Projects required to be undertaken by specific Responsible Parties, within set parameters, so you can measure the results or impact of the Tactics.

There is no limit to the number of Tactics you can include in your Project Plan (beyond the practical constraints of your organization's infrastructure). As long as you can execute the Tactics in a timely manner, feel free to add as many as you need.

Tactics have relatively short deadlines within which they must take place. They may be open to the rest of the team or confidential between you and your KDM. An example of a confidential, sensitive Tactic would be for the director of marketing to solve the problem of an employee on his team whose ongoing, persistent pattern of passive-aggressive behavior is hurting the organization—by terminating the employee. The director of marketing is responsible for implementing this confidential Tactic, which is just one element of the Project Plan shared with the KDM. Another Tactic, less sensitive in nature, might be to hire a new employee with a specifically targeted skills-set, such as social media marketing.

For smaller organizations, it is particularly important that some of the tactical commitments have short (i.e. no longer than 30-day) completion deadlines, so that the employees can see for themselves that some Tactics are in fact being completed.

SIZE AND SCOPE OF WRITTEN PROJECT PLANS

The size and scope of written Project Plans that you go over with your KDM each week should be no more than one hundred words, excluding Tactics. If timelines are being met, your KDM will probably not want to drill down to the level of Tactics during your weekly meeting. There is no word-count limitation when recording and defining your Tactics; whether it is in regards to carrying out a Project Plan or in regards to each of your Project Plan Statements.

MORE ON TACTICS

Don't confuse the Project Plan you review weekly with your KDM with the many Tactic-related assignments to specific employees that must be achieved for the Project Plan to succeed.

Tactics can be assigned to anyone in the organization, although authority for updating tactical due dates is limited to the employee, generally a manager, who is responsible for the specific Project Plan.

The party responsible for the Project Plan must assign and clearly communicate Tactic responsibilities under the Project Plan, as well as all relevant expectations to the parties who are responsible for executing the Tactics. It is important to designate and document the single person ultimately responsible for completing each particular Tactic of the Project Plan.

Each Tactic, like the Project Plan as a whole, should be date-driven. A Tactic that calls for a manager to hire an assistant, for example, must include the deadline for doing so. This must be done in order to verify the Tactic dates are being met.

The following list of questions will show you the type of issues you should be thinking about when you develop Tactics. The questions below relate to a project involving the hiring of sales staff.

Tactic Questions

- Who will create (or update) a job description for the salespeople, and by what date must it be completed?
- Who will conduct the interviewing?
- What selection criteria will be used?
- By what date must the salespeople be hired and start employment?
- By what date must the salespeople start and complete training?
- On what skills or product information will the new salespeople need to be trained, and who will do the training?
- Who will create the training programs, and when is the deadline?
- What minimum sales results are expected from each salesperson, and within what time frame?

LIMITED NUMBER OF PROJECT PLANS FOR EACH STRATEGY

Project Plans identify what needs to be done to satisfy a specific stated Strategy that your KDM understands and personally supports. There should be no more than five Project Plans for each of your Strategies.

This point is worth discussing in depth with your KDM. Even with a large organization, there should be a *maximum* of five Project Plans for each Strategy. I've worked with many KDMs who insisted that five Project Plans were simply not enough to accomplish a particular Strategy. It turned out in each case that it was much more effective to keep to the limit of five Project Plans and instead review the Strategy closely, because it is likely to become too complex. Try instead to break a complex Strategy into two or more separate Strategies.

> **Plans that are manageable are Plans that can happen!**

The smaller the organization, the smaller the number of Project Plans you should assign to a particular Strategy. A small organization may only be able to effectively handle a couple of Project Plans.

Questions To Help You Develop Manageable Project Plans

Answering the following questions, each based upon a specific functional area of the organization, will help you develop your Project Plans.

Operations

- What is needed to differentiate your organization's primary products or services from those of your industry competition?
- How can you lower the risk of product failure, thus lowering buyer dissatisfaction, as well as your cost of returned products?
- How can you improve your product by improving any of the following: appearance, installation cost and/or ease, price, ease of use, versatility, user and/or maintenance cost, durability, speed, size, material quality, accuracy?
- How can you lower your prices based on improved internal efficiency?
- How can costs such as delivery, installation, or financing be lowered?
- How can you process orders faster?
- How can you lower labor costs?

After you have completed a draft of each Project Plan, check to see whether:

- Goals are specific enough
- Expectations are realistically achievable
- Evaluation dates for verifying the Plan is on schedule and on track have been identified
- Clear measurement methods are employed
- Expected results are communicated to specific people or teams
- New equipment and/or personnel will be needed

ALLOCATION OF RESOURCES

The question of resources is an especially important one to consider when reviewing the draft of your Project Plan.

Have all human and financial resources necessary for the Project Plan to succeed been identified? Only after doing this can you forecast and budget your foreseeable financial requirements.

The reality is that the smaller the organization, the more often this budgeting and forecasting is not formally done. If your organization doesn't yet have the wherewithal to do formal budgeting and forecasting properly, you can at least develop a "ballpark" budget and forecast number before finalizing your Project Plans.

Commitment Date Delays

If key commitment dates are being missed, you should know why. If you are not sure why, not knowing should bother you enough for you to want to find out on your own, and with complete certainty. This is another aspect of holding yourself to a higher standard than the KDM—or anyone else for that matter—could possibly hold you.

If things are not going according to plan, then you, as the DR, need to volunteer to tell your KDM that the expected results are not happening. You also need to volunteer why they are not happening and what you plan to do to change things. It is essential that you and your KDM are in Alignment so neither of you will permit a culture in which ignoring key benchmarks, overlooking deliverables, or missing deadlines in a Project Plan is acceptable.

This is not a matter of simply requesting an extension, but rather a matter of personal accountability, of coming to a viable, mutual understanding between you and the KDM about what the "battle plan" really is. Don't go to the KDM too often with "It wasn't done, but I'll do it by such-and-such a date, okay?" If you request extensions too often, the pattern will become an organization joke. More importantly, your KDM will eventually conclude that your commitments are meaningless.

Of course sometimes delays are inevitable and timely revisions to your Project Plans are required. A missed date is bound to happen now and then, but it cannot become the norm!

As the Responsible Party for any Project Plan, you should think long and hard before agreeing to benchmark dates or completion dates. Once you have committed to dates, you will be personally accountable for making sure they are met. In fact, it is a good idea to establish a practice that allows you to be ahead of the schedule rather than behind it. **Insofar as you can do so, your goal should be to under-promise and over-deliver.**

STEP TWO: REVIEW YOUR PRIORITY TO-DO-LIST

Your Project Plan is *not* the same thing as your Priority To-Do list. The Project Plan lays out what is to be done. Your Priority To-Do List identifies what, specifically, *you* will be doing *next*! Your KDM needs to be part of that conversation, as well.

Each week your priorities need to be updated for the meeting, reviewed, and revised per the feedback of your KDM. It is essential you do this, because you want to make absolutely sure the things you are working on are in fact the areas your KDM wants you to be focusing your efforts. To ensure this happens, you must bring a recently updated Priority To-Do List into the weekly meeting so your KDM can review and revise it as necessary.

Bert, a DR, explained at a training session that one of the most beneficial things that came from attending Alignment training and going through this priority review process was a personal plan he and his KDM developed to get him to a point where seventy five percent of his work time would be focused on activities that used his strongest **Aptitudes** and **Passion**, with all his other work-related activities using twenty five percent or less of his time.

As a result of these weekly one-on-one reviews of his priorities (which had never before taken place), he and his KDM shared an Aligned view of where he should spend his time to give the greatest impact to the organization. An additional positive result—and one not to be minimized—was that he was getting more satisfaction from his work!

> **Don't continually request your Project Plan dates be pushed back, because most KDMs believe that completion dates do matter and are set in stone when you commit to them.**

It is quite common for these discussions to result in helpful guidance from the KDM concerning tasks that are currently on your to-do list, but can be safely delegated to other members of your team (I opened this chapter with an example of a KDM who had this experience).

GO INTO THE MEETING WITH YOUR TO-DO LIST UP-TO-DATE

Reviewing your updated priority list supports the type of hands-on management needed in most small and midsize organizations. Make sure the copy you hand over is absolutely current! It should not omit anything of consequence and should reflect what you will actually focus on today, when you leave the meeting.

If you can hold yourself to that standard, you will find these weekly meetings will keep you and the KDM in Alignment on all of your most important priorities. It will help keep you from the type of burnout that can happen when employees feel overwhelmed with too many priorities. These weekly reviews also help you overcome any weaknesses you may have in self-management. When you have discussed something on your list that is important for you to do and then in a later review it becomes clear it did not happen, both you and the KDM will know it is time for you to hold yourself accountable!

WEEKLY REVIEW OF PRIORITIES REDUCES "DROPPED BALLS"

Fred, a DR who served as general counsel in a manufacturing organization, was asked to draft agreements to be signed by current and future employees. These agreements prevented those employees from competing or sharing information about organization technologies and the organization customer list for a specified period of time, in the event they ever left the organization. This is typically called a non-compete agreement. This is a task activity, not a complex Project Plan.

Several months after receiving the assignment, the general counsel still had not drafted the documents, and consequently no employees had agreed to the restrictions. As Fred admitted to me, his KDM simply forgot about the assignment.

Sometime later, an organization manager presented a plan to develop new technologies. The KDM owner and the VP of Operations agreed to development of the manager's proposed technology. Shortly after the technology was developed, the manager quit and, using profit-sharing plan money he had received from the organization, opened a competing organization using all the new technology from the organization and marketing to the organization's customer list! Of course he was free to do so, since he had never signed a non-compete agreement.

This major problem would not have occurred if Fred's To-Do List had been reviewed weekly with his KDM!

A WEEKLY PRIORITY REVIEW KEEPS YOU FROM FEELING OVERWHELMED

Some DRs become so overwhelmed by the multitude of things they have to do each day that they end up avoiding doing much of anything at all. They fill their day with diversions, and their time flies by with no results.

In contrast, High-Impact DRs do not allow themselves to become intimidated or overwhelmed by the size and complexity of the task in front of them. They bring tasks down to size by breaking them into small, manageable pieces, and they make a clear, achievable commitment to finish what is in front of them. During their weekly meetings, these High-Impact DRs are comfortable discussing what they feel to be the three to five top priorities for the upcoming week that will have the biggest impact upon their own time commitments.

You will be far less likely to freeze with inaction if you look at a major task from the perspective of how and when you must accomplish each phase of the process. If it is a task that involves multiple steps, create a detailed schedule listing all the steps involved. Indicate start and completion dates for each step of the task, and separate out things that don't have to be done immediately so each day you are only looking at the part of the task you absolutely have to address. This will keep you from becoming overwhelmed by the magnitude of the assignment.

You will be amazed, upon completing steps A, B, and C of a task, how steps D and E suddenly become comparatively easy! This technique carries benefits well beyond the organization spectrum. When my wife and I were building a house, my wife commented to me that she felt overwhelmed by the task of making so many choices about lighting fixtures, carpet, granite, cabinets, and so on. We sat down and broke the process into smaller steps. We prioritized the decision-making needs according to what had to be decided by what date. Breaking the process down and taking the time to prioritize exactly what decisions needed to be made, and when, allowed my wife to make the necessary decisions without feeling overwhelmed.

During an Alignment training session, Moira, a DR, told me and her fellow trainees that she felt overwhelmed by having too many things to do and too little time in which to do them. She admitted she was not getting things done in a timely fashion and blamed the situation on a list of things that must be done that contained over one hundred items. She claimed there was no way she could ever catch up, let alone get ahead. I asked her to bring her list to the upcoming monthly training session, which happened to be on the topic of one-on-one weekly meeting with her KDM, and told her we would discuss her priorities before she met with her KDM. She arrived with several pages of her To-Do List tasks.

We then did the following exercise to help her prepare for her newly scheduled weekly one-on-one meeting with her KDM, which resulted in her creating a To-Do List she could review with her KDM.

The first step was to create a To-Do List with three different side headings representing separate categories of tasks. The first category on the list stated "**recurring weekly items**", which were for such recurring activities as weekly Strategic Leadership Team meetings with her KDM and her fellow organization DRs. If you start the day without setting up a schedule or a list of priorities for that day, you will likely come up short and find the day stressful due to feeling overwhelmed. Every DR faces multiple tasks they need to do during the business day. That is just the way it is. Manage this situation by identifying and prioritizing the tasks, activities, and decisions that must be done each day. **The key is to get out of your sight, as quickly as possible, all the things that don't have to be done** *today*. That's why I began by giving Moira this category.

The second category on the list identified all Moira's "**Items I absolutely have to get done by the close of business on the next day at work.**"

The third category on the list identified her "**Items I absolutely have to get done within the next week.**" Breaking this down further, I asked Moira to identify the specific day on a day-to-day basis, setting a priority status during the upcoming week for when she should work on each of these items. When these items were spread out on a day-to-day basis, not one of Moira's days had more than ten items that needed to be done that day.

The fourth category on the list identified Moira's "**Items I absolutely have to get done beyond the upcoming week but within the next 30 days.**"

The fifth category was reserved for low-priority items. These were items

Moira felt did not have to be completed within 30 days and that might not even need a completion date at all. They were things she had to get done whenever she could find the available time. While working on this fifth category, Moira recognized items that probably did not even have to be done within the next twelve months and could safely be moved to a file for next year's tasks.

Interestingly, while doing this exercise, Moira was able to identify a number of items that had either already been done or that she no longer needed to do. In all, she completely eliminated 25 of the items on her list.

After going through this exercise, Moira realized there were actually less than fifty tasks on her list. She prepared to discuss them with Fiona, her KDM, so that Fiona could help her set priorities or perhaps delegate some of them to others.

During her very first weekly review meeting, Moira and Fiona shifted many of the tasks to beyond the following week, because Fiona felt they were of a lower priority than Moira had assumed. The result: Moira no longer felt threatened by the things that had to be done, and her anxiety was completely eliminated. Not diminished: eliminated! She had much more clarity and much less stress.

In the process of going though Moira's priority list, both Moira and Fiona agreed to reduce the magnitude of her workload by identifying tasks that could be delegated by her to her subordinates. This is a common outcome of the process—take advantage of it!

Here is an example of a Priority To-Do List.

DONNA TO-DO'S FOR A SALES TRAINING PROGRAM 11/23/2015

Recurring

- Complete online training enrollment requests

Done By Close Of Business On Next Day At Work

- Develop a budget for the following items:
- Design of binders and the material in the binders, such as the DVDs
- Presentation materials, such as PPTs
- Talent for videos
- Recording of video/audio

Done Within The Next Week

- By 11/30/15, produce the proof-version for initial 100 binders, with the DVDs and other training material content for the first three training sessions

- Once proof is ready, get quotes for production
- Leader's Guide #4 complete 11/26/2015

Done Beyond The Upcoming Week But Within The Next 30 Days

- Leader's Guide #5 complete 12/3/2015
- Videos 4-6 to be recorded 12/14/2015
- Leader's Guide #6 complete 12/10/2015

Low Priority

- Videos 7-9 to be recorded 1/11/2016
- Leader's Guide's #7 complete 12/17/2015
- Leader's Guide's #8 complete 12/31/2015
- Leader's Guide's #9 complete 1/7/2016

DAILY UPDATE FOR PERSONAL USE

This Priority To-Do List, with its five categories for priorities, needs to be updated before each weekly meeting with your KDM. For your own best use of time, update the list for your next day at work at the end of each day. This small investment of your time in keeping your To-Do-List up to date will give you a big return of available time in which to conjure the energy and creativity needed for you to make the highest possible impact for your organization.

In determining your priorities for what tasks need to be done each day, ask yourself which tasks, when completed, will bring about the greatest results. Your answer to this question will help clarify the priority of different tasks. I find that getting the most undesirable task accomplished first relieves much of the dread of doing an undesirable task, and allows me to look forward to the rest of the day. You may be able to take advantage of the same approach.

A SAFE ENVIRONMENT WHERE YOU CAN DISCUSS PROBLEMS

Another major advantage of the weekly Plan and Priority Review is worth discussing here. There may be sensitive concerns about areas of potential weakness or other problems in the organization, topics you should discuss with your KDM but are not likely to bring up in a setting in which other DRs are present.

KNOW WHEN TO SPEAK UP

This weekly one-on-one meeting is a time when you can tactfully bring up something involving another DR that you might be hesitant to bring up at a group meeting. The potential issues requiring private discussion are legion, and might range from cultural and performance issues to potentially serious questions of legal liability, such as accusations of sexual harassment.

Sometimes this will be difficult. Yet, as a high-impact contributor, you should be prepared to raise difficult issues, even issues involving the performance of DRs, especially when not speaking up runs the risk of allowing the KDM to make a decision that is not in the best interests of the organization.

It would be ideal if these kinds of situations and threats to the organization were easily shared in Strategic Leadership Team Meetings, but in the real world that's unlikely to be the case, particularly when the person who is causing the problem is present. If circumstances warrant, you must use this private meeting to bring up important, sensitive concerns you feel shouldn't be discussed publicly.

KEY CONCEPTS

Tactfully, persistently engage with your KDM to schedule a weekly one-on-one Plan and Priority Review with you.

Create a uniform Project Plan template that is relevant to your working environment. Use it to create at least one and not more than five Project Plans that connect to projects for which you are personally responsible. Identify the relevant Tactics that support each of your plans, and prepare to discuss these Project Plans one-on-one with your KDM.

Do all the up-front work necessary to make this meeting as efficient as possible. Ask yourself: "What does my KDM need to know, and what do I need to be ready to discuss, so we don't waste everyone's time?"

Your Project Plan is not the same thing as your Priority To-Do list. The Project Plan lays out what is to be done. Your Priority To-Do List identifies what, specifically, you will be doing next! Your KDM needs to be part of that conversation as well. Ask for feedback on your updated list of priorities.

If circumstances warrant, you can also use this private meeting to bring up sensitive concerns you feel shouldn't be discussed publicly.

HOMEWORK: PROJECT PLAN EXERCISE

1. List the Projects on which you are focusing.
2. Narrow down your list to only those Projects of the greatest importance.
3. Select the most important—no more than five—of your Project Plans
4. Complete written Project Plans using the criteria and template approach shown in this chapter.

During the next week, have a one-on-one meeting with your KDM to review the Project Plans for which you are responsible.

HOMEWORK: PRIORITY TO-DO-LIST EXERCISE

- Identify: do a "brain dump" of all your future task items onto a master Priority To-Do-List file.
- Completely eliminate from your To-Do List tasks that have either already been done or no longer need to be done.
- Next, identify items that probably do not have to be done in the next twelve months.
- Put a check mark next to all of the remaining tasks you absolutely have to get done the following day.
- Then put a circle mark next to all the items you absolutely have to get done within the next week.
- Finally, during the next week, break down your final items-to-be-done list into smaller, day-to-day lists for the week based on priority status. Spread these items out on a day-to-day basis. Not one of the days should have more than ten items that need to be done that day.

During your one-on-one meeting with your KDM, review your updated Priority To-Do List and ask for suggested changes.

CHAPTER 4

Align on Weekly Strategic Leadership Team Meetings

EXECUTIVE SUMMARY FOR THE KEY DECISION MAKER

Can you think of any team sport in which the most successful team in the league never holds any kind of all-team meeting? I can't. Pick any sport in which members of a team have to interact with one another to achieve victory: football, baseball, basketball, hockey, cricket, you name it. Now think of the reigning champion within that sport. Did they hold meetings to prepare for an individual game? Of course!

We find that most private organizations whose **Direct Reports (DRs)** have not completed the **Alignment** process, do not hold meetings that support the strategic leadership of the organization. Many of the leaders of those organizations imagined they were using meetings as a strategic tool to support their enterprise; in reality, they weren't. Yet, by following the guidelines laid out in this chapter, they were able to change course and attain "major league" results.

Upon completing this chapter your DR will begin a major undertaking, one that must have your support and blessing: launching a "team meeting makeover" initiative that creates Alignment between you and all your DRs. A **weekly** meeting process separates the champions from the also-rans in virtually any field of endeavor. Fully support that process when your DR shares it with you and asks for your help in launching it!

For a definition of Direct Report and other capitalized terms, see the Glossary (Appendix C).

STARTING OVER

Victorious warriors win first and then go to war, while defeated warriors go to war first and then seek to win. —Sun Tzu, The Art of War

Liv, a DR, mentioned at one of our Alignment training sessions that she was not comfortable expressing her opinions during her team strategy meetings with her KDM, Seth who is a division manager. I asked why.

Liv explained she was reluctant to express her ideas during these team meetings because she was concerned about retaliation from Seth if she made comments about work he or the other DRs had initiated. She was not comfortable disagreeing with anyone in a public setting, much less her boss or colleagues.

Liv also felt there was "no point" in contributing: her ideas had been shot down in the past during one-on-one meetings with her KDM—a sign of what Liv called a "culture that rejects innovation." Good ideas were ridiculed or (worse still) ignored. She was sure that no action would be taken on any of her ideas, even if she did work up the nerve to express them during the team meeting.

After hearing her concerns, I explained to Liv that her division was starting over. Her KDM had hit the "reset" button. He had only recently made the decision to conduct these **Strategic Leadership Team Meetings**. Previously, Seth had held meetings on an "as needed" basis with each of his DRs, but had held no meetings in which they all sat down together, and certainly nothing that was scheduled regularly.

The dynamic for these new meetings, I assured Liv, was very different and could be very positive for both her and her organization. It would, naturally, take a while to get used to the new environment. I suspected that most of the barriers she was experiencing, however, were self-imposed. By taking time to communicate with her boss about how she felt, she would be able to remove some of those self-imposed barriers.

I encouraged Liv to share her feelings about the meeting process—privately, during a one-on-one session with her KDM. She promised to do that.

At the next Alignment training meeting, we learned that Seth had given Liv his personal assurance that she would not have to worry about any retaliation if she expressed ideas that related to his work, or to the work of any of the other DRs or departments. In fact, at the next team meeting, Seth made a point of letting all the members of his executive team know that their feedback mattered to him, and that he would try to quickly implement any and all ideas he felt could be beneficial to the division with practical follow-up and/or changes.

Liv now reports that, after a full year of executing the Strategic Leadership Team Meeting principles laid out in this chapter, Seth lets team members know exactly where he stands on the suggestions he hears from them. There have never, to her knowledge, been any adverse consequences to anyone for sharing ideas during these meetings.

When Seth decides not to go along with a suggestion, he follows up with an explanation of why he didn't use the idea. In some cases he has let the team know that while the idea itself was good, the timing was wrong. He explains the timeline he envisions. This is a common (and quite sound) approach to addressing the good ideas that arise during Strategic Leadership Team Meetings. Very often the implementation of changes must be put off for a while in order to take root and be effective.

The "culture that rejects innovation," that Liv had been so certain of, turned out not to exist. Seth was indeed very interested in good ideas; he gave credit for them where credit was due and was interested in implementing them as soon as it was practical and effective to do so. True to his word, he never subjected Liv or any of the other DRs to any kind of recrimination for speaking their minds.

Most of the obstacles Liv had foreseen in implementing the Strategic Leadership Team Meeting regimen you're about to discover turned out to be entirely self-imposed. That's why I'm sharing her story with you.

> **Effective Alignment among KDMs and all their DRs requires both: "Weekly Strategic Leadership Team Meetings, and annual retreat meetings with the Strategic Leadership Team.**

The weekly meeting system you will learn about here *works*. It has been proven to work in countless settings and countless different industries.

My experience is that the only time the Strategic Leadership Team Meeting system *doesn't* work is when the KDM and DRs entrusted with implementing it decide to live by their own unwarranted perceptions about its effectiveness! There are indeed some cases of self-fulfilling prophecy when it comes to these meetings but your organization does not have to be one of them.

WEEKLY STRATEGIC LEADERSHIP MEETINGS

You are about to become an advocate for an ongoing series of weekly meetings.

These meetings will require the full attention of your KDM, you, and of the rest of the leadership team.

A consistently high level of **Aligned** communication is not possible without weekly meetings. Weekly team meetings are NOT strategic level type meetings, but are instead focused on tactical issues.

Meeting with your KDM and fellow DRs each week is a time investment essential to Alignment of the team and, by extension, the enterprise. Starting this practice of scheduling team meetings should be done as soon as possible. It requires a very modest time investment and offers greatly improved Alignment.

If these weekly meetings are not happening now—and at most of the private organizations we survey, they are not—then it is time for you to start advocating on their behalf!

Who Should Attend Strategic Leadership Team Meetings?

The Strategic Leadership Team should be a group limited to the KDM and the KDM's most important DRs. An employee who reports to a DR should never serve on the team, although these employees may briefly attend the team meetings to give reports and answer questions. If a non-DR member were placed on the team, the DR to whom the non-DR reports would not be able to discuss matters openly. Team members must be peers who can support each other and trust each other's discretion.

Consider, for example, the potential conflict and disruption to the team if both the Vice President of Marketing and the Director of Marketing (who reports to the VP) were to be placed on the Strategic Leadership Team. If the VP wanted to discuss a performance problem of the subordinate, or vice versa, there would be no chance for honest communication.

The team should be limited, ideally, to not more than six people, all of whom report directly to the KDM. I am assuming that you are one of those six. Other people, however, may be invited to attend portions of team meetings, as needed, to share their views and provide feedback on specific areas. Occasionally, organizations have attempted to conduct these meetings with more than six DRs. The results are usually mixed, and I do not recommend a higher number. I recall one KDM attempting to oversee a very chaotic meeting involving ten DRs. The session was less productive and more stressful than it needed to be. An argument can be made that, if there are more than six DRs reporting to the KDM, then there are too many DRs—but that is another topic.

"DON'T WASTE MY TIME!"

One of the biggest complaints employees have about any kind of organization meeting is that of wasted time. Most of these complaints are valid. This is a big part of the reason the number of people in the room should be kept comparatively small, and no non-team member employee should be invited to attend an entire group meeting if that person is only going to be involved in a small portion of the topics being discussed. The team should be small enough and the topic list relevant enough to keep any single member from feeling bored or excluded.

Understanding Your Team Role

All Strategic Leadership Team members need to clearly understand their roles. To bring about this clarity, consider working with your KDM to develop a Strategic Leadership Team charter, such as the following:

"To facilitate success, you, as a member of the team, need self-discipline, perseverance and an ability to focus on what is most important for the organization. You must direct your energies to satisfying the Organization's Critical Success Factors, particularly the Driving Critical Success Factor. No matter how many important day-to-day areas need to be addressed, you have to focus on those areas that most impact the Driving Critical Success Factor. This focus will give you improved, directed energy that will increase your productivity in areas that lead the organization towards attaining its long term vision."

TEAM MEETINGS AND THE CRITICAL SUCCESS FACTOR

Critical Success Factors are objectives that are so essential to your enterprise's success that your organization will not succeed without attaining them.

The most important of these factors is the **Driving Critical Success Factor**, or DCSF.

Following are ideas that will help you and your fellow team members clarify your roles and create a **Manifesto** relevant to your enterprise; one that supports the attainment of your Critical Success Factors. These ideas will shed more light on what you all have a right to expect from the Strategic Leadership Team Meetings you attend.

> **Critical Success factors are always important topics of discussion at Strategic Leadership Team Meetings.**

Team Meetings Should Be Confidential

Information discussed at the KDM/DR meetings must always be held as confidential.

Choosing to confide in a fellow DR always has the potential to create an uncomfortable situation. Brian, a DR attending what he thought was a confidential team meeting, spoke about his dislike for the operations manager, one of his subordinates, and also about the stress level involved in dealing with him. Another DR shared this confidence with one of his subordinates, who in turn told the operations manager. Breaches of trust such as this make the meeting process less effective, and take the entire team out of Alignment.

Team Meetings Should Serve as a Sounding Board and Promote Accountability

All members of the team should be able to look to their fellow DR team members to be their sounding board and help keep them accountable to their plans.

As a team member, you should expect to be challenged. Your fellow DR team members understand the dynamics of the organization. As peers you respect, they should be free to offer advice and differing perspectives. They are there to share your challenges and problems, and the joy of success.

One of the key roles of team members at weekly meetings is to challenge **Organization Action Plans** and **Tactics**. You are not meant to blindly agree with everything. Members must openly and honestly express their views. Don't make the mistake of being a team member who is a "rubber stamp" or "yes man". Team members must feel comfortable sharing differing views about both strategic priorities and tactical decisions.

TEAM MEETINGS AND THE "YES MAN" PROBLEM

The "yes-man" effect is all too common with some DRs, especially those not yet familiar with the dynamics of Strategic Leadership Team Meetings. When you, as a fellow DR, see this happen, think about how you can best get your fellow DR to understand that challenges to ideas expressed at the meetings are both welcomed and expected.

> A good question to pose about one's own projects during team meetings is: "Is there any room for improvement here?"

Weekly team meetings provide all in attendance with a constant flow of information. It's up to the team members to understand how useful the information is to them and to appreciate when they need to act on it.

Team Meetings Should Follow Basic Etiquette Rules of Courtesy and Respect

Team members must adhere to shared etiquette rules, such as the following:

- Interrupting other team members is not acceptable.
- Comments should be given in a way that does not stifle others from giving their views.
- Verbal attacks are prohibited.
- Being defensive (e.g., excuse-making, finger-pointing to deflect blame) is not productive.
- Raised voices or yelling is not permitted.
- Checking of email, text messages, or other digital communication platforms is not permitted during the meeting. Neither is making or receiving calls on cell phones. Wait for the break. To avoid interruptions of the meeting, consider placing a "do not disturb" sign on the meeting room door.

This last point of etiquette is particularly important. It is essential that you, your KDM and your fellow DRs each fully commit—meaning with 100% undivided attention—to focusing exclusively on what is happening in the team meetings. This standard needs to be enforced and *followed* by the KDM. **One of the worst examples of poor team meeting management is when the KDM partakes in non-emergency, non-meeting-related messages, emails and calls during the team meeting.** DRs should tactfully engage to at least attempt to redirect this behavior wherever and whenever it is possible.

During one Alignment training session, Tony, a DR, mentioned that he and his fellow DRs had faced a major challenge at their first Strategic Leadership Team Meeting: they did not have the attention of their KDM, Emily. Despite ground rules being established ahead of time, Emily reviewed her emails throughout the meeting. Both her cell phone and computer were constantly in use with incoming and outgoing messages, all of which Emily excused with the magic phrase "this is important." Tony shared his belief that the team meeting was mostly a waste of everyone's time, due to the fact that Emily did not give her undivided attention to the task at hand. In a one-on-one meeting, Tony discussed the issue tactfully with Emily, and her behavior changed during the next Strategic Leadership Team Meeting. **The process simply cannot work unless everyone, including the KDM, gives it undivided attention.**

Weekly Team Meetings Should be Conducted at a Brisk Pace

Small and mid size organizations need to react faster, with more flexibility and aggressiveness, than their competition. This requires Alignment at the top. Strategic Leadership Team Meetings need to mirror this requirement and play out at a fast pace.

The pacing of the meeting is more important than you might think. A brisk pace can help bring about the Alignment needed to execute agreed upon changes with a fast reaction time, rather than delaying action or postponing it indefinitely (which is what happens at many organizations where the senior leadership team is out of Alignment).

Team Meetings Must Maximize the Value of the Participants

Most meetings bring the worst out of people, because they are poorly conducted. They often leave participants feeling they have contributed and received little or nothing of value. You can make sure this meeting is different by consciously maximizing your own value and supporting the value of others. **Your perceived value as a team member during team meetings will go up if you:**

- Employ good (non-threatening) eye contact and attentive body language.
- Test your assumptions before you recommend any course of action. When you're assessing a situation, don't assume you have all the right answers.

- Employ the Socratic method of questioning by asking questions that elicit well-thought-out answers instead of "yes" or "no" answers (for example, ask "why" things are not going as planned without trying blame or confront, which can only be counterproductive). Also, ask "what" and "how" type questions because they often elicit fresh ideas.
- Stay "on topic" and help others to do the same. Diversions and side discussions have their place, but not in this meeting. Frequent "off topic" diversions lower everyone's value.

WRITE YOUR OWN CHARTER

The guidelines you've just read have been proven, from direct experience, to support Strategic Leadership Team Meetings. Consider using them as part of a one-paragraph **Charter** that can help to guide and focus your meetings. Share the Charter with your KDM and get his or her feedback.

Let's look now at some of the operational specifics of the weekly team meeting.

What Makes For a Successful Weekly Meeting?

Weekly Strategic Leadership Team meetings are a "thirty thousand foot" reality check. They keep the KDM and all of the DRs in touch with what is happening—or should be happening—in the organization at a very high level. This meeting is not an excuse to review all the operational details of all current projects. If any team member starts going into deep levels of detail, some other team member should tactfully intervene.

This weekly team meeting is a platform for DRs and their KDM to share concise summaries of the situations they feel their fellow DRs and the KDM need to know about and talk about. Although the weekly meeting must, by definition, address some tactical issues, the purpose of this meeting is NOT to delve into all the details and resolve narrowly defined, "granular" operational problems. This session must not turn into a "rat-hole" meeting—where the team spends a great deal of time drilling down into minutiae, and suddenly two and a half hours have passed with only a fraction of the agenda items having been addressed. The facilitator needs to be vigilant (particularly during the first few meetings) about the importance of a) keeping the discussion on a high level, and b) making sure everyone stays engaged.

This meeting is about updates, yes, but it is also about creating appropriate, high-level solutions within an accelerated, real-time setting. With this much "fire-power" assembled in one room, it would be a lost opportunity not to create such solutions!

Therefore, each Weekly Strategic Leadership Team Meeting has a twofold objective:

1. Primary objective: share status updates on key initiatives.

2. Secondary objective: make decisions or resolve issues on high impact initiatives.

IMPORTANT: If an issue or question excludes most members of the team, and consumes a significant portion of the time allotted for discussion, then, by definition, it is not "high-impact"

If the discussion ever veers into a protracted "problem solving" mode that leaves most members of the team staring at the ceiling, then the facilitator must intervene and change course.

SCHEDULE A FOLLOW-UP MEETING!

These follow-up meetings may include some members of the Strategic Leadership Team. It is extremely important to respect the time of team members so they do not get "drafted" for problem-solving (or ignored while someone else solves a problem) during the weekly meetings.

> **Weekly meetings are not intended to solve "granular" problems, but often clarify the need for in-depth follow-up meetings to solve specific problems.**

Keep It High-Level

The topics the KDM and DRs present during this meeting should help all team members to become familiar, at a *high level*, with what the other team members are doing. They should give the opportunity for all team members to share their thoughts about what is working and not working within the organization. You'd be surprised at how often people in this elite group of senior managers have absolutely no idea what's going on in other departments!

Over the years, while sitting in on these weekly team meetings, I have frequently heard the comment, "Oh, I didn't know that was happening," or some similar statement. You will probably hear something like this—and say it—at your own weekly meeting.

You should be prepared to find out just how much you didn't know. It's more than you think. You should also be prepared to ask questions like, "How does that fit in with our Driving Critical Success Factor?"

The Weekly Meeting Must Go On

Strategic Leadership Team Meetings are an essential Alignment tool and must be treated as a high priority commitment by you, your KDM, and any other DRs who are invited to participate. It is essential that team members not miss weekly team meetings without a very good excuse. Attending these meetings faithfully needs to become part of the organization culture—for the KDM and the DRs.

There may be rare circumstances, such as severe weather, or other emergencies, that keep the meeting from taking place during a given week. But the Weekly Strategic Leadership Team meeting should never be canceled two weeks in a row.

On the rare occasions your KDM is unable to lead the weekly meeting, **the meeting must go forward anyway.** It should be facilitated by you or another DR designated by your KDM.

The selected facilitator of the meeting should at all times act on behalf of what he or she believes to be the views and values of the KDM. After the meeting, the facilitator should give the KDM a summary of the key issues discussed, and all the situations where the presiding DR tried to act in accordance with the KDM's values. This philosophy of facilitating is important, because it will help bring about a feeling on the part of your KDM that things are being handled as they should. **In the KDM's absence, the watchword should be, "What would my KDM do, say, or decide in this situation?"**

Your Time in the Spotlight

Each week's team meeting has one member with allocated time to share updates and major non-project activities with other team members. I call this time designated specifically for these updates "the **Spotlight Update.**" The **Spotlight** time does more than just keep other team members in the loop. It also brings about in-depth discussion relating to the updates and greater personal accountability regarding progress with **Project Plans** and major non-project activities.

Alignment on a culture of self-accountability cannot happen if DRs feel that certain DRs are not held accountable. Ignoring these violations destroys the desired Alignment with a self-accountable culture, regardless of what your KDM says he/she wants the culture to be. The Spotlight update is an effective method to build Alignment in this area.

Accountability helps build Alignment

The weekly Spotlight Updates should be on a regular scheduled rotation among all the Strategic Leadership Team members, including the KDM, so everyone knows well in advance when they will be "in the Spotlight."

Prior to the meeting, the team member giving this update, or the "Spotlight member," should distribute a spreadsheet identifying each of the high level activities for which he or she is responsible, as well as some of the most important related Tactics. This information should indicate the completion dates and whether each Project Plan or activity listed has a high, medium, or low impact on attaining one of the organization's Critical Success Factors, and if so, which one.

When preparing this spreadsheet for your Spotlight Update, meet with the parties who are driving specific Tactics that connect to the Project Plans for which you are responsible, and get an update on their progress. You need the "thirty-thousand foot view" from them so you can share it with the Strategic Leadership Team when you are in the Spotlight.

> **If it's your turn to be "in the Spotlight," be prepared!**

The Weekly Agenda

Prior to the weekly meeting, some team members may request that topics they feel warrant a high-level discussion be added to the agenda. To manage these requests, your KDM should select one person to create the Weekly Strategic Leadership Team Meeting agenda. This person will be responsible for keeping track of the requests, reviewing them with the KDM, and updating the agenda as necessary.

The meeting agenda, following the format outlined below and with clear time allotments for each item, should be distributed to all team members twenty-four hours before the team meeting. This provides time to review and/or offer changes or additions to the agenda items.

Let's look at the agenda format of the Weekly Strategic Leadership Team Meeting:

1. One team member should be responsible for keeping track of the specific commitments made during the meeting. At the beginning of the meeting this person, the scribe, reviews commitments from the previous team meeting. This is followed by a very brief report by the responsible parties on the status of the commitments. This brief status report 'closes the loop' for commitments made. This should take about one minute per update.

   The scribe maintains the commitment list by deleting completed commitments and adding any new commitments made during the current meeting.

2. Next is the **Spotlight Update** by the Spotlight member. The update and related discussions should never be more than forty-five minutes.

   The Spotlight member should update the status of his or her major Project Plans, as well any major non-project activities that are designated as "high impact", on the spreadsheet prepared for this update. The Spotlight member should also refer to any parties who are driving key Tactics within that activity or project plan.

   After the update, the facilitator of the team meeting should call for comments and facilitate discussions by the team. These discussions should be interactive and focused specifically on the high-impact topics *directly* related to the Spotlight Member's update. If there is time available after these discussions, within the allotted Spotlight time block, the Spotlight member can briefly discuss the status of medium and low impact items shown on his or her spreadsheet.

Discussions relating to points brought up during the Spotlight often result in ideas or questions that may not have been brought up or discussed previously. For example, a team member may ask the Spotlight member who gave an update why he or she thinks certain specific projected results for Project Plans in his or her area of responsibility aren't tracking as projected.

3. **Brief update from each team member** on issues he or she feels other team members should be aware of, and opens the discussion on items they requested to have added to the current meeting's agenda. Time varies with the need for discussion.

4. **Identify the following week's Spotlight member**, who will give the next Spotlight Update.

5. Before the meeting concludes, each member should share the most important "**takeaway**" that he or she received from the meeting. This brief statement should take no more than thirty seconds. Here are some examples of what good takeaways might sound like:

I didn't understand some of the key dynamics of the program until I heard the measurable benchmarks we discussed today.

I didn't know about all of the items that John had on his plate, and now that I know, I think I have some information that will help him with some of those items.

While not part of the weekly meeting agenda, the scribe's final responsibility for the meeting is to distribute the updated commitment list to team members within twenty-four hours of the team meeting.

Facilitating the Weekly Team Meeting

At most organizations, Weekly Strategic Leadership Team Meetings are scheduled for a maximum of two and a half hours, at the same set time and day of the week (for instance: each Tuesday afternoon, from three to five-thirty). An efficient facilitator will make sure the weekly team meeting always starts on time, even if a member is late. Timeliness should become part of the organization culture, and it should begin (and be reinforced) with this weekly meeting.

A "constructive feedback culture" must also be established during these meetings, a culture in which suggestions are welcomed and rewarded. One essential way for this to happen is for the

> The Spotlight time block should never get bogged down with excuses or defensiveness regarding timeliness that are not being met; the motto here is "just the facts."

meeting facilitator to encourage team members to give feedback, and praise and compliment them each time they do.

A "get to the point" culture is just as important to encourage and reinforce during these meetings. The facilitator must tactfully keep attendees from spending too much time sharing too many details and discussing minutiae.

Even if your KDM is serving as facilitator, you can help keep these meetings on track. At one organization's Weekly Strategic Leadership Team Meeting, Frank, the director of the sales division (a DR), brought in a spreadsheet with the names of fifteen to twenty key accounts that required special action. Creating awareness of the situation at this meeting was correct. Unfortunately, the "awareness" led to a lengthy discussion involving Frank, the KDM, and two other team members about the history and future prospects of only five of these key accounts, a discussion that eventually grew to embrace tactical issues, allocation of resources, and complex decisions about who would do what and when. The conversation went well beyond its allotted time, and excluded half of the room ... but since it involved the KDM, no one said anything. This discussion was a complete waste of time for the other members of the team.

After thirty minutes, Tara, one of the other DRs, pointed out that this type of discussion should take place at a separate meeting, one limited to those involved in addressing those specific key accounts. **This was exactly what the group needed to hear.** Gary, the KDM facilitating the meeting, recognized what had happened and stopped the discussion, making a commitment to schedule a separate meeting with the DRs involved with this project. It is safe to say that most KDMs will need a polite reminder of the kind Tara gave.

> **The facilitator is responsible for keeping the discussion of agenda items within the time allotment.**

The weekly meetings need to finish no later than the scheduled time on the agenda. If a pattern exists where meetings are not finished by the scheduled time, it's important for the team to discuss the factors that have caused the meetings to run over schedule. Think about such things as whether too many interruptions and conversational "detours" take place, and, if so, who or what needs to change for this pattern to change. **You and your fellow DRs may, at times, need to help your KDM keep attendees on track.**

A Safe Meeting Environment

Many organizations never achieve their true potential because suggestions never make it to the KDM. Why do these suggestions not make it? Because their DRs do not feel safe expressing their opinions.

It's extremely important that, during these scheduled weekly team meetings, DRs feel completely safe in expressing their questions and views, as well as in making any suggestions they feel are appropriate.

> **Some DRs find it less intimidating to express their views in weekly team meetings than in one-on-one meetings, due to a belief that at the team meeting, other DRs will be supportive of their views.**

For some KDMs, it is hard to facilitate in a way that brings about this culture. For certain KDMs, it can be hard to hear DRs challenge their strategies or question what is happening in another department without responding defensively or aggressively. As a DR team member, you should do whatever you can to help your KDM see that when you and your fellow DRs know for certain that even frank suggestions are welcome, you will all be able to contribute more honestly and effectively about what will make the organization succeed. Words like these may help:

"Before I present my views, I want you to know that I consider all of us to be on the same team. I think looking at this situation from different angles will help us make the best decision for the organization."

These are not "magic words," but prefacing sensitive observations with something like this will help you set a good example and point the team in the right direction. A culture of providing a safe environment for team feedback during these weekly meetings will help create the kind of Alignment that will make everyone's work time less stressful and more productive. In fact, a feeling of complete safety and complete confidentiality during these meetings is one of the most important tools for Alignment among the members of the Strategic Leadership Team.

Diplomacy Matters!

An etiquette observation is in order; I am placing it here because it is equally relevant to the environment of the weekly meetings (which we have just covered) and the annual meetings (which we are about to cover).

Your comments and suggestions may involve creative ideas for things that are the responsibility of other DRs, even down to the level of Tactics that are not directly within your area of responsibility. There may be some things you want to express that are simply not suitable for a team meeting. Use discretion; avoid those parts of your report that may be politically charged and not suitable for sharing at team meetings. Part of your decision must be based on your own best-educated guess about how the other DRs will react to what you have to say.

Miriam, a DR, told her **AlignUp** training group about a "bottleneck" she felt had been caused by Vivian, her fellow DR. She felt Vivian cultivated a pattern of delay and inefficiency that impeded the progress the organization needed to make towards achieving its **Organization Strategic Direction** goal.

Miriam told us that during a Strategic Leadership Team Meeting, she mentioned the "obsessively hands on" behavior of the operations manager, who reported to Vivian, was causing the organization's production problems.

She gave as an example that the operations manager had demanded to see the first draft of a set of drawings. The drawings then sat untouched on the operation manager's desk for weeks because he was too busy to look at them. The delay in reviewing the drawings resulted in setting back the production schedule by several weeks. Miriam suggested to the team that someone needed to send the operations manager a message that it was time to change his ways.

Raising the issue during the Strategic Leadership Team Meeting removed the obstacle—the problems with the operations manager vanished—but this progress came at major political cost. Miriam now had to deal with Vivian's resentment at having been made to "look bad" during the meeting (for the record, Miriam informed us she had tried to deal with the issue by means of one-on-one discussions with Vivian for over a year, and had gotten nowhere). Fences needed mending after the meeting, and some long-term diplomacy was in order. Once the air was cleared, Miriam and Vivian became better colleagues, and even allies, but it took some work.

These are the potential consequences of frank discussions during the Strategic Leadership Team Meeting. I mention them not because I believe Miriam did anything wrong—I don't believe she did—but because you should know how complex interpersonal issues can sometimes be with fellow DRs, especially during team meetings.

KEY CONCEPTS

- Effective Alignment among KDMs and all their DRs requires Weekly Strategic Leadership Team Meetings.
- A consistently high level of Aligned communication really is not possible without these meetings.
- Weekly team meetings are NOT strategic level-type meetings, but are focused on tactical issues.
- If your organization does not set aside time for weekly team meetings, it is operating at a significant strategic and competitive disadvantage.

HOMEWORK

- Develop a strategy for advocating on behalf of Weekly Strategic Leadership Team Meetings to begin as soon as possible. These meetings are to be limited to the KDM and the KDM's key DRs—ideally no more than six. Scheduling and managing these meetings, according to the principles laid out in this chapter, is an extremely important personal and organizational Alignment priority. Without them, Strategic Alignment for your organization cannot be fully achieved.

- Before the first weekly meeting, help your KDM become familiar with the guidelines laid out in this chapter. The advice on etiquette and effective facilitation are likely to be particularly important points of discussion.

CHAPTER 5

Align on Annual Strategic Team Meetings

EXECUTIVE SUMMARY FOR THE KEY DECISION MAKER

This month, your **Direct Report** will share certain initiatives concerning a special strategic gathering for you and the other members of your **Strategic Leadership** Team. This is the **Annual Strategic Leadership Team Meeting**, and the key issue this month is to avoid making the most common mistakes regarding this meeting. There are three common errors.

The first mistake is to treat this meeting as being essentially the same as your weekly team meeting. It is not. it must address different issues in an entirely different setting. Its purpose is to allow you to step back from operational details, from the daily task of "putting out fires," and address critical longer-term issues affecting your organization.

The second common mistake is to postpone this meeting until a time when things are less hectic. Things are never less hectic. It is common for organizations to skip this element of Alignment, intending to "come back to it later," and never hold an Annual Strategic Leadership Team Meeting. Don't do that!

The third common mistake is to imagine that you, the **Key Decision Maker**, can facilitate this strategic meeting yourself. In reality, you need someone who is familiar with the process of conducting this meeting, and who has enough distance from your organization to pose important questions that others on the team have not considered. You are too close to the game. Follow your Direct Report's lead when it comes to scheduling and participating in this important meeting, but find a qualified third-party facilitator. Do not try to lead it yourself.

ANNUAL STRATEGIC LEADERSHIP TEAM MEETING

Once a year, the Strategic Leadership Team should meet in an away from-the-office series of meetings that I will refer to as the **Annual Team Meeting**. During the Annual Team Meeting, the team will review, re-examine, and reassess all strategic aspects of the organization's operations. Properly facilitated, this annual meeting brings about a consistently high level of "long term" Alignment that is not possible otherwise. This Annual Team Meeting is an extremely important tool for bringing about, improving, and maintaining Alignment among all organization employees, even though it only involves the DRs who attend the weekly team meetings and the KDM. This meeting sets the course—and the Alignment standards—for the whole organization!

Move Beyond "Putting Out Fires"

The Annual Team Meeting is an opportunity for all members of the Strategic Leadership Team, specifically the KDM, to **get some time away from their day-to-day efforts of "putting out fires,"** and to focus instead on high-level, longer-term strategic thinking. Let me repeat: **this meeting is not about "granular" project plan issues.**

The objectives of this meeting are very different from those of weekly team meetings, which are focused on tactical issues. By definition, Annual Team Meetings are strategically focused. During this meeting, the Strategic Leadership Team has uninterrupted time for significant, deep conceptualization and uninterrupted discussions. These discussions involve looking at, challenging, removing, modifying as needed, and even adding to your organization Critical Success Factors, as well as the **Goals** and **Strategies** of your **Organization Plans**.

The Annual Team Meeting will help your organization respond more creatively, more effectively, and in a more timely manner to the many high level challenges it faces, both inside and outside the enterprise.

"Can We Change Course in Time?"

You've no doubt heard the true story of the Titanic: a collision with an iceberg took the ship that was supposedly unsinkable to the bottom of the Atlantic. If the ship had better information, if the captain had known just a few minutes ahead of time where the iceberg was located, the great vessel could have changed course in time. The decision to change course, however, was made too late.

There's an important lesson here for both KDMs and DRs. **A strategic planning decision that is made too late can be just as bad as a wrong decision.**

Translation: organizations that don't hold these annual meetings, or procrastinate about scheduling them, are less likely to adapt in time to the "icebergs" awaiting them on their journey!

Pre-Annual Team Meeting Protocol

There are a few basic tasks that need to be completed before your Annual Team Meeting can begin.

1. **Determine the Meeting Location**

   Hold your Annual Team Meetings at locations away the office. This is a mandatory requirement!

   This meeting has to take place in a physically different setting from the one where you normally work, even if it is only a mile away. The setting does not have to be exotic, but it must be free from distractions.

   The "away from the office" venue frees the team from day-to-day distractions and allows team members to completely focus their creative energy and attention on the objectives of the meeting. It helps members move past thoughts of other commitments so they can focus, for a limited time, exclusively on *this* commitment tapping into their deepest creative resources to bring new ideas and solutions to the forefront.

   > **Team members are much more likely to avoid conscious or unconscious thoughts about putting out day-to-day "fires" when meeting in an environment that is different than their daily workplace.**

2. **Determine Blocks of Meeting Time**

   Allocate between twelve and sixteen working hours for your Annual Team Meeting. This can be spread over two consecutive full days, or a series of half days. Most effective Annual Team Meetings for small and mid-size organizations take place in a series of half-day meetings. This minimizes any strain that may occur due to the absence of the organization's KDM or any of the DRs—if they miss one meeting, they are likely to be able to get to another one. In larger organizations, the meetings are usually scheduled for one and a half to two consecutive days, at least one of which is a weekend day.

3. **Preparation before Annual Team Meeting**

   Regardless of your job title, you should review all the functional areas of the organization using the questions that appear in Appendix B of this book. Do this several days prior to attending the Annual Strategic Leadership Team Meeting. These questions will stimulate your thinking about issues you will want to discuss during the meeting.

   In addition, each person planning to attend should identify specific ideas and proposals he or she intends to bring up at the team meeting. Before you propose an idea, research whether other organizations (in particular your competitors) are doing things that are in line with the thinking you intend to propose at the meeting. There is much to be learned from looking at both the successes and failures of other organizations.

Of course, all participants should carefully review and reflect upon the organization's current working plans before attending the annual meeting.

Identify and share information relating to your ideas or proposals before the meeting by sending it to all the members of your team to review. This will minimize time-wasting in the meeting while people read the information for the first time. It will also give other team members time to prepare questions, challenges, and suggested changes relating to your ideas and proposals.

4.   **Select the Meeting Facilitator**

Important: The individual who presides over this meeting should be a professional **Facilitator** who is NOT employed by the organization. **Even if your organization KDM is an effective facilitator of group meetings, you should still bring in an outside Facilitator** who does not have a personal stake in the issues being discussed and the decisions being made.

You can secure a professional Facilitator for your meeting through any number of sources. Be sure to share this chapter of the book with your chosen Facilitator well in advance of the meeting. An in-depth discussion of all of the chapter content is essential to the professional who is facilitating your Annual Team Meeting.

THE ANNUAL TEAM MEETING AGENDA

In order for the team to get maximum results from this meeting, the Agenda must follow a specific sequence. This sequence should include all of the following main elements. They are:

- Opening Comments by Facilitator
- Temenos Exercise
- Sharing by Each Team Member of His/Her Behavior Styles and Values
- Discussion of Organization Critical Success Factors
- Discussion of Organization Goals and Strategies—Strategic Direction Initiatives
- Discussion of Project Plans/Action Plans to Achieve Strategies and Ownership of Each Plan—time permitting
- Takeaways

Timing is an important part of the agenda, too. Each element of the meeting should have a target start time and a target end time sufficient for the purpose of that particular section of the agenda. This is not about speed! Even the most creative organizations' leaders are hard-pressed to come up with their best creative ideas, solutions, and methods for "making it happen" when they are working under severe time pressures.

During the weekly team meetings you read about earlier in this chapter, team members typically get used to addressing and resolving issues in a brisk, fast-paced way. That's fine for the weekly gatherings—but this is a different kind of meeting. There is no point setting aside the days and reserving the space if you do not encourage members of the team to take the time necessary for creative thought during in-depth discussions.

> **To allow for creative thought during the Annual Team Meeting, allot sufficient time for in-depth discussions.**

Opening Comments By Facilitator

At the beginning of the meeting, the meeting Facilitator will briefly walk through the Agenda, explaining each Agenda element and briefly describing his or her expectations for the members with regard to their roles and responsibilities at the meeting.

The Facilitator should then make the point that at the end of each discussion area there *must* be Alignment with the decisions the KDM makes after hearing all the points made by team members. That conversation should begin with remarks that sound something like this:

"During this Annual Team Meeting, I expect to get your open feedback. I'm going to listen to what you have to say. We're all going to discuss the various items. Ultimately, Jim (the KDM) may or may not agree with you. But this doesn't mean he hasn't listened. At the end, it's the job of all DRs to get into Alignment with what is decided by your KDM."

The Facilitator must cover another important preliminary issue. **The guidelines for behavior during this meeting must be discussed explicitly, and all participants must agree ahead of time**. Why? Because, unless the Facilitator sets and enforces a hard boundary on the guidelines for mutual respect, you're unlikely to have a good session. To this end, the Facilitator must lay out ground rules, specifically about the use of information technology. Those ground rules ought to sound something like this:

"During our meeting sessions, your computer is to be used only for things directly related to what we're discussing. This may be a Word document you use to keep notes, or it may mean going on the Internet to research something discussed at this meeting. There is to be no looking at emails and other files that aren't related to what we're doing here. There is to be no making phone calls or looking at phones to check who is calling you. There is to be no looking at or sending text messages. Those are the standards I will be holding myself to while we work here, and I expect everyone in this room to show the same courtesy to every other member of the group. That's what mutual respect looks like during this meeting. Can we all make that agreement, to show each other that mutual respect?"

A "reminder" of these ground rules may need to occur during the meeting if violations of this agreement take place. Violations are quite common during the first meeting. Reminders should be issued as soon as the violation happens, rather than waiting until later.

The person who sees the violation, whether it's the Facilitator or any of the team members, should politely but firmly bring to everyone's attention that someone is violating the agreement on Mutual Respect. **It is important that this standard be applied equally, to all members of the team.**

Facilitator Conducts Temenos Exercise

The annual meeting must support an atmosphere of complete openness that encourages members to speak frankly and honestly with each other—an environment that unleashes the inventive genius inside each member. A key prerequisite for creating this type of atmosphere is for the Facilitator to set openness and mutual support as a clear expectation during the initial stages of the meeting. The best way to do this is to conduct what we refer to as the Temenos* exercises, which help team members lower their "verbal armor" during the meeting. The Facilitator must conduct these exercises very early in the meeting or, where appropriate, review past agreements arising from them if everyone in the room has previously conducted the exercises.

You will find instructions for conducting Temenos communication exercise in Appendix A of this book.

Sharing by Each Team Member of His/Her Behavior Styles and Values

After the Temenos session, the Facilitator will allow each team member a little time to discuss his or her basic behavior style and motivators. This sharing will help you adapt how you communicate at the meeting with other team members, based upon their respective behavioral styles and values. You will recognize, for example, such things as who has a dominant nature and who is reserved; who is very process-oriented and who is not.

There are many computerized assessment programs that will identify this information. These are easily researched on the web. I recommend one of the many so-called DISC programs for behavioral surveys, which identify on a scale of 1 to 100, the natural and adaptive style of each person relating to Dominance, Influencing, Steadiness, and Compliance. I also recommend the

---

*   See glossary for definition and Appendix C for further information on Temenos

use of one of the available surveys that help you identify personal motivating factors such as personal Interests, attitudes and values.

At Team Meetings, I recommend a placard be created for each team member that concisely summarizes each member's DISC natural behavior styles, as well as the members' top two personal motivators. Whether you use a DISC based survey or any other survey system, each team member should share these types of interpersonal dynamics so all team members can better understand the distinctive blend of personal motivators and communication styles unique to each team member.

The following is an example of how this can be handled with a brief introduction at the beginning of the meeting:

> "My natural D (for dominance) is a 37, I (influencing) is 54, S (steadiness) is 69, and C (compliance) is 47. My top motivating values that drive me are theoretical and aesthetic."

When communicating with someone with those types of DISC numbers and motivating factors, try to take your time when communicating, be clear, keep things in order, and leave time for questions.

Discussion of Organization Critical Success Factors

As a step towards identifying the organization's Critical Success Factors (CSFs), the Facilitator should start by asking each team member to share what he or she believes to be one of the **Organization Strengths**. This is followed by each member sharing one **Organization Weakness**. Then each member shares one **Organization Opportunity**, and finally each member shares one **Organization Threat**. It is very important for team members to have a real handle on the organization's Strengths, Weaknesses, Opportunities and Threats (**SWOT**).

The scribe of the meeting should identify all of these SWOT points on large sheets of a flip chart. The sheets should then be torn off and affixed to a wall for a team discussion of the organization's SWOT points. The sheets should remain visible throughout the meeting because they help team thinking when discussing your organization's Critical Success Factors (CSFs) and other topics that arise during the annual meeting.

Your organization CSFs must be conceptual, non-measurable factors that are truly critical to the success of your organization, such as "improve the organization infrastructure to support greater growth." If your organization Critical Success Factors have been previously identified, it is time for the Facilitator to hand out hard copies of all the current written organization Critical Success Factors. But remember: this discussion of organization CSFs needs to be based upon the realities that exist as of the day of the meeting. **Team members should not lock themselves into the view that the CSFs in existence prior to the meeting will**

be exactly the same as those that exist as a result of the CSF discussions.

The Facilitator, after emphasizing this point, should request round-robin contributions from each member of the team as to what each member feels are the Critical Success Factors currently facing the organization. Since your organization Goals are intended to satisfy organization Critical Success Factors, you should take some time to properly discuss and evaluate the suggested CSFs. Consensus should emerge as to the most important CSFs.

After your team has mutually agreed upon no more than three to five organization CSFs, it is time for the team to discuss and identify which of the CSFs should be your organization's **Driving Critical Success Factor** (DCSF). The **DCSF** is the organization CSF that is most critical to the success of your organization. The organization DCSF should be your organization's most important, dominant, and overarching Critical Success Factor.

Changing organization factors, such as the emergence of a major new competitor, may require removal or revision of one or more organization CSFs. This may lead to a change to the organization's DCSF.

Identify the Organization CSFs and the Organization DCSF.

Every team member at the annual meeting must be clear on and in full Alignment with the answer to this question: "What, specifically, are our Critical Success Factors, and what is our organization's Driving Critical Success factor?"

Discussion of Organization Strategic Direction Initiative: Goals and Strategies

Now is the time to identify no more than five organization Goals that each lead to achieving one of your organization's CSFs. Ideally there should only be one Goal for each CSF. The first Goal the team focuses on should support the attainment of the DCSF to be achieved. There will typically be many alternative Goals suggested by team members, followed by discussions that will narrow it down to only one Goal for achieving the DCSF. Once this Goal for achieving the organization DCSF has been identified and agreed to by the team, the team will focus on identifying the conceptual strategies necessary to achieve that Goal. What financial and human resources must be allocated or added? What additional skill-sets are needed to attain the Goals?

There are also likely to be in-depth discussions on whether to eliminate one or more of the organization Goals that have been previously identified but have not been achieved. Of course, once a previously identified Goal has been achieved, the Strategic Plan focused on that Goal will be eliminated.

After extensive discussions, the team, including the KDM, should agree to the exact language of each written organization Goal before starting the discussion on Strategies for achieving each Goal.

ANATOMY OF A DRIVING CRITICAL SUCCESS FACTOR

- The Goal and its Strategies relating to a specific CSF together make up an **Organization Strategic Direction Initiative.**
- At a later time, Project/Action Plans will be added to the Strategic Direction Initiative.
- The Strategic Direction Initiative plus the Project/Action Plans collectively make up each of your Organization Strategic Plans.
- These Project/Action Plans are essential to making the Strategic Plans happen.
- The Project/Action Plans will be discussed later during the Annual Team Meeting.
- Each Organization Strategic Plan should lead toward satisfying a specific
- The most important Strategic Plan—the one you create or refine first—should lead to the fulfillment of your organization's Driving Critical Success Factor.

> **The fewer Organization Strategic Plans a small or midsize organization is working on at one time, the more likely it is the organization will accomplish them.**

AVOID LOCKING ONTO THE PAST

Discuss in depth what has worked—and what hasn't—during this annual meeting. Modify strategies as needed, so that strategies that created failure in the past are not repeated. These kinds of intelligent "course changes" are a major benefit of the discussion time allotted.

The team should discuss, in depth, the important question of whether the time and energy being spent on a current Strategic Direction Initiative could be better invested in accomplishing one or more other organization Strategic Direction Initiatives that might be more important. The team may, upon review, determine the organization simply does not have the resources needed to focus on all the current organization Goals, and may decide to eliminate one or more Goals.

Adding a new Strategic Direction Initiative is serious business. The team should only add a new Strategic Direction Initiative if there are adequate resources to develop a Strategic Plan for it that will succeed.

There are organizations we've worked with that were making great strides in accomplishing a Organization Strategic Plan when they focused on only one at a time, but lost their focus and saw results drop significantly when they added additional Strategic Plans. Your organization should never have more than five organization Goals at a time. With smaller organizations, their chances at succeeding with Goals are greater if they only have one to three organization Goals on which to focus.

New opportunities can certainly be tantalizing, yet your team must consider the limitations of organization resources. Any new opportunity for which a Organization Strategic Plan is developed will require resources: money, additional employees, or new skills to take advantage of the opportunity, to name just a few. The fact that a great new opportunity exists doesn't necessarily mean you should "go for it." The upside must justify diverting resources from other Organization Strategic Plans that have previously been launched—or could be launched now.

No matter how appealing a new opportunity may be, if it diverts your organization from projects that are more critical, don't take it on. Shifting resources from a critical area to a new opportunity less critical will have a demoralizing, negative "domino effect" throughout your organization.

Discuss The Specific Project Plans/Action Plans

At Annual Team Meetings, if time is available, discuss at the "thirty thousand-foot level" Project/Action Plans needed for satisfying each written organization Strategy agreed to for achieving the corresponding written organization Goal. Focus first on those Project/Action Plans that support the organization's DCSF. If time at the meeting is available, you can discuss Project/Action Plans for Strategies that support other CSFs identified at the annual meeting.

Let me give you an example. Suppose the team agrees on a strategy to "develop a new compensation program to attract more talented salespeople," as a way of achieving a specific department Goal of "increasing next year's sales by ten percent." Assume this goal connects to the department DCSF of "significantly increasing department sales results." The DR to whom the department salespeople and/or sales manager report would typically be the DR taking on responsibility for this Project/Action Plan.

This high-level discussion of an individual Project Plan is like a broad brushstroke on a canvas. That canvas must, after the Annual Team Meeting concludes, be painted in by the responsible DR with finely detailed strokes. After the meeting, the DR responsible will identify the specific Tactics and timelines. In the process, he or she will answer questions such as, "What are the reporting dates necessary to verify the process is moving at an appropriate pace toward its targets?" The detailed Project Plan the DR develops must also identify the measurable results reasonably expected from the project.

PROJECT PLANS/ACTION PLANS

One of the major challenges KDMs commonly face during Annual Team Meetings concerns the allocation of limited organization resources between the DCSF Organization Strategic Plan and the other Organization Strategic Plans. It is important to focus first on resources necessary to satisfy the

organization DCSF so you know what
resources are available to satisfy other
CSFs. You will not know how much
time and resources need to be devoted
to achieving the organization's DCSF
Plan until all strategies have been developed and the Project/ Action Plans that
support those Strategic Initiatives have
been created.

> **The KDM has final decision making authority for every key area resolved at the annual meeting, however, it is imperative for Alignment that every DR on the team be included as part of the decision making process.**

Each team member should closely
consider the amount of time and
resources that need to be devoted to
the individual Project/Action Plans for
which he or she will be responsible. From a practical standpoint, this information will not be fully known during the annual meeting. There will be discussion to flesh out the Project/Action Plans between the DR and the KDM at
their one-on-one weekly meeting, which takes place after the annual meeting.

If there are not sufficient resources available after considering what is needed
to succeed with the Strategic Plan, the organization may not be able to handle
other Project or Action Plans.

On Adding a New Organization Strategic Plan

When the KDM and the team are ready to add a new organization Strategic
Plan, they should be sure to create it in the same way all good organization
Strategic Plans are created—by identifying the Goal of the Plan then identifying the Strategies necessary to achieve the Goal. The team should also look
closely at which Goals, if any, need to be changed, and if so, changed to what?
Sometimes the timing for achieving the Goal turns out to be wrong. During the
meeting, the team needs to be open to the possibility of revisiting and changing
timelines in Goals as needed. Such changes will, of course, lead to discussions
about what new organization Plans need to be developed.

No ideas should be discouraged; everything a team member wishes to share
during this part of the meeting should be shared, big or small, brilliant or less
brilliant. No one should score points at anyone else's expense during this discussion. Remember, creative ideas don't always have to be astonishing, brilliant,
or world-changing. They can be practical and built on a small scale and still
be powerful.

Realities of Meeting Dynamics

Final decisions relating to organization Strategic Plans should be based upon
the best possible deployment of human and financial resources. Inevitably,
these kinds of decisions affect different team members differently, because

> **When things are going right at the Annual Team Meeting, team members build on one another's thoughts, bringing about ideas representing collective Aligned thinking, and consensus becomes easy to build.**

they finalize the resources that will be available for their own departments. These discussions may, consequently, become intense. That is okay as long as the intensity remains respectful and all team members have the opportunity to speak freely. This is essential during this critical part of the meeting. A DR can still be committed to Alignment, even if they don't agree with every decision made at the meeting. When discussions are over and the Plans finalized, all team members must be in full Alignment with the finalized Plans, even if individually they would have preferred something different.

Clarity Requires Written Statements

Each factor in an organization's Strategic Plan needs to be clearly and concisely identified in writing. The final wording must be collectively developed and clearly defined to ensure all team members understand the final document. This will minimize or eliminate the possibility of a lack of full support and Alignment.

TAKEAWAYS

The Facilitator closes the meeting with a go-round in which each member briefly shares his or her most significant Takeaway from the meeting experience. Each Takeaway should be concise, as in "thirty seconds or less." An example of such a Takeaway would be, "I have a much better understanding of our Driving Critical Success Factor."

KEY CONCEPTS

A consistently high level of Aligned communication really is not possible without annual strategic team meetings.

The annual team meeting is strategically focused. It allows more time for creative thought and discussion, is held in a different venue, and must be led by an outside Facilitator.

The annual team meeting will help your organization to respond more creatively and effectively to the many changes it faces, both inside and outside the enterprise.

HOMEWORK

Advocate for and get a clear commitment from your KDM to schedule and hold an annual retreat with your organization's Strategic Leadership Team, which of course has to include the KDM. Prior to attending, both you and your KDM should read the guidelines to ensure the Annual Strategic Leadership Team Meeting is successful.

Once you're familiar with the guidelines, establish a process to select a facilitator, then schedule the dates and location for your organization's Annual Strategic Leadership Team Meeting![†]

[†]   Questions that will help you to prepare for the Annual Team Meeting appear in Appendix B.

CHAPTER 6

Align on Working Dynamics

EXECUTIVE SUMMARY FOR THE KEY DECISION MAKER

This chapter of The Aligned Workplace is a little different from the other portions of the book.

In most of the chapters, we begin by briefly summarizing the key takeaways for which your **Direct Report (DR)** will be responsible. Then we outline what your (minimal) time commitments are likely to be in supporting his or her efforts while working on that chapter.

This chapter takes a different approach.

In order to fulfill the critical objectives of this book, it is essential that you BOTH read this chapter in its entirety, and that you BOTH complete the end-of-chapter assignments you will find here. This effort from both sides is necessary in this chapter—because two-way communication and a mutually respectful relationship are the foundation of all the productive achievement you and your DR will collaboratively deliver in the other chapters. In order to work together effectively to support your vision for the organization, you and your DR should invest the time and attention necessary to collaborate and complete what follows to the very best of your ability.

A TALE OF THREE MONOLOGUES

Assumptions are the termites of relationships. —Henry Winkler

I once sat in on a meeting of store managers of a major regional retail chain in the Northeastern United States. These managers had driven in from all corners—some from a significant distance—after receiving an invitation to "discuss an important new strategic initiative" with the founder of the chain. I'll call him Frank.

Frank had launched the very first store in the chain some twenty years earlier, in his hometown. He was extremely proud of the organization he and his team had created over those two decades. According to the e-mail he had sent, Frank had called this meeting for one reason, and one reason alone: to discuss an exciting expansion and promotional plan that he had for the organization, a topic that all nineteen of his managers were eager to explore with him.

Frank opened the meeting by speaking for thirty straight minutes about miscellaneous unrelated issues that had nothing—and I mean nothing—to do with expanding and promoting the chain. He talked about the weather, the planning process for finalizing the location of the upcoming organization picnic, his grandkids, and he talked about why his partner, Bill, could not be in attendance. He talked about baseball. He talked about his early days in the organization. For half an hour, he talked, it seemed, about everything under the sun except the expansion plan the meeting had (supposedly) been called to discuss.

Those thirty minutes were downright deadly for the store managers in attendance. I know. I was there, and I made a point of watching them. As Frank rambled on, you could see some of them fighting to keep their eyes open. By the time he got around to presenting the plan and requesting feedback on it, the store managers' enthusiasm, and level of interest, was just a fraction of what it could have been, and should have been, given the importance of the plans Frank had put together.

* * *

Melanie, a marketing executive in her mid-twenties, proudly boasted that she was "all about connection." Melanie was a true "social media queen," and that was a big part of the reason Tim, the founder and CEO of the advertising agency where she worked, had recruited her. She was to head up the agency's digital communication initiative.

Tim, born in 1955, was only intermittently interested in channels like Facebook and Twitter, but he knew he needed someone with deep social media competency on his team. Tim didn't text. He didn't tweet. And he didn't even know what a blog post was. He was very glad that Melanie did, though.

During Melanie's first week on the job, Tim (who traveled a lot) told her, during their first one-on-one meeting, that he would prefer to keep in touch with her the way he kept in touch with all of his key people. He would leave her voicemail messages. Tim liked to say that his agency lived or died based on whether people had checked their voicemail. That phrase, in fact, was an important part of the onboarding process at the agency Tim led. He made a point, from day one of their working relationship, of sending that signal clearly to Melanie.

Melanie, however, missed that signal.

Correction: she missed part of that signal. She got the part that said she was supposed to listen to her voicemail every day, and she did that, just as instructed. What she had not picked up on, however, was the crucial, unspoken preference Tim had for receiving updates from key staff via voice-mail when they could not reach him voice-to-voice (which was quite oft en).

Melanie, like a lot of people of her generation, considered voicemail kind of old fashioned. She loved to text people. She loved real-time access. She loved to share great ideas in real time, too—the more ideas the better. Now, there's nothing wrong with that instinct in theory. With a younger, more tech-savvy CEO, Melanie's habit of sending her boss ten to twenty text messages a day might have been a perfect fit. With Ted, however, it was not.

Ted quickly "tuned out" her messages, literally ignoring them without reading them. For her first two critical weeks on the job, Melanie assumed that Ted's silence signaled consent with every new initiative she had texted. She soon found out otherwise. In fact, the total absence of response to her texts meant only that Ted was focusing on other issues with other people in the organization—typically, someone who used voicemail as the primary means of interacting with him. This perpetually on-the-go, old-school CEO needed to hear the voices behind the good ideas. Not aware of this, Melanie found herself out of the loop, eventually realizing that her working relationship with Tim had needlessly gotten off to a bad start.

* * *

Chris was a manager of a trucking organization. He had devised a new compensation plan for his 200 drivers, a plan he was certain would not only lead to significant cost savings, but also create a major competitive advantage for his organization. He convened a meeting of five of his DRs to "ask for feedback" on his new plan. After reading the details of his plan, all five executives told Chris that it was unworkable and uncompetitive, would create significant morale problems, and would generate instant mass defections among the drivers. Convinced they were "looking at the glass like it was half empty," Chris informed his DRs that the memo he had distributed outlined a payment system that would reduce labor costs and catapult their firm to the top of the industry. He ignored their objections, ordered the new payment plan implemented exactly as written, and headed off for a one-week vacation that was not to be interrupted—because, he said, he wanted his team to learn to "implement good ideas without wasting energy complaining about them."

When Chris returned a week later, his organization was in crisis. Half the corps of drivers had quit, and finding replacements who would drive the routes under the new compensation system was proving to be a major challenge.

* * *

Frank, Melanie, and Chris all imagined they were engaging in *dialogue*. The dictionary defines a *dialogue* as "**an exchange of ideas and opinions about a particular subject.**"

In reality, these three people were all engaging in the very different activity known as *monologuing*. To *monologue* means to go on and on at length, without requiring a response of any kind from the person, or people, one is addressing.

Unfortunately, it takes conscious effort, and quite a lot of practice, to engage in a true dialogue. It's extremely easy, and takes hardly any effort at all, to start a monologue. You might even say that most of us are preprogrammed to start monologuing. Most of us love to talk. But we shouldn't be under the impression we are communicating every time we do.

There's an old joke that says: "Conversation is more than just waiting for your turn to speak." There's a whole lot of truth to that joke.

MESSAGE IN A BOTTLE SYNDROME

Frank, Melanie, and Chris were victims of a disorder I call "Message In A Bottle Syndrome." This is a mysterious affliction that can disable not just an organization's leaders, but all of those who report to them as well.

You've probably seen at least one "Message In A Bottle Scene" in one of those old black-and-white movies. In these films, someone stranded on a desert island might write down a message, seal it in a glass bottle, hurl it into the ocean and watch the waves carry it away. In the movies, time might be collapsed in some creative way, and we might next see that character standing on the beach when the bottle washes back up on the shore. Who knows how much time is supposed to have passed? Inside the bottle, though, is proof the tactic worked: a written response that says help is on the way. In the movies it might look like a good approach to communication.

In real life, it doesn't work that way.

In real life, we can stand on the beach, throwing bottle after bottle into the waves, and we can wait for years, for decades, for the rest of our lives, even—and get absolutely nothing back. In real life, communication is collaboration. In real life, you need at least one identifiable partner if you want true communication to take place. You need to make sure that the person with whom you're trying to communicate contributes something that constructively affects the direction of the conversation. In real life, a bottle, a piece of paper, a pen, and an ocean are not enough. In real life, you need ears.

If we've got the choice—and most of the time, most of us do—we really don't want to fall victim to "Message In A Bottle Syndrome." If we do, we'll just find ourselves staring at the ocean for hours, wondering why nothing is coming back. What a waste!

GET OFF THE BEACH

This chapter is all about finding better ways to communicate than standing on the beach, throwing bottles into the distant waves.

Now, there are some very simple steps that Frank, Melanie, and Chris could have taken to get off the beach and improve the quality of their communication. I'll share those steps with you in just a moment. Before we review any of that, though, we need to focus our attention on a profound observation about workplace communication. If it is internalized by both the Key Decision Maker (KDM) and the DR, it can keep both of them off the beach, and, in extreme cases, literally save the organization. The saying I'm talking about comes from that noted management consultant, George Bernard Shaw, who said:

The single biggest problem with communication is the illusion that it has taken place.

Shaw might have gotten precisely the same point across, and might have connected it more directly to the experiences of privately owned organizations, if he had said this:

People in low-performing organizations often say they want a dialogue but don't realize they don't really mean that. In fact, what they're actually after is a chance to do some monologuing, even if that monologue is interrupted occasionally by other people monologuing. People in high-performing organizations, on the other hand, tend to MEAN it when they say they want a dialogue.

That paragraph is this whole chapter in a nutshell. Here's an even more concise version of the same principle. If you just remember these three words, you'll be able to stay off the beach and avoid "Message In A Bottle Syndrome" entirely:

MONOLOGUING KILLS ALIGNMENT!

The three examples I've already shared with you—Frank's tedious opening remarks, Melanie's failure to notice that her communication channel was not working, Chris's "request for feedback" that was really a demand for validation—are not the only potential obstacles to effective two-way communication. They are only examples of some of the ways that monologuing can kill Alignment between the KDM and the DR.

ALIGNMENT MEANS TWO-WAY COMMUNICATION

True Alignment between the KDM and the DR, in any and all of the areas discussed in this book, depends on communication. This communication must occur in two directions—not just one. The moment two-way communication stops, Alignment begins to wither and die. If two-way communication is not restored, the death process accelerates.

Let me repeat the point for emphasis: two-way communication does not always come naturally, but Alignment is simply impossible without it.

> **Without two-way communication, Alignment dies.**

What exactly do I mean by "two-way communication"? I mean **the free, respectful exchange of views and opinions—in both directions.**

The challenge we face when it comes to communication is double-edged. First and foremost, the kind of interactive communication that supports Alignment is actually quite rare in the workplace (and elsewhere)—so rare, in fact, that we usually don't get exposure to very good role models in this area.

Second, we often *think* we're supporting the free, respectful exchange of views and opinions in two directions, when we're actually placing obstacles in the way of such communication. Usually, we do this without even realizing. In other words, both the KDM and the DR typically put up unconscious barriers to the free exchange of views and opinions. The result: each side may believe they are *supporting* two-way communication when, in fact, both are simultaneously *sabotaging* it.

As a veteran of this course once put it: **"People barely communicate ... but they don't always realize that."**

OBSTACLES TO TWO-WAY COMMUNICATION

Please note that the three stories I have just shared are not intended as a comprehensive list of communication challenges. There are as many different potential obstacles to two-way communication as there are pairs of people trying to communicate.

Obstacles to communication can, and usually do, arise between KDMs and DRs because of unconscious, subconscious, or semi-conscious choices made by each party. These are choices we make, typically without even realizing it, that sabotage the free flow of ideas and quickly take both sides out of Alignment.

I realize it's possible you just read this part about subconscious or semiconscious

choices with skepticism; it's possible you felt it might be accurate, but it applies to others, not you. If this is how you feel—and rest assured that's how most people feel when I raise this topic for the first time—let me ask you a few questions.

- Have you ever spoken before a group (small or large) and eventually realized your "impromptu" remarks had left the audience feeling restless and disengaged—as Frank's remarks did?
- Have you ever tried to communicate with someone through a particular channel, such as text messaging, e-mail, or printed memo—communication channels that seem perfectly natural to you—but ended up alienating the person with whom you wanted to communicate—as Melanie did?
- Have you ever asked for feedback about something, but then realized you didn't really want to hear it—as Chris did?

Most of us, if we are honest with ourselves, have to answer "yes" to each of these questions (I certainly must). None of these obstacles come about as a result of a conscious choice to make it difficult to communicate with someone else. Yet there they are.

Let me repeat. These obstacles to two-way communication arose not because we wanted them to, but because we built the obstacles into the exchange unconsciously. Once we notice the pattern, then we can do something differently—but until we do notice the pattern, and do something about it, two-way communication suffers.

By the way, if Frank had taken the simple step of **creating and following a concise, bullet-point *meeting agenda***, then shared that agenda with his audience at the very outset of the meeting and stuck to it carefully, he would have done a better job of engaging and winning support from his audience of key stakeholders. Agendas are extremely important in such settings. I'll share some more insights about agendas a little bit later in this chapter.

As for Melanie, if she had **noticed early on that her favorite communication channel was not her partner's favorite communication channel**, she would have gotten her working relationship with Ted off to a much better start. Her first clue should have been that Ted never responded to her texts. Channel selection, too, is incredibly important. We'll cover that subject in more depth a little later in this chapter, as well.

And Chris could have saved his organization, and himself, much difficulty if he had made his request for "feedback" the starting-point for a **true "give-and-take" session about the pros and cons of his plan.** The key to generating this kind of discussion is to learn to follow, and help others to follow, a simple process I call Receive, Internalize, Act. You'll learn about that here, too.

ARE YOU A ROLE MODEL?

In any situation where two-way communication is impaired, it is a mistake to believe that "the other person" is the one who needs to do the work. Specifically, if you are a DR and you know there are communication issues, you can, and should, learn to "coach" your KDM, in subtle, tactful but persistent ways, on processes of communication that support both of you. The best way to "coach" is simply to serve as a good role model for communication—by listening without preconception, for instance, and by changing communication patterns that you know cause others to "don their verbal armor" (the Temenos exercise, discussed later in this chapter, will help you identify what these patterns are).

PUSHING BACK?

At some point in this discussion about two-way communication, I usually get a little "push-back" from the people who have reached this part of the course (more often, truth be told, this resistance comes from KDMs rather than the DRs, for reasons I'll explain in a moment). I'll hear complaints that sound like: "Look—Frank, Melanie, and Chris each made a big communication mistake. I'll buy that these mistakes were unconscious. I'll buy that they were serious. I'll even buy they're the kind of mistakes I might make. But, once I make a mistake, I fix it then move on. Case closed."

Unfortunately, it turns out the case is not quite as open-and-shut as all that.

UNINTENTIONAL BARRIERS

Most relationships between KDMs and DRs are out of Alignment. The single biggest reason for this lack of Alignment is that the relationship is not built on the principle of a free, respectful exchange of views and opinions between the two parties.

The reason they're not built on that principle, more often than not, is that **KDMs put up subconscious or semi-conscious barriers that make it very hard for DRs to share views and opinions without fear of reprisal.**

KDMs do this while maintaining, usually with the very best of intentions, that they're actually promoting good two-way communication. And they are sincere when they say that. The problem is, no matter what they may say out loud, and no matter how deeply they may mean those words about having an open-door policy, wanting to hear all viewpoints, or keeping an open mind, **the words do not match the reality experienced by their DRs.**

These DRs have learned, from careful observation, and perhaps from direct experience, there is a point at which the free expression of their views and opinions is not welcome. They have learned there are subtle signals a KDM sends but rarely acknowledges sending, to let DRs know they have reached that point. This is why I so rarely meet with resistance from DRs when I share the point that **obstacles to two-way communication are often put up without the person creating the obstacle even realizing he or she is doing so.**

DRs have usually seen this pattern play out countless times, witnessing their own KDM "draw lines"—verbally and nonverbally—that shut down communication, even as the KDM professes to support the free exchange of ideas. Let me give you just one extremely common example of this phenomenon before we move on.

It's quite common for a KDM to pose the following query near the end of a topic being "discussed" with a DR: "Are there any questions?" These words, when written on a sheet of paper, would seem to indicate the KDM is trying to determine whether the DR has any unresolved issues he or she wants to discuss. Yet the vocal tonality used by the KDM may send a very different message to the DR: "There had better not be any questions." **The problem is that the KDM may actually believe he or she is supporting an environment in which questions are welcome—when the exact opposite is what the DR actually experiences.**

So now we know: KDMs sometimes send messages that sabotage good communication, messages they often don't realize they're sending. DR's do this too, of course—sometimes while they are face-to-face with the KDM, and sometimes when they are in other settings (such as when they talk about the boss behind his or her back to another employee). It's part of the all-too common pattern of ineffective, and even dysfunctional, communication.

This state of affairs should not come as a huge surprise to anyone. Most employees are trained over a period of months, years, or even decades to assume that "speaking your mind to the boss" can entail significant career risks. Most of the people we see on TV, or in the movies, who tell the boss exactly what's on their minds end up getting fired or quitting.

In most real-life organizations there are complex political and cultural pressures that dictate employees' interactions with the KDM. It makes perfect sense that the majority of DRs would want to avoid exchanges that might threaten their livelihood or future prospects. Often, they simply don't feel safe expressing their views. The result is that communications from the DR to the KDM are usually sanitized, and typically do not accurately reflect the entirety of the DR's feelings or opinions.

Yet KDMs generally do not operate under such restrictions of self-censorship.

In fact, when it comes to communication, most KDMs live on a "one-way street" in which they share insights, ideas, and goals, and DRs say what they think the KDM wants to hear. **Even if the KDM is unaware of this dynamic (which is often the case), it is, nevertheless, the predominant model.**

Yet without open, two-way communication, there is no true empowerment within the relationship on the part of either the KDM or the DR—and no chance for Alignment. Both people are simply standing on separate continents, on different beaches, facing separate oceans, flinging their own bottles into the sea.

For many years, I was asked whether there was a simple way to tell whether a KDM and a DR were in Alignment with each other. It was only recently I realized that, in fact, there is a way to figure out whether the relationship is functioning in a healthy way, at the level of Alignment. When these two individuals are in Alignment, **they both feel enough safety to express their real views and opinions freely to each other.** When they are out of Alignment, a wall arises between them that prevents this free exchange of insights, opinions, and ideas.

Effective two-way communication means you share relevant information with each other in an open, timely, thorough and, of course, honest manner. This helps both parties make better organization decisions and higher-quality contributions to the success of the organization.

In truly high-performing organizations, KDMs and DRs are in Alignment—and you can tell they're in Alignment because of the quality of their communication. You can reach that level of trust and connection, too.

One particularly critical factor that will affect the level of trusting two-way communication in any relationship is the other person's perception of your intentions. So let's begin there.

Choose, right now, whether or not you really do want open, two-way communication with the person who is completing this chapter assignment with you. Are you willing to take the steps necessary to create that bond of trusting, open communication? I hope so.

Only a minority of organizations' leaders are actually willing to take the steps necessary to hear others out, especially when it is obvious there is the possibility of disagreement on something. *Share your intentions verbally with your partner.* State specifically what you want to be different between the two of you once you finish working on this chapter. Use words, spoken out loud, that your partner can hear.

* * *

Once you do that, and follow through appropriately on your verbal commitment to your partner, you will join the ranks of the most effective organizations' leaders. This principle of sharing good intent is a particularly important one for KDMs to observe, though—as with so many aspects of communication—both parties in any relationship can stand to benefit from adopting it. Having stated your intention, of course, you then have to prove it.

You can begin with words. If you are a KDM, you might say, "I want and need two things: your very best effort—and your honest input about the decisions we are facing. If I've ever made it hard for you to share your feelings and opinions about what we're doing, I want you to know it's a priority for me to change that, starting today." Then—back it up.

KDMs can come across as harsh or dismissive when they encounter opinions they do not want to hear. If you are a KDM, plan to reverse that trend. Simply thanking someone for sharing an opinion, or for making an honest effort on your behalf, goes a long way here.

21 WAYS TO SAY "WELL DONE"

Sometimes, offering praise is harder than it should be. In a busy office, it's easy to forget to compliment and voice appreciation. But praise can really make any team-member's day. Here are some reminders of how easy it really is to say, "Thanks; well done."

1. I'm proud you're on my team.
2. Congratulations on a terrific job.
3. You're so helpful. Thank you.
4. You keep improving. Well done.
5. Thanks so much for your consistent effort.
6. 1 really admire your perseverance.
7. Your mood always lifts the team's spirit.
8. You're a champion.
9. Wow, what an incredible accomplishment.
10. Great effort. You make us all look good.
11. I have great confidence in you.
12. You've grasped the concept well.
13. Your customer service skills are sensational.
14. Your sales results are outstanding.
15. You're a valuable part of this team.
16. Your efforts are really making a difference.
17. You are a bonus.
18. You continue to delight our customers.
19. You make the team's vision come alive.
20. Your accomplishments inspire the team.
21. Customers are noticing the efforts you're putting in.

It is just as important to avoid the temptation to criticize, ridicule, or simply ignore a contribution that seems off-base to you—all very common points of complaint and dissatisfaction among the DRs with whom I have spoken.

RECEIVE, INTERNALIZE, ACT

The main goal of all communication in the KDM/DR relationship (or any constructive relationship between peers, for that matter) is for each party to be willing and able to receive a message, take the time to internalize it and then act on it.

That's what "two-way communication" actually means: the willingness to:

1. STEP ONE: receive (understand) and
2. STEP TWO: internalize (consciously consider) the other person's message, and then
3. STEP THREE: take appropriate action on the message—knowing

all the time that the other person is similarly committed to receiving, internalizing and acting upon what you choose to share.

This takes practice. It is not what usually happens in working relationships.

Everyone says open communication is important. A minority of us go out of our way to do what is necessary to support two-way communication. That means memorizing, using, and constantly re-using the simple three-step process I just shared with you. Look at it once again.

STEP ONE: RECEIVE the message. Very often, we rush past what the other person is trying to say so we can get to what WE want to say. The first step in effective two-way communication is to make sure we do the opposite. There are many, many ways to make sure that you receive and actually understand another person's message. All of them involve WAITING and LISTENING, rather than talking about what you wish the other person knew or understood. For instance:

- Frank could have circulated an agenda at the very beginning of his meeting and then asked the group whether they felt anything needed to be added to it.
- Melanie could have asked her boss, early in her tenure, how he felt about receiving text messages.
- Chris could have suggested to his DRs that they begin the meeting by each writing and signing one brief comment about his proposed changes to the compensation plan for drivers. Then he could have read each one aloud for the group as a whole.

Another time-tested strategy for ensuring you have actually received someone's message is to "play back," or restate in your own words, what you just heard the other person say, and then ask whether or not you got it right.

STEP TWO: INTERNALIZE the message. This is probably the most difficult step if you are a newcomer to this process, or are still practicing it. Until it becomes second nature for you to do so, you should make a conscious effort to STOP TALKING and ask yourself, silently, questions like: "What is most important about what this person just told me?" and "Why did this person choose to share this with me?"

So for instance:

- Frank could have carefully considered any suggestions about the agenda his managers had. If one of them mentioned he needed to leave the meeting a little early to attend a family obligation, for instance, Frank would have known how important it was to condense his opening remarks and get right to the point.
- Melanie could have picked up signals from her boss that he had been confused by, and eventually simply ignored, her flurry of text messages.
- After reading each of the initial comments from his DRs out loud, Chris could have stopped to ask himself what was really behind the broad consensus of skepticism he was hearing from his team.

STEP THREE: TAKE ACTION on the message. This means taking appropriate steps to do something constructive with what you have just learned. It does not necessarily mean agreeing with what the other person has just told you (although, of course, it may!). Following this step may mean implementing your decision, postponing a decision until later, thanking the person for sharing his or her views, or any number of other things.

- For Frank, taking constructive action could have meant skipping the chitchat and moving directly into his vision of the chain's next five years, focusing on his expansion strategy and the promotional plan necessary to back it up.
- For Melanie, taking constructive action could have meant changing course by matching her communication strategy to her boss's preference, i.e. leaving him updates via voice mail rather than texts.
- For Chris, taking constructive action could have meant pausing to consider all the implications of his team's objections to the new compensation plan—and tabling its implementation until the plan could be thought through.

IS IT SAFE TO COMMUNICATE?

Trusting, two-way communication is open and regarded as safe by both sides. This kind of trusting interaction only exists when both sides are committed to proving, again and again, that it really is safe for each person to share what is important, and there will be no adverse consequences for sharing. You can improve the level of perceived safety in your discussions by:

Asking the other person what he or she thinks.

Hearing the other person out, at length if necessary, before attempting to close the subject.

Thanking the other person for sharing opinions that differ from your own, and meaning it.

Explaining exactly what actions you plan to take now that you have heard and internalized what the person shared with you.

"WHAT DO YOU THINK?"

Wherever and whenever it seems appropriate, ask what the other person thinks, listen carefully to their answer and comment respectfully on whatever you hear.

If you show people you care enough about them to actually process and internalize what they say before moving on to the next item on your own list, you will prove you trust and value their thoughts and ideas. You will demonstrate you are, indeed, committed to establishing a functional two-way relationship. They will be able to trust that they do not need to fear being open with you, and they will also know you will have no hesitation about being direct and respectful with them.

Once you have established this trust, you must never betray it.

By the way, there are also cases where one-way communication arises because KDMs are simply not clear enough. Often, this happens because they do not want to offend or belittle an employee by asking one or two additional questions. They may feel that being "too direct" or "too specific" about every little detail would make the DR feel uncomfortable. As a result, they may over-rely on phrases like "You know what I mean," and be genuinely surprised when it eventually turns out that the DR really had no idea at all what was meant. Words like "You know what I mean" may be intended positively—as a sign of respect. Yet they may leave out critical information. An effective two-way communicator would add, "Just to be sure we are both on the same page, tell me what you think about (X issue)..." or even, "I know that I can sometimes be vague regarding expectations on details, so tell me what you're thinking about doing in (X area)...."

WE ARE POWERLESS WITHOUT TWO-WAY COMMUNICATION

Choosing two-way communication over one-way communication takes a little more (initial) work and practice, but it leaves both the KDM and DR empowered to accomplish truly great things. Choosing one-way communication may seem easier, but, in fact, it entails a great deal more work and leaves both the KDM and the DR disempowered. To get a sense of just how devastating the choice to rely on one-way communication can be, consider the following true story.

Julian, an organization's leader I worked with, enlisted my help to find out why the sales and success goals he had set for his organization had not been met. For three straight years the numbers had been dropping sharply, despite what the owner considered outstanding, highly competitive pricing and state-of-the art technology.

After speaking to several of his employees, I learned the products Julian felt were state-of-the-art were, in fact, far behind the times. What Julian believed to be cutting-edge technology was at least a generation behind what was now hitting the marketplace. **His employees did not feel safe about expressing their views to him.**

The DRs never challenged any of Julian's constant statements about their products being cutting-edge and state-of-the art, because, in their experience, questioning Julian on such points was not good for their careers or sanity. Julian's employees believed he simply did not want to know the truth, and they believed such honesty might cost them their jobs. The unfortunate reality was they had plenty of evidence to back that belief up.

Julian was quite disturbed when I relayed his employees' comments to him. He told me what shocked him most was finding out his employees did not feel safe enough to let him know how they felt. He literally did not realize he had placed obstacles in the way of good communication, and he even felt anger that his employees had (in his words) "let him down" by not sharing their true opinions with him.

The problem was not that the DRs had let Julian down. The problem was that trusting, two-way communications had never been established between this organization's owner and his DRs. Julian had never demonstrated that he valued people's input. In fact, his actions proved quite the contrary.

THE ROLE MODEL

This leads us to another issue. Most KDMs who do not realize they have "ground rules" problems also do not realize their own patterns of information-sharing serve as the primary behavior model for the DRs who work with them. So, in addition to sending signals of potentially imminent disapproval, disconnect, or demotion when they hear feedback they don't like, they may share information on a highly restrictive "need to know" basis—a standard that perpetuates itself throughout the organization and often ends up keeping the people who really do "need to know" in the dark.

Let me emphasize: Most KDMs, Julian included, don't consciously intend to hold back necessary information. They may, however, have developed an outlook over the years that "the person who has the most information has the most power," and, as a result, they may lose sight of just how important it is to give their DRs all the facts they need to do their jobs at the best possible level. In some cases, these KDMs give far less information than is needed by their DR and may communicate in such a way that the DR really doesn't get a sense of the importance, or even the timing, of the project in question ("Remember that assignment I gave you? It's late"). It's not all that surprising that a DR who is repeatedly placed in such a position will, eventually, decide not to go out of his or her way to keep a KDM up to date—especially if doing so carries negative consequences. That is dysfunctional "communication." And that's what was happening in Julian's world.

The first thing Julian had to do was come to terms with the reality that his DRs had not "let him down." If anything, he had let them down. He had sent messages of disapproval, both subtle and overt, whenever his DRs attempted to share their opinions with him, and he had trained them, by his own example, not to share necessary information. Now his organization was at least a year behind the competition, maybe more. **Poor communication had left him and his DRs seriously disempowered.**

The critical point I want you to take away from this story is that all of Julian's poor communication choices were made as a result of **unconscious,**

subconscious, or semi-conscious instincts. He honestly thought he had made it clear to every one of his DRs that his door was open, he wanted to hear from people, had an open mind, and that sharing information was essential—he had even said those words out loud. But his behaviors and his example told his DRs a very different story. Changing those behaviors takes more than happy talk. It takes conscious effort; not just from the KDM, but also from the DR. In the next part of this chapter, we'll look at the single most effective tool for beginning and sustaining that effort.

A SAFE PLACE: BUILD TRUSTING TWO-WAY COMMUNICATION WITH TEMENOS

A powerful technique, called Temenos, can quickly help you create open and trusting two-way communications. I try to use it with all the KDMs and DRs with whom I work.

The word Temenos is derived from the ancient Greek word Temenos, which means sanctuary. Temenos creates a sanctuary—a safe place—for two-way communication. It does so through a series of interactions that effectively lowers the natural defenses people raise in response to perceived attacks from others. Once both partners in an exchange start lowering their defenses, communication can, and does, improve.

This simple exercise, successfully completed with your chapter partner, is the heart of everything else you will accomplish in The Aligned Workplace. It is not elective. It is mandatory. DO NOT SKIP IT. You will find this exercise in Appendix A.

Very often, there are complex emotional, personal, and social factors to consider when DRs and KDMs communicate. Temenos builds up the trust necessary to help you and the other person address these issues sensitively. One executive I worked with, someone who was a key factor in making many of my plans succeed, was perceived by her co-workers as having a strong air of overconfidence, of being condescending, and of considering herself incapable of error. In one-on-one meetings, I found even the slightest hint of criticism thrown her way caused her to lose focus and become overly defensive. As soon as she heard me say anything she interpreted as criticism, her facial expressions and body language clearly changed to indicate her focus on what we were discussing had been lost, and she was instead thinking about how she was going to protect herself against perceived criticism.

Because we had conducted the Temenos process together, we were able to identify that part of the problem was my making certain comments that caused her to don her "verbal armor." Together, we had gotten much better at avoiding these polarizing exchanges. In private discussions, though, we were able to determine that, even though these kinds of comments were a problem, they weren't the entire problem.

At one point, I had a lengthy heart-to-heart chat with her about these issues. She said the problem stemmed from her childhood, and that her air of over-confidence was, in fact, a cover for problems she had with low self-esteem. This explained why she was so sensitive to perceived criticism. I had to decide what communication style would be most effective to use with this executive so she would not feel threatened and lose her focus.

From that point on, whenever I felt she was approaching something in the wrong way, I always tried to begin my communications with her by mentioning something she was doing right (and she did most things right). Then I would talk to her about the things she was doing that did not satisfy me. I made it a point to criticize her actions, rather than criticizing her as a person. This is an important communication principle for all relationships, but it took on special importance with this particular executive, who was, I must emphasize, an extremely important and valuable member of our team.

After I began using a communications style better tailored to her personal-ity, most of the barriers to our trusting, two-way communications disappeared, and we had a very productive working relationship from that point forward. **The changes we made to establish a pattern of trusting, two-way communi-cation simply would not have been possible without the Temenos process.**

Let's look next at some additional, important points relevant to two-way communication.

"YOU'RE NOT LISTENING." ("NO, I'M NOT *AGREEING* — THAT'S DIFFERENT.")

Up to this point, I've spent a lot of time examining some of the most unpro-ductive communication patterns of KDMs. In a chapter such as this, the initial emphasis has to be on KDMs, because they control the dynamics of commu-nication within the relationship in virtually all cases, and because meaningful changes in behavior are extremely unlikely to occur until they "make the first move." DRs, however, present many unproductive communication patterns of their own. One of the most common of these is the "You're Not Listening!" syndrome. Take a look at how it may play out in your organization.

Jane, a DR who worked at a commercial real estate firm, had what she thought was a great idea for revamping the organization's compensation program for its sales team. She was very excited about the idea, and she asked for a meeting to talk about it with Kyle, her KDM. Kyle agreed to the meeting.

Jane told Kyle she wanted to implement the plan right away. She felt certain that doing so would have a substantial positive impact on the organization's fiscal performance that year.

The plan, however, was quite complex. Kyle paid close attention as Jane walked him through all the details. He spent an entire hour discussing the ins and outs of the plan with her.

At the end of the meeting, Kyle told Jane that he appreciated her initiative, and he realized she'd put in a lot of work on the plan, but he just wasn't comfortable with it. He didn't like the idea of switching up the rules on the sales team mid-quarter. What's more, he would be bringing on a new sales manager soon, and he wanted to be sure to get his input before making any decisions with such far-reaching implications. He asked Jane to table the idea and bring it back in three months so he and the new sales manager could consider it for the next fiscal year. Jane was crestfallen.

The next day, she made the rounds with all the other DRs on the team, intending to form a "consensus" that would persuade Kyle to change his mind. To each of the DRs, she made the same appeal: she'd had a great idea, shared it with Kyle, and he hadn't listened. Could they work together to change his mind while there was still time?

Unfortunately for Jane, Kyle happened to overhear her while she was conducting one of her "consensus-building" conversations. He immediately called her into his office for a private meeting.

"I hear you're sitting down with everyone, telling them how you're not being listened to," Kyle said, behind closed doors. "That's not quite correct. You're not being agreed with. There's a subtle difference." End of meeting.

Jane was off base here. The lessons for the DR are pretty obvious: once your KDM gives you a fair hearing, the job of deciding belongs to the KDM, not you. And if you think you're not being listened to, take the issue up with your KDM, not with anyone else.

CHANNEL CHOICES

A lot of apparent communication problems between KDMs and DRs are actually instances where the DR has not yet identified the KDM's preferred communication channel, has not yet gotten used to using it, or has resisted using it (recall Melanie's over-reliance on text messages). This problem is easily remedied by the adoption of a very simple principle: *the DR should try to master whatever communication channel the KDM prefers, not the other way around.*

If the KDM is more comfortable using Skype than talking on the phone, the DR should make an effort to learn how to use Skype. If the KDM prefers meeting in person each day, rather than exchanging dozens of e-mails, the DR should come into the office. Of course, there may be situations where compromise is possible and desirable, and if it's appropriate to do so, DRs should try to discuss compromises that seem likely to make sense to both sides. The guiding principle remains the same, however: don't assume the communication channel that feels like second nature to you will feel like second nature to your boss. Very often, it won't.

NO PUBLIC CRITICISM

Keith, an entrepreneur I worked with, assured me that the reason for his high rate of staff turnover was simply that the competition was recruiting aggressively and paying higher wages. A little digging on my part, however, revealed another factor to be considered. Each and every one of the DRs reporting to this entrepreneur related to me, with varying degrees of courage, that this gentleman was not particularly mild-mannered in his dealings with employees. His impatience for measurable progress toward key goals often resulted in public "explosions." He usually targeted a single employee he felt had made a mistake and publicly humiliated them

Employees were leaving the organization not just because they were underpaid, but also because they had become tired of the highly charged, unfair atmosphere the founder had created with habitual, sustained verbal abuse. This abuse took place both in one-on-one sessions and in public settings. In fact, the employees seemed to think Keith looked forward to the inevitable sessions of public abuse.

The way KDMs respond in public settings to things like mistakes and unorthodox suggestions will greatly affect the enterprise's ability to support trusting, two-way communication. If part of your public communication pattern routinely involves some kind of negative reaction to the comments or actions of others, you will need to learn to be more careful about how you express yourself, and learn quickly. If you are not sensitive to this issue and not willing to find a way take your feedback behind closed doors, you will probably find the person with whom you find public fault, and all the others who witness his or her humiliation, are less open to giving feedback you can benefit from in the future. Public "explosions" like Keith's may well lead to mass departures of talent and/or other major problems, such as vendettas, feuds, and liability problems for harassment.

Few people respond positively to public criticism. If this kind of attack has ever happened to you, it will help to recall that you probably took the humiliation personally and felt a long-term resentment to the person who criticized you publicly. Why perpetuate that cycle?

AGENDAS

As I have already mentioned, Frank, the retail KDM with whom we began this chapter, should have developed and circulated a written agenda for his meeting—and then followed it carefully. This one simple step could have kept the meeting on target, preventing it from going off on tangents that took away from the primary focus of the meeting.

A written agenda is an essential management tool, one that you can, and should, be ready to use in any meeting, whether it is a one-on-one or group meeting. The act of preparing the agenda will force you to think about the main points you are trying to communicate. An agenda will help you emphasize positive matters, point out major areas where you have concerns, and help you strike a balance between the two.

Of course, an agenda can assist you in allotting the available time intelligently; something Frank failed to do. Decide in advance roughly how much time is needed for communicating each point on your agenda, and present your points in a concise manner that keeps to your time schedule. Be sure to include a question and answer time for each major point to reaffirm your communications have been fully understood by all at the meeting.

FAMILY MATTERS

Family communication skills within a private organization are often quite poor. In a family organization, family members are more likely to make inappropriate remarks to each other than they would if they were employees of an outside firm. Quite honestly, they sometimes communicate with each other in exactly the same way they did when they were children. This attitude does not always lead to support for the goals of two-way communication, which, as we have seen, are to hear the other person's message, take time to internalize it, and then act on it.

Complicating the matter is the common complaint of "different rules" for family members and non-family-members who work for the same family-owned organization. The result, all too often, is a completely dysfunctional communication system. A family organization culture that accepts poorly executed communication may create a working environment where resentments build, tensions mount, relationships suffer, and results are subpar.

The goal of both the KDM and the DR in this situation (whether or not they are related) should be to have the type of communication culture between family members and others in the organization that minimizes these resentments. Making expectations for improved communication a cultural reality among family members usually requires some kind of proactive step on the KDM's part.

Things work better in the family-owned organization if there is a culture, agreed to among family members and others, in which everyone feels safe and comfortable in expressing their views in an open and honest manner. This can be achieved by using the Temenos process, which should be considered just as mandatory for family-owned organizations as it is for other organizations.

MUTUAL RESPECT IS THE FOUNDATION
FOR ALIGNMENT

Effective two-way communication is essential for creating and supporting mutual respect. Mutual respect is the foundation upon which an **Aligned** relationship between the KDM and the DR rests.

If there is no mutual respect, there can be no Aligned relationship! It's that simple. Unfortunately, there are certain common destructive behaviors that lead to a lack of Alignment between a KDM and a DR. If such behaviors aren't addressed constructively, communication will suffer, problem-solving efforts will become less and less effective, and the relationship between the two will become progressively more stressful and unproductive. This is the downward spiral of the relationship without mutual respect.

Of course, it is possible for the DR to experience disrespect without the KDM intending to send a disrespectful message (and vice versa). In fact, this is usually what happens: someone perceives an unintentional signal of disrespect, internalizes it, and a repetitive pattern of lower and lower quality two-way communication emerges. If the cycle worsens, the two can become frozen in place, as it were, focusing mostly, or only, on perceived slights, regardless of what is said aloud. Alignment becomes impossible.

The eleven most common Destructive Behaviors examined here are particularly dangerous because they can create and reinforce feelings of instant disrespect. In extreme cases they can cause instant contempt, which is the polar opposite of Alignment. Yet we must always remember that, as a rule, these behaviors are not intended as gestures of disrespect. In fact, many of the people with whom we work are deeply surprised to learn that their actions lead to these feelings of disrespect. It is one of the ironies of the human experience that we so frequently engage in behaviors that lead to strong emotional feelings in others, without realizing what we're doing.

If they are not eliminated or neutralized, these eleven Destructive Behaviors can rapidly lead to complex patterns of dysfunction within the KDM/DR relationship and, eventually, throughout the whole organization. They can literally destroy relationships and organizations. That's why I call them Destructive Behaviors.

As we shall see, habitual Destructive Behaviors can be major obstacles to the productive collaboration between KDMs and DRs. In too many situations, these behaviors result in the DR finding subtle ways to retaliate—for instance, through the kind of passive-aggressive "support" of the KDM's initiatives that features lapses in follow-through, or even covert sabotage. Instead of using his or her full efforts to achieve the KDM's desired results, the DR finds various ways to obstruct the KDM, sometimes without full awareness that this is what is happening. In other cases, DRs respond to Destructive Behaviors by providing biased information based on what they feel the KDM wants to hear, rather than what they believe to be best for the organization. This, too, can be a form of passive-aggressive behavior.

Even when DRs are not being unsupportive or subversive, Destructive Behaviors will definitely prevent them from giving their best efforts to support the KDM's vision.

DESTRUCTIVE BEHAVIORS ARE TYPICALLY "ONE-WAY"

It is not surprising that the behaviors I am talking about are virtually always "one-way" in nature, from KDM to DR. Direct Reports are less likely to exhibit any of these behaviors when working with the KDM, but don't go patting yourself on the back about this just yet. It would certainly be nice to be able to say that DRs are naturally disinclined to engage in these destructive actions. But it wouldn't be true. To the contrary, many DRs engage in one or more of these types of behaviors with the employees who report to them!

The reason a DR does not exhibit these actions with his KDM is that the DR has learned to use a "brake" on these behaviors during interactions with the KDM. Displays of any of these types of behaviors to the KDM tend to place the DR's job in jeopardy.

ASSUME GOOD INTENT

If your KDM displays any of the eleven behaviors discussed below, your first job is to remind yourself that the behavior in question is probably viewed as benign by your KDM, regardless of whether or not it appears hostile to you. Assume good intent on the part of the KDM. Many of the behaviors discussed in this chapter are attributable to simple uncertainty or lack of experience.

Discussing such matters can be complex, and a good intuitive understanding of your KDM's preferred communication style is essential. The most important question to ask yourself here usually concerns pacing. What is the rhythm of the most successful conversations you have with your KDM?

Some DRs find they need to dialogue at a pace somewhat faster than they usually employ because that's "how the boss operates." Even though they may have sent a written message to prepare for the private meeting, these DRs have learned to recognize that such KDMs might not actually read and/or comprehend the message in advance.

Other KDMs, of course, will have very different communication styles. Many DRs report during Alignment training that they need to "slow down a little" during important conversations like these. If you find that to be the case in your situation, you will need to be just as careful to follow the KDM's lead. It's possible you will also have to deal with other aspects of this person's communication style, such as the fact that your boss's willingness to take risks may be a lot lower than your own.

WATCH YOUR OWN RESPONSES

It is sometimes quite hard to remember, but your response to these Destructive Behaviors has just as serious an effect on Alignment as the behaviors themselves. Some DRs "let off steam" to friends and colleagues about these exchanges, a habit that carries a negative cultural impact. Other DRs learn to tolerate these behaviors and accept them without judgment, which gives the KDM the impression this behavior is acceptable. Some think they have learned to ignore these behaviors entirely, but eventually find they are harboring deep resentments about the way they are treated.

At the end of the day, what matters most is not which of these categories describe you, but how well you and your KDM communicate about these kinds of events. Destructive Behaviors are bad for an organization on multiple levels. If they are not reversed, the entire daily working culture of the organization will suffer, and the organization as a whole will not be able to perform to its full potential.

Working with someone who consistently engages in any of the eleven behaviors means both of you are facing a pattern that is always counterproductive to the task of producing positive organization results. In fact, one of the most common reasons DRs decide to leave the organizations they work for is that they come to view the relationship with their KDM as adversarial. This is typically the result, at least in part, of the KDM's habitual reliance on one or more of the Destructive Behaviors.

An important side note: when you look at each of the common types of behavior I have listed below, consider not only whether your KDM displays any of these behaviors while interacting with you, but also whether *you* display any of these behaviors while interacting with the people who report directly to you.

> **Both parties must take action over time to reverse the dynamic established by Destructive Behaviors, even though these behaviors typically originate with the KDM.**

\WHAT IS REALLY HAPPENING?

KDMs and DRs need a clear understanding of what is actually taking place in the relationship, and what can and should be done to improve that relationship. For the sake of the organization (and each other) each should be able to meet the responsibility of being open to what needs to be done next, rather than being held back by the emotional baggage that inevitably accompanies Destructive Behaviors.

Eliminating these behaviors requires sustained effort by both parties. Although this often requires tact and patience, it is not impossible.

Identifying Destructive Behaviors

For a trusting, Aligned relationship to exist between a KDM and a DR, negative patterns of behavior that arise must be identified. Only after recognizing the specific problematic behavior can you work on transforming it into something more constructive.

Begin by studying the eleven classic Destructive Behaviors I share below, each of which can move your KDM/DR working dynamics into areas of stress, emotional exhaustion, and poor results. After you finish reading, ask yourself whether you are facing even one of these dynamics over the course of a typical week with your KDM.

If your answer is yes, you will need to employ techniques that minimize and eventually reverse these behaviors. The techniques you will find in this chapter have been used successfully to bring about trusting, cohesive working dynamics—the kind of working dynamics that make an organization more successful and actually reduce stress between KDMs and DRs.

> Don't waste energy resenting a KDM's disrespectful behavior if you know for sure you can't fix it, or don't want to try – let go of the problem and move on.

These techniques will show you the steps to take to improve communication and bring about the respectful working dynamics needed for alignment between you and your KDM.

THE 11 MOST COMMON DESTRUCTIVE BEHAVIORS

The following Destructive Behaviors were first identified in a 1987 survey of DRs as the most common negative behaviors of their KDMs. A quarter of a century later, each of these negative behaviors showed up again in another survey of DRs! That tells me these eleven behaviors will always be relevant. **Study them well.**

Freedom goes hand-in-hand with mutual respect.
—Kay Rala Xanana Gusmao

Destructive Behavior Pattern #1: Responding Poorly to Stress

The ways we react to frustration and disappointments—such as lost sales, missed deadlines, and other common challenges—has a major impact on the level of Alignment between the KDM and the DR team. The ability of you and your KDM to operate effectively together is, predominately, a result of how well the two of you have learned to respond jointly to stressful situations.

Even if a DR does not agree with a KDM's chosen course of action in addressing a potentially stressful state of affairs, the relationship must be strong enough and trusting enough for the DR to voice an opinion. However, having stated the opinion, the DR *must then implement* the KDM's eventual decision, even if it is contrary to the opinion he or she has expressed. This kind of commitment is in the DR's job description, but what is oft en overlooked is that it must be reciprocated. The KDM, for his or her part, must commit to a respectful dialogue that elicits the DR's perspective within a truly collaborative decision-making process. **This mutually respectful decision-making dynamic must play out even in very stressful situations.**

So: If something has gone wrong and you feel your KDM is stressing out, try calming things down by explaining that you recognize your KDM's feelings and understand that your KDM is angry. You can do this by saying something like, "I can tell you're upset about what's happened." Then let your KDM know you, too, would be angry if you were in his or her position.

Next, you should try to restate your KDM's perspective before you try to inform him or her about how you see the facts. Explain what you think your KDM's point of view is in a calm, even tone of voice: "Let me see if I've got this straight. You feel that...." Restate what you believe to be your KDM's major "hot buttons" *without editorializing.* Your words should bring about a confirmation of how your KDM sees the situation. For instance: "So, if I'm hearing you correctly, you feel like the schedule is not being managed effectively and the project is out of control."

It's hard to overstate the importance of restating your KDM's viewpoint in words that he or she would actually endorse. Even if you feel your KDM is over-reacting to a problem, let your KDM know you understand how he or she is feeling about the situation. **This one simple step will resolve many of your problems with this behavior pattern.**

> **Not all emotionally intense responses by the KDM are off base!**

If you think every complaint from a KDM is inappropriate, you are wrong. Sometimes, there is a legitimate, significant mistake made by a DR that fully warrants an impassioned and direct response from the KDM. In such situations, the DR needs to be mature enough to handle negative feedback if he or she has let the KDM down on an important initiative.

Once you master the essential tactic of restating your KDM's viewpoint, you will want to expand your repertoire and look for additional ways to help your KDM "de-stress" in potentially stressful situations. For Andy, a DR I worked with, it came down to understanding his boss's patterns. Andy shared with me how his whole life changed when he realized that the times his boss would blow up in anger seemed to be when certain difficult things were happening in his boss's personal life. He realized his boss's anger was never really about Andy. As a result, he stopped caring quite as much about the externals, did a better job of helping his boss redirect emotion in a more constructive direction and found a much greater comfort level with his KDM. The quality of his interactions with his boss improved, and his stress level decreased dramatically.

Destructive Behavior Pattern #2: Mood Swings

Some KDMs have a pattern of erratic, hard-to-predict swings in demeanor: the outlook is great, then the outlook is terrible; the organization is destined for triumph, then the organization is doomed. These feelings and pronouncements may alternate with astonishing speed. Such emotionally fickle KDMs can be hard to predict . . . like a squirmy child, they don't offer you a lot to hold on to. That makes it hard to know whether the two of you are in Alignment.

Begin by recognizing it is important that you not take the mood swings of your KDM personally. Remember: it's not about you. There's probably a whole lot of stuff you know nothing about that's making your boss act that way.

One of the best ways to make a relationship work with a "mood swing" KDM is to try to limit communications to only the most urgent matters, especially when you know your KDM is on edge.

Janice, the CEO of a software organization, was emotionally fickle. Sometimes Mel, her Director of Sales, could ask her a question and receive an enthusiastic, detailed answer. At other times, Janice would practically bite Mel's head off if he dared ask her a question. These "answers" would sound something like: "Mel, there is absolutely no way we are making any changes to any of our sales materials, so don't even bother talking to me about it." Mel learned to test Janice's mood before asking any questions. If she was in a bad mood, his tactic was to wait for that mood to pass before making his inquiry.

A KDM who overreacts, typically has the problem of listening to you without really hearing what you say. If your KDM has problems with mood swings, try sending a concise written message that clearly lays out your points before you discuss the topic.

Another effective tactic is to say something like this to the KDM: "It's ok to react this way to me behind closed doors, but you would really hurt the morale of the office if you took this same position with the team at large." This may cause the KDM to better compartmentalize" negative moods, and also consider the effect these "down" moods may have on you.

Destructive Behavior Pattern #3: "See Me First"

Another type of KDM with whom Alignment is difficult is the habitual "see-me- first" KDM. Nothing you ask about ever seems to get decided; instead, you are asked to clear whatever next step comes up, personally, in a future conversation with the KDM—a conversation which is often difficult to schedule. This KDM may be sending you the message that he or she doesn't value your ideas.

Such KDMs have convinced themselves the only way they can really manage effectively is to be personally involved in literally everything that goes on (of course, that is not really management, and it is usually impossible as well). They must see all reports and memos. They must sit in on every meeting. You must see them first before you make any decision, which, of course, means you are not really making the decisions.

This is a challenging and unsustainable state of affairs for anyone aspiring to be a **High-Performing DR**. The best remedy is to **engage assertively**. Assuming you have, or can aspire to, the kind of personality that allows you to do so, it is best to assert yourself by asking for a one-on-one meeting. During the meeting, explain why you feel the performance results of the organization are being hurt because of the KDM's "see me first" response to your requests. Calmly, respectfully, but directly, without getting emotionally involved, let your KDM know that you believe this behavior is a bad reflection on him or her in the eyes of organization executives.

Many DRs tell me they are not well suited to such a direct approach to the problem. A more indirect way to address this challenge would be to show your KDM a specific situation that illustrates how the behavior is hurting the organization and let the KDM connect the dots.

Another technique I recommend is for the DR to request specific decision criteria that can be used to make the decision without him or her coming back to the KDM. Let's say the DR is recommending a vendor's proposal be approved, and the KDM is uncomfortable with this recommendation. The DR can ask the KDM, "If I get the vendor down to $75,000, do I have your support to go forward with this proposal?" This way, the DR has autonomy to proceed within certain parameters the KDM is comfortable with.

It is possible your KDM will still resist, in which case you may have to take a more direct approach. Lisa, a DR who served as her organization's comptroller, got her CEO to change his "see me first" ways by pointing out that the CEO's policy had resulted in senior executives (including her) simply not making decisions because they knew that nothing they "decided" would ever be a "real" decision until the CEO okayed it. No one was even bothering to make decisions until meeting with the CEO—they had been conditioned to believe that making decisions wasn't their responsibility! Lisa then pointed out instances where the delays in getting various crucial decisions made had hurt the organization. The pattern changed!

Destructive Behavior Pattern #4: Taking the Credit

Most of us have encountered the "credit hog" KDM at some point. This KDM takes credit for your ideas or hard work in creating a successful solution to a complex problem. The question is; how should you respond when you see this pattern?

During one Alignment training session involving DRs from several organizations, Melanie, a DR in a manufacturing government division, shared her personal experience with the "credit hog" syndrome. She told of her strong feelings as she watched her KDM take sole credit, at a division's **Strategic Leadership Team Meeting**, for a cost-saving strategy that she alone had developed. It had taken her months. When she'd proudly shared her suggested strategy with her KDM, he'd said he thought it was a great idea, and he would take the steps necessary to bring it into the division strategies for the government division-wide plan. The first step, he'd told her, was to introduce it at the next weekly Strategic Leadership Team Meeting. Naturally, she expected him to acknowledge her in front of the team for developing the strategy. He didn't. Instead, he presented the idea, and all of her work, as his own.

Melanie expressed to all of us at the Alignment session just how disappointed she was about her own decision to stay silent and allow her KDM not to recognize her contributions. She said she had justified her silence—at that meeting, and in the past—by telling herself it was "just the way the game has to be played." She explained she was quite sure he would do this again in the future. As a result, she admitted, it was hard for her to motivate herself to give that extra special effort.

There are a lot of DRs who have had to deal with KDMs like that. I was one of them, although I have to point out that my response to the situation differed from Melanie's! From the beginning I have always advocated tactful, assertive engagement to address this problem.

A KDM who demonstrates this type of behavior is likely to be an insecure person and, as a result, must be dealt with in a special way. Begin by praising your KDM tactfully and honestly for specific instances of effective managing. Do this in a private meeting. Yes, I want you to put aside your resentments about past or future credit-hogging episodes, and I want you to think carefully and clearly about the KDM's positive contributions. Surely you can come up with something this person is doing right as a leader. Identify that positive attribute in your own mind and then **offer heartfelt praise to him or her for the good work of subordinates**. The point you are making, of course, is that a good leader does get acknowledged for the (properly credited) achievements of those who report to him or her. During these conversations, you can easily move on to talking about how important it is to you to receive recognition when you do a good job.

If you have one or more such private discussions with your KDM and still find that the "credit hogging" issue is a problem, then it is time to set boundaries and make decisions about whether it makes sense to continue to work with such a KDM. In my case, I decided it was time to move on, and I have never regretted doing so.

Destructive Behavior Pattern #5: Constant Complaining

Complaining is calling attention to a problem without making any effort to help solve it. All of us complain from time to time, but the KDM who consistently engages in this behavior seems to find fault with everything and everyone.

This person often seems to be having a bad day. Even though his or her own work may not be affected, the complaining "virus" will affect you and your fellow DRs. It may also become contagious, with some of the other DRs becoming chronic complainers ... though, of course, the complaints tend to filter downward, toward subordinates.

I have found that most "constant complainers" have a need for attention. My approach is to look for a positive outlet for that need for attention. Usually, for the DR, this means finding an area where the complaining KDM can get his or her need for attention met in a constructive way. Note: be aware that some complaints from your KDM may be valid and can be solved by ascertaining the perceived issue and addressing it.

Mariana, a DR at an electronics firm, shared with me how she dealt with this problem. She scheduled a private lunch with her KDM away from the office. There, in a secluded booth, she asked her KDM why she was always complaining about her and the other executives working for her. A bit taken aback, the KDM had no good answer but asked Mariana to elaborate. That was the opening Mariana wanted. Calmly, but purposefully, she expressed her feelings about how the KDM was hurting her opportunities for getting a team spirit developed because she spent so much time and energy complaining.

Mariana told me it was remarkable how her KDM's attitude changed after their talk. The KDM did not become an effervescent, positive office personality overnight, but she did start to display a much more positive influence on those around her.

Not all stories about constant complainers have a happy ending. Still, I believe it is worth making the effort to help your KDM become more aware of the real-world consequences of complaining as a way of life. Many complainers I have worked with turned into some of the most effective and admired KDMs, but for that to happen, you must do something! Once again, the key is tactful, assertive engagement.

What is the alternative? Listening to more constant, de-motivating

> **To ignore the constant complainer is to guarantee a lack of Alignment because eventually you will not want to help the KDM or, in some extreme cases, even see the KDM succeed!**

complaining, knowing that any complaint you address will be succeeded by another? There are no benefits in reinforcing this pattern because the KDM comes to associate perpetually negative, complaining behaviors with getting solutions from his or her staff.

Destructive Behavior Pattern #6: Meddling

The world is full of meddlers: people who want to jump in when they see you going about your organization in a way that differs from the way they are used to.

"Meddling" is not a pretty word, but unfortunately there is no other word in English that does the job. When your KDM meddles, the action not only implies that your KDM always knows how to do things better than you, but also that there is one, and only one, way to complete a task. Indeed, some KDMs seem to operate under both assumptions. Neither of these assumptions reflect reality. Your KDM may even see his or her meddling as sensitive and compassionate. Most DRs, however, see these efforts to "help" in a negative light.

This type of KDM doesn't mean to come across as a know-it-all, but that is how he or she is likely to be perceived. Unless you have enough self-confidence to engage tactfully and assertively and defend your right to do your job in the way that makes the most sense to you, the meddler KDM will have a detrimental effect on the way others view you within the organization, and perhaps even on the way you view yourself.

The best action for you to take, as a DR, is to request a private meeting and then, within that meeting, assertively let your KDM know that, without meaning to, he or she is creating problems. Your goal should be to sensitively help the KDM understand that his or her "help" is not only not wanted, but counterproductive because of the deep resentments it causes.

Sometimes the meddler even meddles with things that are not organization-related. An extreme example involved Jane, the operations director of a restaurant chain. The organization's owner (her KDM) gave Jane the unsolicited advice that it was time for her to leave her husband! Not exactly a good formula for Alignment.

Rather than ignoring the problem, Jane took assertive action. She told the manager, in private, to stop giving personal advice to her, and calmly but frankly set some boundaries: "I know you have good intentions, but none of us executives want your personal advice."

The good news is that the KDM's meddling dwindled down to a tolerable level within weeks. At the same time, Jane was able to channel a greater amount of her energies into new tasks. The result was a more fulfilled, happier and effective KDM/DR team.

Destructive Behavior Pattern #7: Lack of Accountability

"It's not my fault!" Deflecting blame to someone or something else is a classic annoying behavior, one that is certainly not limited to KDMs. To be sure, many DRs also keep themselves very busy avoiding blame.

This disrespectful behavior displays a pattern of not accepting responsibility for being wrong, and in extreme cases, an inability to ever admit making a mistake at all. Some people will use every method imaginable, and some you may not have imagined, to avoid accepting personal accountability for problems. Effective Alignment requires respect that will not be there for an organization's leader who tries to deflect accountability for his/her mistakes.

The "blame game" described in this behavior pattern is often based on replaying past mistakes (real or imagined), in an effort to avoid personal present responsibility. If you report to someone who is playing this blame game, your attitude will inevitably become one of self-protection, which can lead to a "me against him/her" mentality, problems of factionalism within the organization, or both. If you know your KDM would be quick to place public blame on you if things didn't work out, you are unlikely to feel like part of a winning team.

"Don't blame me" behavior erodes productivity and hurts the morale of those who work around anyone who engages in it. **To achieve a high level of Alignment, the "blame game" must be abandoned, and the destructive "me-versus-you" mentality that accompanies it must be left behind.** This requires work—and the assumption of good intent—from both sides.

Mike, the KDM of a drug-packaging nonprofit organization, was great to work for when things were going smoothly, but when something got messed up, he put up a smoke screen. He seemed to think whatever problem had arisen would go away if he talked fast enough and loud enough about it not being his problem. His DRs all learned to recognize when trouble was brewing: Mike would come by in a huff trying to find someone he could pin the blame

on whenever a mistake was made. This unwillingness to accept responsibility for a problem became part of the daily working culture and the cause of serious dissension within the organization. It also made the DRs less likely to want to manage the changes necessary to bring about better results.

Arnie, the chief operating officer who reported to Mike, had a private meeting with the KDM in which he tactfully but persistently showed his "blameless" KDM all the ways in which he or she was directly or indirectly responsible for a particular problem that had been the subject of a recent blame-fest. Such a private meeting may become essential and is a challenge to conduct. When dealing with a "blameless" superior, maintaining the right balance between what must and what must not be said can be exceptionally difficult. This type of meeting calls for you to keep your temper while you are setting the record straight, even if the KDM does not keep his or her temper. Fortunately, Arnie was able to do this; he kept returning calmly to the point that leadership means accountability, one that Mike could not dispute. Eventually, Mike began making better choices about accountability (I think this was due, in large measure, to the personal respect he had for Arnie before this difficult discussion took place).

Once you have identified your KDM is engaging in this behavior pattern, ask yourself what motivates these actions. Often, it is a lack of inner confidence or self-esteem. Ask yourself what, if anything, you can do to help your KDM overcome this lack of confidence or self-esteem.

One important cautionary note is in order here: only DRs who are themselves willing to be accountable are in a position to expect their KDM to be more accountable. As the adage goes, consider your own shortcomings first before finding the shortcomings in others. If you are personally accountable for your work, you will be in a position of strength when discussing accountability issues with your KDM.

> **Play it smart when it comes to calling attention to anything that could make your KDM look bad in front of others – communicate sensitive matters to your KDM privately.**

Greta, a DR at a lawn service organization, told us, during an Alignment training session, that her boss's blaming behavior was rooted in a "paranoid" concern about whether she or one of the other DRs was doing something against his direction. To be found guilty of disobeying instructions was to invite another round of the "blame game." Greta's approach, whenever she was blamed for such things, was to acknowledge what had happened and then move on.

There is a tendency among some people to believe they will lose face if they ever admit their decisions and choices are not always right. They are committed to avoiding ever saying those dreaded words, "I was wrong." What they don't realize is that this causes people around them to lose respect for them. A good leader must be willing to accept responsibility for being part of the problem. In the real world it's the act of trying to deflect blame for something you did that really results in loss of face.

Destructive Behavior Pattern #8: Duplicity

A KDM who is engaging in this behavior will say something positive to you when you're face-to-face, and then, when talking to other employees, will work to undermine you or your work when your back is turned. The KDM who does this creates DR resentment, often without realizing it.

Your job, as DR, is to neutralize these actions. One way to do this, of course, is simply by calling attention to behind-the-back comments that have gotten back to you. As usual, you will need to maintain a tactful, emotionally balanced demeanor when you talk about this. Simply make it clear you are aware of what is happening and ask (without turning your question into an attack) for clarification about what the KDM wants you to work on improving.

When you meet to discuss the problem, keep discussions professional at all times and focus on facts, not emotions. Mention you want to avoid problems stemming from miscommunications. Be sure to separate your personal ego (which might take offense at mean-spirited remarks) from your "executive" persona (which is eager to avoid even the possibility of miscommunication and knows that remarks are sometimes misreported).

Your job, with this and all such behavior, is to stand up for yourself in a diplomatic and respectful manner.

Share your assessment of what the real problem is of your being undermined by restating objectively how you see things. Hopefully your assertive action now leaves you with the issue of how to solve the problem (which is something you and the KDM can work on together) rather than whether the backstabbing behavior actually happened (which doesn't really matter, because once it stops you're both happy).

You should be sure to document the duplicitous comments that get back to you. Keep a private "paper trail" of these incidents. If necessary, you can show the KDM this list of all the times he or she appears to have spoken inappropriately about you to others (if any of the remarks cross the line into sexual harassment or any other kind of harassment, your KDM will have a strong incentive to curb his or her behavior, because these remarks could conceivably lead to serious liability issues for the organization. However, sexual harassment is a very serious accusation, and you probably shouldn't raise this issue unless you're absolutely certain that that is what you're dealing with. In other situations, it's best to talk about what makes you feel comfortable and uncomfortable).

You may never create a friendship with the KDM who engages in this behavior, and you probably shouldn't expect to. You should, however, expect to be able to work productively with the KDM in an atmosphere of mutual respect.

Destructive Behavior Pattern #9: Bullying

A KDM who engages in this behavior pattern will humiliate you; either privately or in front of others.

Managers who use bullying as a tool to get what they want cross a "bright red line" in the workplace. They move from "being a bit of a jerk sometimes" (which most of us are guilty of, or could be) to berating you on a toxic level that has a clearly negative impact on your relationship and the culture of the organization. Your job as DR is to notice and engage assertively once you know for sure that the line has been crossed.

There are a number of different ways that a KDM may bully a DR. One common way is yelling at the DR.

Your major challenge when a KDM is yelling at you is to bring the volume of the KDM's voice down to an acceptable level. Your best approach here is to try to send verbal and nonverbal messages that smooth over the anger being vented, and tactfully let your KDM know that calming down is the best way to solve the problem at hand. One technique that has worked well for many DRs is to ask specific questions to clarify the situation and bring it into an objective realm of fact and action, rather than a subjective emotional realm. For instance, "Should we schedule a meeting with this customer who decided not to renew the contract with us, so we can hear directly why they made this decision?"

Try to determine the underlying cause for your KDM acting this way. It may be that your KDM literally does not realize he or she is yelling (this is the case more often than you might imagine). Your KDM may simply have developed a bad habit of shouting to get across an important point and may not be trying to be a bully. Some DRs have reported that their KDMs seemed to be totally unaware of their yelling. If this is the case, it should be relatively easy for the KDM to change the behavior once he or she recognizes it exists.

> If your KDM is yelling, the one thing you definitely don't want to do is yell back.

More often, however, bullies do their yelling because they either simply like the feeling of power they associate with bullying, or they hope the bullying behavior will intimidate the other person. Sometimes the bully has underlying anger issues.

It is common for KDMs to respond to complaints about bullying behavior by saying things like, "Yes, I sometimes yell or behave inappropriately, but most of the time I don't do that." The reality is that the unpredictability of the negative behavior by a KDM is itself part of the problem.

Mean-spirited behavior, even if it only happens a small portion of the time, destroys the potential for true loyalty and committed support for the KDM's initiatives. This kind of behavior can have a devastating, negative impact on organizational culture.

Some DRs come to feel threatened by bullying episodes and will do virtually anything to avoid mistakes that could trigger it. Often, this problem worsens over time. As a result, these DRs become less and less likely to make critical decisions or take necessary risks on behalf of the KDM's vision, and more and more likely to question the direction or decisions of the KDM behind his or her back. This behavior is virtually always the result of unresolved conflicts with the KDM. As hostility, spoken or unspoken, smolders and intensifies, there's a much greater likelihood these DR's actions are not only inconsistent with making a plan succeed, but are actually counterproductive to the success of the plan.

Many KDMs have discussed such "sabotaging" patterns with me in an attempt to offer the "real reason" for the departure of a DR; they often put forward some kind of assurance that the organization is somehow "better off" as a result of the DR's exit. In virtually all of these cases, however, the KDM's responses before, during, and after the departure are part of a larger cycle of non-Alignment within the relationship; typically one with bullying, mean-spirited behavior from the KDM at its core.

KDMs may not always realize it, but the whole organization is usually *worse* off when a qualified DR heads for the door because of a cultural problem that tolerates bullying behavior. By the same token, the organization is usually *better* off when a DR defends a productive working culture by drawing the line (appropriately, in private) with a KDM who has problems with bullying.

Gina, a diminutive DR at a publishing organization, shared with me how she asked for a private meeting with her KDM, during which she flat-out told her burly 6'5" boss, "You are a bully and I resent it."

The story stands out in my mind because Gina is a petite woman who describes herself as "four feet, eleven and one quarter inches tall." The point to remember here, of course, is that physical size is immaterial when it comes to

> **Even if bulling behavior by a KDM doesn't happen all the time, not knowing when the uncivil behavior is going to happen destroys trust and creates a stressful working culture.**

dealing with bullying behaviors. Gina had no problem engaging assertively to redirect a boss who was exhibiting bullying behaviors. The outcome was very good for both of them because, thereafter, her boss "stopped trying to manage me and the other executives with his loud bullying style ... and became a real leader."

In one family manufacturing organization, an executive named Brent was in charge of manufacturing and reported directly to his father-in-law, who owned the organization. The father-in-law, Tom, had a bad habit of berating his son-in-law, both in private and in front of other employees. He would yell at him and humiliate him for almost any reason. Because of the public nature of so much of the bullying, it was not surprising that the son-in-law was unable to garner a great deal of respect from his subordinates.

The public bullying didn't stop until Brent and his wife Tina sat down with the organization's owner and explained exactly how the bullying was affecting the productivity of his department.

A footnote is in order here: Although the bullying only eased up in private, the public bullying stopped right away. The son-in-law was thus able to gain the respect of his employees, and as the department performed better and better over time, his father-in-law also showed respect for his son-in-law. Eventually, the cycle of bullying stopped altogether as the cause-and-effect relationship between less bullying and better results became clearer. This is a common pattern.

Ignoring bullying does not work, nor does just giving in to it. One way or another, you must find a way to deal assertively with the problem. As with the other behaviors we have examined in this chapter, you should find a way to calmly raise the subject during a one-on-one meeting. By discussing the problem calmly and not getting emotionally engaged, you will make it clear you are not intimidated. Once that critical "defusing" step has been accomplished, and it is obvious the bullying has not caused you to lose your composure, you should have the opportunity to explain your position.

In many cases, bullying behavior has been dramatically reduced simply as a result of the DR's calling attention to the bottom-line negative impacts of the behavior. Once bullying behavior stops, there is typically a dramatic improvement in alignment between the KDM and their DRs.

Many DRs who are not comfortable with "cold" face-to-face discussions of bullying behavior have effectively expressed their concern via confidential written communications they sent to their KDMs before taking part in a private meeting. This provides an opportunity for the KDM to process the DR's concerns and work through any instincts to have emotional "explosions" before meeting in person. This type of communication generally explains the DR's belief that he or she cannot do a good job in the current work environment and identifies a few of the specific instances of the KDMs de-motivating behavior.

For DRs who simply cannot raise the issue in any way, it is probably time for the DR to find another KDM to work with.

If the bullying behavior by the KDM does not stop, the behavior will not only cause greater and greater Alignment problems between the KDM and the DR, it will also "trickle down" through the organization. Managers who are verbally abused by the KDM are likely to exhibit the same bad leadership behaviors when interacting with those who report to them.

Destructive Behavior Pattern #10: Second Guessing

Jim, VP of Marketing for a sporting goods organization, found himself having to reverse some of his decisions after he had already communicated them to his subordinates and clients. The reason? His KDM, Amanda, had undermined his authority by making him reverse course in these areas, including terms for major contracts he had negotiated. Amanda then required Jim to communicate that reversal to people who had trusted his word.

This was not an isolated incident, but a pattern of behavior on Amanda's part. Jim commented during an AlignUp training session that he had "all the responsibility and none of the real authority" for his department. The result of all this second-guessing was that Jim simply stopped making decisions and negotiating terms in critical areas that were (supposedly) his responsibility. He would wait until his one-on-one meeting with his KDM and then let her make all the decisions.

As a result of discussing this point during his Alignment training, Jim committed to have a heart-to-heart conversation with Amanda. In a private meeting, Jim stated to Amanda that he was no longer making decisions in certain areas because he was tired of appearing foolish when Amanda reversed them. Jim pointed out that even though he didn't always make the decisions Amanda would have made, or secure the terms she would have negotiated, most of the time, things worked out just fine when Jim was given real authority to carry out his job.

After many discussions, Amanda realized the error of her ways and agreed to adopt a "hands off" policy in the areas where Jim was supposed to make decisions and negotiate terms. As Jim had predicted, everything worked out fine.

Very often, second-guessing involves, not reversal of a decision, but "twenty-twenty hindsight" that is meant to discredit the DR. Assertive engagement is particularly important when hostile criticism has occurred as the result of a KDM's second-guessing. When there is a difference of opinion about a KDM's decision to overrule you, you can deflect the most negative results by being smart enough to admit any error you have made.

At one weekly Team Meeting, Jack, the CEO, accused Norma, a department head, of making the wrong decision on a recent purchase (I was sitting in on the meeting in a coaching capacity). It seemed obvious to me that a power play was taking place. Jack, the CEO doing the accusing, was clearly playing to the other executives in the room, in much the same way a youngster will make a point of accusing a sibling within earshot of a parent.

Norma, the woman who stood accused in this meeting, deflected the hostile criticism by relating the situation that had led to her decision and admitted that, now, with the benefit of hindsight, she realized her choice had been wrong. She ended her remarks with an open question to her peers: "Given what we now know about the situation, would any of you have done anything different?" It was her way of saying to her KDM, "I respect your opinion, but we can only do the best we can based on the facts we know at the time we make the decisions."

Instead of reacting defensively, and possibly digging herself into a deep hole, Norma pulled everyone in the management team into her court. By being honest and admitting her mistake, she also gained respect from her KDM.

A consumer products nonprofit president, during a similar meeting I sat in on, closely reviewed the activities of one young executive and concluded by telling him he had made a big mistake in judgment on a project. He really laid into the junior executive—in front of the team. When the president finished, all eyes focused on the young man, and his response was, simply, "You're right, I blew it." After taking a minute to recover, the president laughed and said, "Just don't let it happen again."

The young man's honesty was refreshing, but it probably isn't a good idea to make a habit of responding this way on a regular basis!

Of course, DRs cannot expect to be treated as prima donnas; if you only want your positions to be confirmed, you will not make much headway for yourself or your organization. The KDM brings a certain perspective to initiatives the DRs cannot always fully appreciate. Therefore, the KDM's input into all efforts should be valued. It is naïve to think that one's decisions should never be challenged. A mature DR will accept input with an open mind and will utilize the very best ideas, regardless of whose ideas they are.

Destructive Behavior Pattern #11: Micromanaging

There is a literary stereotype known as the Old Ship Captain who perfectly embodies the behavior pattern of the micromanager. The Old Ship Captain is a stern, bearded, intense figure who "runs a tight ship" and keeps a tight leash on everyone and everything on board. The Old Ship Captain perpetually looks over the shoulders of everyone who works on the ship and may drive the crew insane during the course of the voyage. The Old Ship Captain "manages" everything happening on "his" ship down to the very last detail (note the quote marks around the word "manages").

If you report to a KDM with this type of behavior, your KDM is sending a message to you: Your opinions or suggestions aren't worth listening to or considering. He or she knows best, in all situations, and will take all the necessary steps to ensure that everything is carried out precisely to his or her specifications, first time, last time, and every time.

The sad fact is, this disrespectful behavior may well drive you crazy. The sadder thing is that it may not matter much to your KDM (the Old Ship Captain, after all, doesn't really care how many deckhands can't handle life on his "tight ship").

What should matter to your KDM, though, is the reality that many organizations stagnate at levels of success far below what they're capable of because the Old Ship Captain unwittingly sabotages the voyage. Their KDMs spend far too much time micromanaging the affairs of their organization and far too little time orchestrating them.

Micromanaging is not only a bad use of your KDM's time, but it also interferes profoundly with your productivity and that of your fellow DRs. The message you need to get across when dealing with a KDM who shows micromanaging behaviors is that every truly great leader makes the transition between doing all the tactical things him/herself, and facilitating getting things done through his/her DRs.

This transition is never easy, and some KDMs never make it. In fact, it is best for me to acknowledge here that this is one of the most challenging destructive behaviors of them all—for the simple reason that it is almost always keyed to a KDM's commitment to personal growth and the development of leadership skills. Micromanagement is usually not intended to convey a feeling of disrespect, though, of course, you are likely to feel disrespected by it.

If you wish to change your KDM's behavior, that means finding some way to support his or her growth as a leader. The reality, though, is some KDMs are more eager to explore strategic growth in this leadership area than others, even when the success of their organization depends on that personal commitment to growth.

Your goal is to move things in a direction in which you, as the DR, are managing things and simply keeping your KDM in the loop about anything of importance. Achieving this goal can be extremely difficult for both parties. One reason is many KDMs who are micro-managers are in a state of denial about their reliance on micromanaging behavior. Others acknowledge the behavior but argue they need to engage in it in order to stay in their comfort zone—"That's just how I work," is a common explanation.

If you report to a KDM who micromanages some, or every, aspect of the organization, your challenge is to get your KDM to understand that he or she cannot have a great management team unless that behavior changes. As DR, your challenge is to earn and maintain the trust of the KDM by operating effectively with no missed deadlines and with full attention to detail, as the KDM agrees, step-by-step, to ease up on certain areas of micromanaging.

Before you begin this process, it makes sense to look closely at two factors.

One is the breadth of time availability you have. The second are the skills you have: Will they really allow you to take over some of your KDM's responsibilities and complete them as well as, or better than, he or she does? If there are problems in either area—time or skill-set—it might make sense to enlist the help of other DRs before you start negotiating for items on your KDM's to-do list.

Whenever you're trying to get your KDM to feel comfortable delegating more responsibility and authority to you, it's extremely important that you show your KDM exactly how this decision will enable him or her to improve his or her performance as a leader—and thus make it possible for the organization to achieve measurably better results, perhaps within a more desirable time-frame. If your KDM does not see the benefit, or does not trust that you have the skills and tenaciousness to take on these tasks, the behavior will not change. This is the time to "step up to the plate" and find the opportunity to prove you're worthy of the trust you are asking your KDM to give you. The more convincingly you demonstrate that trust is justified, the more likely it is that your KDM will add additional areas of responsibility and authority and move away from the micromanaging pattern.

CHANGING THE PATTERN

Interactions about any of these behavior patterns will give you the chance to discuss the important subject of accountability at the highest levels of the organization, accountability that goes well beyond the "blame game". On the strategic level, the KDM and all DRs must set the example here. In the KDM's case, that means holding himself or herself personally accountable for articulating the vision and the strategic intent of the enterprise; for getting the major priorities straight; for creating an innovative organization; for being persistent and not letting obstacles distract the organization from moving forward; for setting appropriate goals; and for maintaining healthy personal relationships. In each of these areas, a high-impact DR can sometimes serve as a powerful, and subtle, role model.

Now that you know the eleven common Destructive Behaviors, here are six important guidelines to follow before any meeting with a KDM intended to raise and examine a pattern of disrespectful behavior.

1. Once you really are certain the meeting is necessary, don't put off scheduling it. If you avoid confrontations with your KDM for any of the behaviors mentioned above, you are probably holding resentment within you. It is better to make sure your KDM is aware early on than it is to let resentments get to a boiling point. The only exception to this is the situation where you are not sure you are yet able to view the situation objectively (see 2, below).

2. Prepare to focus on the facts, not the person. Remind yourself your main goal is to keep the discussion objective and unemotional. This will be easier if you identify:

   - The specific behavior that concerns you. Focus on the action, not the individual. You do not want to tear into the KDM personally during this meeting, nor do you want to use labels (such as "meddler" or "backstabber") to describe him or her.
   - The timeframe. How long has the behavior been a problem?
   - The history. What, if anything, have you tried so far to do to fix this?
   - The bottom line. What is this behavior choice costing the organization in terms of dollars and cents? How do you know?
   - The affected parties. Who else besides you cares about this? (Your answer to this should include relevant descriptions of affected employees, customers and stakeholders.)
   - The consequence. What happens if you don't fix this? What are the benefits to each of you and the organization if the disrespectful behaviors could be fixed? What are the negative results you see on the horizon if the disrespectful behavior continues?
   - The plan. What are the positive steps you recommend to fix the problem? What, if anything, are you personally committed to do to correct the problem? (For instance, what responsibilities are you ready to take on in areas where you have time and know you can commit to quality?)

3. Pick the right time and place for the discussion with your KDM. Never initiate a meeting on this type of problem at a time when you are emotionally upset about the situation. Avoid public settings unless there is a very high level of privacy (such as a secluded booth in a secluded corner of an empty restaurant).

4. Prepare to start with the positives. When you finally meet, consider beginning the conversation with an approach you've worked out ahead of time. This approach should begin with something you like about something your KDM did, and should then tactfully segue into the reason you've asked for private time. It might sound like this: "Tom, I have to say I admired the way you managed the new research project. But I also want to tell you that, when you took that project on, I think you hurt me by not letting me be personally responsible for the project, which is, after all, something that falls within my department. How do we solve the problem of your taking on things like this? What can I do to help you take more of an organization big-picture focus? I can take these types of projects off your back." This approach will neutralize some of the natural defensiveness that may exist on the part of your KDM, Tom, because you are addressing the actions that have taken place, rather than attacking your KDM.

5. Practice listening. You may want to do a brief role-play of the meeting with a friend or trusted colleague. Your goal in these role-plays is to practice listening. Be open to opposing views, and do not leave the impression that you feel your views are the only right ones. If the KDM raises the issue of disrespectful or inappropriate behavior on your part, listen carefully to his or her perspective and do not "put up walls." (Many DRs are surprised to learn that behaviors they consider completely benign are seen as gestures of hostility and disrespect by their KDM.)

When you do speak in the role-play, be as specific as possible. Don't make inflammatory personal attacks like, "You blew it by second-guessing my judgment in front of the team." A confrontational approach can (and usually does) backfire. Use the role-play to practice a different way of stating your case: "I think it may undermine my ability to get work done with my team when you give me certain kinds of feedback in front of them."

6. Know when to end the meeting. If, despite your best efforts, emotions get out of control, it is probably time to end the meeting. Emotions have the effect of closing minds to logical attempts to resolve a problem. If you find the conversation is becoming circular because either you or your KDM is acting defensive, plan ahead of time to disengage and set a date to resume your discussion. Know the backup date and time you will propose before you begin the meeting with your KDM. This approach will give each of you time to think of new ways to eliminate the problem.

A calm, resourceful attitude on your part really can help bring about mutual respect between you and your KDM—but for this change to take place, both sides need to understand that there is a problem.

> At some point, every DR needs to accept that the KDM has the last word – don't go to battle over the little stuff and draw a line in the sand that, in hindsight, you wish you had not drawn.

Sometimes conflict is unavoidable in these conversations. Once you accept this, you are much more likely to be in control of your emotions. Mutual respect is essential for Alignment. If you avoid dealing with the subject, you will sabotage your relationship with your KDM and your effectiveness as a leader

Bringing up the subject of disrespectful behaviors and their negative impact may cause some short-term resentment, but using the techniques shared in this chapter will minimize that resentment in the long term, and will help establish mutual respect that will benefit you, your KDM, and the organization over time.

KEY CONCEPTS

- A dialogue is "an exchange of ideas and opinions about a particular subject."
- Often, we think we are engaging in a dialogue, when, in fact, we are monologuing—communicating in one direction only.
- Monologuing kills Alignment.
- True Alignment between the KDM and the DR, in any and all of the areas discussed in this book, depends on two-way communication.
- Choosing two-way communication over one-way communication takes a little more (initial) work and practice, but it leaves both the KDM and the DR empowered to accomplish truly great things.
- Our unconscious and semi-conscious responses to others can be major obstacles to two-way communication.
- Being listened to is not the same as being agreed with.
- The Temenos process makes it easier for KDMs and DRs (and everyone else) to lower defenses and support effective two-way communication.
- When addressing Destructive Behaviors, assume good intent on the part of the KDM. Many of the behaviors are attributable to simple uncertainty or lack of experience, and may be viewed as benign by your KDM, regardless of how it appears to you.
- Eliminating Destructive Behaviors is not impossible, but it requires tact, patience, and sustained effort by both parties.

HOMEWORK

Complete the †Temenos process mentioned in this chapter with the person who agreed to read this chapter with you. Devote at least sixty minutes of uninterrupted "face time" to this exercise.

Discuss the contents of this chapter with your KDM (if it helps, you can share the Executive Summary that appears at the beginning of this chapter). Discuss any obstacles you each see to the respect needed for Alignment between you and your KDM. The behaviors do not have to be limited to the 11 common disrespectful behaviors discussed in this chapter.

- Identify the negative consequences or impacts that exist because of the behavior(s) you identify, and any conflicts related to them.
- Discuss the best ways to eliminate behaviors so that mutual respect can grow.

At some point, you may want to consider sharing with your KDM instances where you have employed behaviors that triggered disrespect in your relationships with people who report to you.

As you work on this assignment, remember that changing the dynamic of any Destructive Behavior requires noticing, caring about, and being sensitive to whether or not the other person feels respected. The whole reason these behaviors are destructive is their effect on our perception of the other person's intentions. Turning the behaviors around requires learning to assume good intent, which is a prerequisite for any effective, respectful working relationship.

> **You and the KDM don't have to be friends in order to work productively together, but you do have to respect each other – mutual respect leads to a more effective management team.**

Please see Appendix A for full details on how to complete the Temenos homework.

CHAPTER 7

Align on the Organization's Values and Working Environment

EXECUTIVE SUMMARY FOR THE KDM CULTURAL ALIGNMENT

In any organization context, "the organization's culture" is the shared values and practices of the organization's employees. It is "how we do things around here." It is "the unique way our employees interact with each other and the world."

The Organization's Culture should be the practice of clearly articulating the organization's values (for instance, timeliness, honesty, and commitment to finish the job).

Culture can make or break your organization. Organizations with a positive culture, a culture that is Aligned to its organization goals, typically outperform competitors that lack such a culture by substantial margins. Some studies report the difference at 200% or more in key metrics! To achieve such remarkable positive results for your

> **Creating and sustaining an effective, Aligned culture of an organization can drive truly great results in any organization.**

organization, both you and your **Direct Report (DR)** will have important roles to play in bringing about true cultural **Alignment**—the kind of Alignment that goes beyond "lip service." This cultural Alignment will not happen overnight, but if you work together in good faith, *it will happen.*

129

Why invest time and other resources in Alignment? Because **a fully Aligned organizational culture is an invisible force that propels great organizations** forward; an unaligned culture, on the other hand, is an invisible barrier holding the organization back from fulfilling its true potential. Most private organizations operate from an unaligned (dysfunctional) culture.

The culture of virtually every privately owned organization can be directly linked to the founder's values. When successful culture endures within a private enterprise, it is generally handed down through the generations in a way that ensures continued success. It is worth noting, though, that an organization's leaders other than the founder can and do shape the organization's culture in constructive ways that capitalize on the founder's influence and help to adapt the culture, as needed, to ensure continued success well beyond the founder's generation.

In this chapter, your DR will find out about the critical role workplace culture plays in the organization, and about how the whole executive team can help hone the culture to bring about increased competitive advantage for your organization. Your DR will also learn the difference between an Aligned and an unaligned culture, and will identify five simple ways to clarify, refine, and strengthen the commitment to an Aligned culture—one that can become the engine of extraordinary achievement for your entire organization.

THE WAY WE DO THINGS AROUND HERE

Jan, a Key Decision Maker (KDM), had eight DRs reporting to her. She became friends on a social level with one of those executives, Irene. This friendship reached a point where Jan and her husband took vacation trips together with Irene and her husband.

A few years down the line, Irene experienced personal problems that frequently resulted in her not showing up to work on time. Beverly, one of Jan's other DRs, noticed there were grumblings in the organization about Irene's habitual tardiness; she also couldn't help noticing Irene's behavior was in conflict with the organization's written Culture Statement. Jan had asked Beverly, Irene, and all the other DRs to help create this document. It included a clear reference to "on-time arrival for work nineteen days out of every twenty" as a requirement for all employees.

For several months, because of her strong friendship, Jan defended Irene to the DRs who complained, directly or indirectly, about the tardiness issue. One morning, to stop what she called "personal attacks," Jan called a meeting with all the members of executive team (with the exception of Irene, who was late).

Jan explained to the group that Irene was going through a "problem period," one that, "with a little luck," would be resolved soon. That would be all. A strained silence concluded the meeting. The eight executives went back to their work areas.

The next day, Beverly asked Jan for a private meeting. One-on-one, she explained her view of the situation, making sure to do so patiently and respectfully. She told her boss that Irene's lateness had gotten out of hand and had lasted for more than three months; that everyone on the executive staff knew that she, Jan, was ready to make excuses for Irene's tardiness; and that these were excuses Jan would not have made for any other employee, much less a senior manager. Beverly also explained this double standard had led not only to deep resentment among the DRs, but to a potentially serious morale problem throughout the organization. Seven DRs were attempting to implement the no-tardiness standard, and one was not only not implementing it, but personally violating it on a regular basis. "That's not the way you asked us to do things around here," Beverly said.

Jan, Beverly said, was now in a difficult position. She was in the leadership position: the position of deciding what should be done about the problem. Without losing her composure, appearing to challenge Jan or being disrespectful toward her in any way, she waited patiently for Jan's answer.

THE CULTURAL MOMENT OF TRUTH

Jan's position during that difficult conversation with Beverly might not be an enjoyable one, but it is the kind of cultural "tight-spot" where most entrepreneurs and organization founders eventually find themselves in. I'm not talking about the specific challenge of having a "protected" employee who does not live by the stated culture, although that syndrome is quite common. What I mean is that, when you're growing an organization, you eventually encounter some cultural "mismatch" or other that, if left unaddressed, has the potential to damage relations with a critical constituency: your DRs. In fact, this is something all successful private organizations go through at some point. What matters most is not whether or not this moment occurs—it will occur. What really matters is how the KDM responds when it happens. For Jan, the choice awaiting her at the conclusion of her discussion with Beverly was what I call a *Cultural Moment of Truth*.

By the same token, Beverly's decision to raise the cultural issue in the first place was certainly not an easy one. Easy or not, however, it was an example of the kind of discussion that the most effective Direct Reports learn to address with **tactful, persistent** engagement. This is the kind of engagement that distinguishes **High-Performing Direct Reports** from other executives in the organization.

The point is: there is always a first time for every big cultural discussion with the KDM to whom one reports. Beverly's brave decision to raise the issue sparked that first conversation. As such, that decision, too, definitely counts as a *Cultural Moment of Truth*.

During that discussion, Jan politely deflected the issue Beverly had identified

> A Cultural Moment
> of Truth represents an
> opportunity for a serious
> discussion about "how
> we do things around
> here," and about whether
> what we say matches up
> with how we actually do
> things around here.

for her. She thanked Beverly for her insights, told Beverly she would think about the issue and let her know of her decision then moved on to the next item on the agenda.

Two weeks went by, however, and nothing changed. Irene kept coming in late.

Then, the fateful meeting. During another one-on-one meeting, Beverly brought the issue up again.

Just as tactfully, just as patiently, and without any sense of "raising the stakes," Beverly asked Jan if she'd had any thoughts on how best to deal with what she referred to diplomatically as Irene's "tardiness challenge." Jan said she hadn't. Beverly quietly pointed out that the problem within the executive ranks was growing: Every time Jan tolerated culturally unacceptable behavior from Irene, she demonstrated a lack of respect for her other DRs. Of course, this had an effect on their work performance.

By framing the issue as a cultural one, without drama or scorekeeping, Beverly was able to navigate safely around the landmines that surround sensitive issues, such as how to work with close friends. Calmly, purposefully, Beverly kept the discussion professional, reminding Jan of her obligations to the organization.

This time, it worked, in part because Jan sensed and respected the depth of Beverly's determination to keep the discussion productive and professional. After that second conversation, Jan accepted two realities: first, that Beverly understood and was supporting the desired culture in a way that she wanted all of her Direct Reports to do; and second, that the issue wasn't going away. She told Beverly she would have a one-on-one meeting with Irene later that day and resolve the problem once and for all.

Jan met privately with Irene and told her that while she valued her friendship, she, Irene, was no longer free to come in late in the morning. No excuses. No exceptions. A continued pattern of lateness would mean Irene would need to find employment elsewhere. The conversation was not easy, but it was one that needed to happen, and it allowed everyone to move forward in a constructive way.

The next day, and at least nineteen out every twenty days thereafter, Irene showed up for work on time.

FIXING A HOLE

I have gone this far without giving you a formal breakdown of what, exactly, a productive workplace culture is and how it functions because I want to emphasize the point that most of us already know, intuitively, what it is.

The productive workplace culture is what was undermined when Jan allowed a double standard to create a conflict between "what we say we do here" and "what we really do here." The productive workplace culture was what was restored when Beverly showed **tactful, persistent engagement** on behalf of cultural values she believed in and wanted to sustain. Now it's time to extend the definition further. **The right workplace culture is like a roof that protects your organization when rough weather rolls in.**

If you've ever felt a disconnect between the way someone says decisions are going to be made, and the way they are actually made, then you have personally experienced a **hole in that roof:** an unaligned workplace culture.

There's probably something else you've experienced firsthand—the kind of collapse in trust that causes people to "opt out" of a relationship instead of supporting it. That eventually translates to a drop in competitiveness, which is **rain pouring in through the hole in your roof.**

If you've experienced any of that, then you've experienced an **unaligned, dysfunctional workplace culture.**

For both people in the KDM/DR relationship, there eventually comes a Cultural Moment of Truth like this one, a situation where you must decide whether or not you are willing to fix the hole in the roof. Unfortunately, these kinds of roofs spring leaks quite often, and the holes left unattended only grow bigger, never smaller. The roof will always be strongest if you and the KDM decide to patch the leak together.

The key word here is "together." When, like Beverly, you decide to take action on a cultural problem, it's important to remember that you're doing so to protect and repair something, not to dismantle something. Notions of "right" or "wrong" may need to be set aside while you and the KDM diagnose what is actually happening and what the right response is. It's certainly true that Jan's tolerance of a double standard was indeed an example of a problem. That double standard was clear evidence of an unaligned culture—a mismatch between the stated, desired culture and the actual culture. But that problem, major though it was, was not a justification for an attack, direct or indirect, from Beverly, or from anyone else. **Even as you are seeking to fix a problem that relates to workplace culture, it is essential to *support* the right workplace culture.**

It is quite common for DRs to shy away from engaging with the KDM during Cultural Moments of Truth, simply because they fear making some

> **The Organization's Culture reﬂects the values of the KDM but is always inﬂuenced by the organization's executives and other managerial employees, because their roles in decision-making and strategic direction continually define the organization.**

kind of mistake when raising the issue. Here, as elsewhere in the book, there are some clear best practices to follow. Before we go any further, let's notice what Beverly did correctly in engaging Jan to take action and help her "fix the hole in the roof."

Beverly raised this sensitive cultural issue in a private meeting.

Especially when you're exploring a cultural issue that connects to something that your boss has done (or not done), it's imperative you begin the discussion in a one-on-one setting. If you have any doubts about whether an issue should be raised publicly or privately, err on the side of caution and raise it privately.

Beverly raised the subject directly.

Especially when dealing with one's boss, it can be tempting to make vague references to serious cultural challenges that demand specific examination and a clear commitment to change. In this case, dropping a hint or two about how "some people" might need to "look more closely at the issue of timeliness" would not have been sufficient to fix the hole in the roof.

Beverly focused on behavior, not people.

Notice there was no blaming of individuals in any of Beverly's discussions with Jan. She didn't provide a list of "faults" or "mistakes," because she knew that such a list would only provoke conflict. She talked about which actions and choices were causing cultural challenges. She declined the opportunity to pass judgment on anyone.

Beverly kept her tone neutral and nonthreatening.

She knew that how an issue is raised is often more important than the facts that connect to that issue. Beverly communicated tactfully and calmly to Jan about an issue that was important to both of them.

Beverly raised the issue more than once—without escalating.

There are times in any person-to-person relationship when it becomes necessary to raise an issue more than once. The trick is to do so without "raising the stakes" in the relationship. It is quite common for emotions to become strained when we feel our point has not been addressed. With your KDM, however, the "default setting" must be one in which we are certain **we are not perceived as setting an implied or explicit ultimatum by raising the issue a second time.** It takes practice to master this aspect of tactful, assertive engagement, but this practice is essential for any High-Performing Direct Report.

Beverly remembered that the decision about how (and whether) to move forward on the Cultural Moment of Truth belonged to her boss.

Rather than trying to dictate a specific course of action she felt was appropriate, Beverly identified the key issues and waited patiently for a decision.

WHY IS THIS MY JOB?

It's quite common for DRs to ask, "Why should I bother with any of this? Isn't setting and protecting the culture the job of the top person in the organization? Isn't the founder, the entrepreneur, the CEO supposed to embody and reinforce the right workplace culture?"

These are all valid questions.

First and foremost, you should pay attention to the cultural issue because **everyone gets wet when there is a hole in the roof.** In fact, the bigger the hole, the wetter and unhappier everyone is going to be. To protect yourself, your career, and your own stake in the viability of the enterprise, you have to protect the workplace culture.

Second, identifying and protecting a productive workplace culture is indeed the responsibility of the top person in your organization. **Like many such responsibilities, however, this one is literally impossible for him or her to fulfill without the support of DRs like you.**

Third, the KDM is indeed responsible for personally embodying and acting in accordance with, a positive workplace culture. However, you should know that it is a universal trait of High-Performing Direct Reports that they, too, choose to **embody this productive culture,** to live it daily in their own interactions and choices and to serve as a cultural role model for the entire organization.

That's not all. **The single most important relationship when it comes to strengthening or weakening Alignment with the stated culture is the relationship between the KDM and the DR.** That means, you have a personal and an organizational obligation to make the right cultural choices—on a daily basis—in your interactions with your boss!

> **Model and demonstrate the kind of world you demand to live in.— Chuck Palahniuk**

Now you've had a look at the basic issues relating to workplace culture, it's time to examine this extremely important subject in a little more depth (this, too, is an obligation of High-Performing Direct Reports: to commit to a course of continuing education on the subject of workplace culture).

Here's another example of a "hole in the roof." One DR, going through AlignUp™ training, mentioned to me that his department manager had a facilities policy that specified all equipment within 450 feet of his office, and all the offices of senior management, was to look great and be kept in top working order at all times. The rest of the department's equipment did not have to meet this high standard! As a result, the department manager saw a smoothly running operation that rewarded technical excellence, but eventually had to admit that most of his employees saw neglect and carelessness. This was an example of a cultural mismatch. Changing this, to bring about positive cultural Alignment throughout the organization, was one of the benefits of the DR attending the AlignUp™ training program.

WORKPLACE CULTURE 101

The following are some highlights of what Professors Ken Thompson (DePaul University) and Fred Luthans (University of Nebraska) identify as important characteristics of workplace culture.

Culture = Behavior. Our culture is reflected in what we do, and the standards of behavior we accept. Some parts of our workplace culture are more likely to support organizational success and progress than others. A culture that emphasizes a strong commitment to meet or exceed the expectations of internal customers, for instance, is more likely to lead to positive external customer satisfaction scores than a culture that views internal customers (also known as colleagues) as rivals or obstacles.

Culture Is Learned. We adopt certain cultures based on our experiences within a group. We learn to rely on certain workplace behaviors based on the positive or negative consequences of those behaviors. If a certain behavior is rewarded, we tend to repeat it, and the repetition makes it more likely to be accepted as part of our daily working culture. The same is true in reverse—if a behavior is connected with punishment, or any intense negative emotion, we are less likely to repeat it. We can see from this how something seemingly simple, like receiving a heartfelt "thank you" from a senior executive whenever we complete a job at a high degree of competency, can carry immense cultural implications.

Culture Is Learned Through Interaction. We learn our most important lessons about workplace culture when we interact with other employees. We usually figure out what the culture is, and how we can fit into it, based on the exchanges we have with other people. This means things like sarcasm, backbiting, gossiping, and jokes that come at the expense of other people have major negative effects on our working environment and careers.

Sub-cultures Form Through a Lack of Rewards. If we don't reward positive behavior in a positive way, subgroups will form in the organization in which people fulfill their needs, social or otherwise, by sabotaging corporate objectives.

THE ORGANIZATION'S CULTURE STARTS AT THE TOP

Culture starts with the KDM and proceeds through all the DRs in the organization.

The clothes worn at the office by these people, for example, send powerful signals to the rest of the organization about how formal the workplace is or isn't. The way your KDM talks to you will send signals about what is and isn't an acceptable and expected way to communicate ... and also about what is and isn't permissible in terms of one-on-one communication with employees. By the same token, the way you interact with the rest of the organization will send signals to others in the organization. If you respond abusively to mistakes or feedback with which you don't agree, that inevitably affects the workplace culture in a negative way. If you are quick to congratulate the team for good work, this action inevitably shapes the culture in a positive way. And if your KDM, or you as a DR, keep erratic work hours, and are gone from the organization for long periods of time, that sends the rest of the organization important signals about the expected work ethic.

In the final analysis, the organization's everyday working culture is based primarily on what the KDM and the DRs do—and not on what they say the culture should be. What is said is important, but if what is said doesn't match up with what's done, there's a disconnect—a hole in the roof.

STATED VALUES, BEHAVIORAL VALUES

The Organization's culture—"the way we do things around here"—is inevitably the result of certain VALUES that drive behavior. If our stated values match up with what we do, and the decisions we make, we can say our workplace culture is in Alignment. Our stated values are also our behavioral values. That's where we want to be!

Let's look at what's possible when a small organization successfully aligns its stated values with its behavioral values. The huge on-line retailer Zappos.com, now owned by Amazon.com, used to be a much smaller, private organization. One of the breakthroughs in that new organization's history came when the founder, Tony Hsieh, decided to create a list of "hiring values" that would help the organization hire and retain the right people. Hsieh considered the top contributors in his organization—his DRs—and asked himself what values united those people. He came up with the following list, which is now quite famous:

- Deliver WOW Through Service
- Embrace and Drive Change
- Create Fun and A Little Weirdness
- Be Adventurous, Creative, and Open-Minded
- Pursue Growth and Learning
- Build Open and Honest Relationships With Communication
- Build a Positive Team and Family Spirit
- Do More With Less
- Be Passionate and Determined
- Be Humble

Without really meaning to, Hsieh created a powerful written summary of his organization's driving cultural values—a roadmap of the best culture he could envision for his organization. He did this by taking a "snapshot" of the values that were already supporting his organization. Zappos's extraordinary success in the years since has often been attributed to the organization's culture that emerged from the successful reinforcement, and the daily expression, of those values. When taken together, when lived together, those values constitute Zappos's culture.

It's worth noticing that Hsieh worked in the opposite direction from many of the organization's leaders in creating a cultural document. **He looked for what was already working in the organization, and then identified the existing positive values he wanted to reinforce and champion as the core of the workplace culture.** He didn't simply post a sheet of paper that said, "We believe in X, Y, and Z as cultural values," and demand that everyone agree. He had specific role models to point to, and he had clear hiring standards he wanted everyone to follow. He made sure the organization's stated values were also its behavioral values.

It's also worth noticing that, at Zappos, these values are not just hiring guidelines, but also firing guidelines. If you work for Zappos, and you consistently fail to uphold one or more of these values, you can be terminated for not supporting the culture.

In your homework for this chapter, you will be asked to work with your KDM to create a list of "hiring and firing values" that reflect the good stuff that is already happening in your team. These values should be ones that you and your KDM share and can personally model for the rest of the enterprise. When the values are pasted on from the outside, and there are no role models to follow, a list of stated values could do more harm than good!

MORE ON VALUES AND CULTURE

One of the shortest, most effective culture statements by an organization out there is Google's "Don't be evil." It's a great example of how an organization's culture statement can be easy for employees to use to guide decisions. One value drives that culture statement: ethics. Zappos's, as we've seen, goes into more detail. Both were essential tools these organizations used to move from small, private startups to major forces in the organization and cultural landscape. Strong values fuel a strong workplace culture, and a strong workplace culture fuels strong growth.

Here are some more examples of effectively stated core values from successful privately owned organizations.

- Employees must keep their word, be truthful, and not mislead or misrepresent anything.

- We will succeed as a team. This success requires direct communication that embraces respect and is without hidden political agendas. One of the advantages of working for a privately owned organization is that one's career path can be highly rewarding—without the internal politics so common in publicly owned organizations.
- When an employee is wrong, the employee is expected to acknowledge that he or she is wrong, rather than make excuses.
- Employees must keep in confidence all internal communications.
- Employees must recognize the importance of and fully support organization systems, processes, procedures and protocols.
- T.E.A.M. (Trust, Engagement, Acceptance, and Measurement)

The point here is not that your organization must adopt these specific values, or any other list of values written by someone else. The point is that you and your KDM must be in explicit agreement about which values constitute your organization's unique culture, and how those values will be expressed on a daily basis, in actions and words the entire organization can understand. **The words chosen should be unique to your organization. They should serve as the "compass point" by which goals are evaluated, tactics vetted, and disputes resolved in the one-on-one setting experienced by you and your KDM, and in the larger context of the organization as a whole.**

Just as there are functional and dysfunctional families, there are functional and dysfunctional teams. Think of the last time you went to a supermarket on a very busy shopping day. Doubtless, you saw many families in the aisles. Some of those parents and kids interacted harmoniously and made decisions, about where to go next and what to buy, with little evident conflict or hard feeling. Other groups fought loudly and openly, spoke inappropriately, or even had major public meltdowns (and I'm not just talking about the toddlers). The difference: some families have established a functional system of values—also known as a culture—that supports both their relationships and their decision-making. For other families who go out shopping, it's evident the system of values is still, shall we say, a work in progress. It's exactly the same with teams and organizations.

FIVE CORE VALUES THAT SUPPORT A PRODUCTIVE WORKPLACE CULTURE

No matter what the stated values or culture may be, there are five Core Values you can model as a DR that will strengthen your organization's workplace culture and improve your relationship with your KDM.

These values can (and should!) be defined in words that make sense to both you and your KDM. Even if that formal statement of values hasn't yet been written, you can help move your organization closer to cultural Alignment by adopting and living these five values, which always show up somewhere in the working culture of successful organizations. Although they will eventually need to be given names that match up with your KDM's (and the organization's) personality, I have assigned these five values the following provisional labels, so we can evaluate them here:

- Execution Commitment
- Respectful Conflict Resolution
- Timeliness
- Continuing Education and Personal Development
- Integrity

Yes, the KDM is responsible for setting the organization's culture; yes, the KDM has prime responsibility to ensure that key organization goals and strategies integrate, and are consistent with, the culture of the organization. Ultimately, however, it is the DR who will be responsible for making it all happen. The process of cultural Alignment will be quicker, smoother, and less stressful for both you and your KDM once you make a personal commitment to live by these five values, all of which are hallmarks of High-Performing Direct Reports. Let's look at each of these five **Core Values** in detail now.

CORE VALUE #1: EXECUTION COMMITMENT

We start here because this value represents an easy point of buy-in for the KDM. Whatever difference in terminology or interpretation may exist with regard to other values, you may rest assured that your KDM really does want you to adopt, live by, and evangelize this value. If you have to choose any one value to model, build your career around, and begin the cultural conversation with, it should be this universally implemented trait of all High-Performing Direct Reports.

Execution Commitment is the value that connects directly to setting goals and achieving. An organization's leader with an endless supply of "great ideas" will only be a high-performing executive if he or she also has a strong personal commitment to **Execution Commitment**: the ability to produce a tangible result and not get caught up in abstractions.

Too many organizations' leaders are wrapped up in their great ideas without understanding the real-world need to bring about an end result. They are leaders only in name. Both KDMs and DRs need to be able to convert ideas into plans, and plans into actions that bring about achievement. The idea is not the key. The solution is the key. Both partners in this relationship should be committed to converting ideas and knowledge into end results. **This value should be considered non-negotiable, and must be a central component of the relationship between the KDM and the DR.**

Success is measured by execution, not inspiration. Many managers sound great, but somehow repeatedly fail to execute their goals, even though they are clear about what those goals are. My experience is that this is either because they are distracted by too many goals, and thus unable to focus their commitment to achieving the goals, or they know if they don't achieve the goals, there is no accountability.

Sticking with a project until it's achieved is something that some people, for whatever reason, simply don't do. They don't make a habit of executing their goals. That problem is, at its most basic level, a cultural one. If the organization says one of its core values is goal orientation, achievement, or the ability to deliver positive results, yet keeps rewarding (or at least keeps tolerating) those who don't have a strong execution commitment, this is a major Alignment gap. That gap is unacceptable, both on the individual and organizational levels. Make sure you are not one of those people contributing to the gap!

If a DR cannot prioritize, neutralize personal fear, minimize or eliminate low-value-add activities and execute on goals, then he or she is likely to be a failure as far as a productive organization culture is concerned.

Many employees are smart but simply lack the tenacity to set objectives and pursue them tenaciously. In order to stand apart from such employees, you should be ready, willing, and able to push back whenever you find yourself bogged down with endless meetings or too much administrative reporting. Both the KDM and the DR need to be able to discuss the most direct, practical way to bring about a given result. This, too, is part of tactful, assertive engagement.

Many low-impact DRs seem to know what to do but just don't get around to accomplishing the right goals. Very often, this is the result of a weak "execution commitment" muscle. It takes discipline to stick with a plan until execution brings about the goal you desire. Of course, KDMs need to support the development of this kind of discipline, and they must be open to the possibility that the DR may go about doing things in a different way than they would.

In the organizations I have led, I've tried to establish a culture in which all my DRs understood that if they saw something they really did not like doing, or weren't good at doing, there could be discussions about getting help from another DR who was good at that part of the job. I believe this kind of DR transparency is an undervalued cultural value, one that is essential to developing execution commitment on the individual level—and without reinforcing execution commitment at the individual level, you cannot build a high performing organization.

Transparency goes both ways, of course. KDMs need to keep DRs "in the loop" if they expect them to execute their goals. KDMs are usually quite comfortable adjusting their approach and finding new ways to solve problems. That's because they tend to be ready, willing, and able to change tactics when it comes to executing on goals!

EXECUTION COMMITMENT

Years ago, I had the opportunity to meet Dr. Stephen Covey. We discussed many issues and found there were certain values we shared. One of them was the second habit expressed in his classic book, The Seven Habits of Highly Effective People (1989). Covey describes the second habit as "Beginning with the end in mind." This is precisely the same value I describe as Execution Commitment.

> An organization that does not reward and value execution commitment is an organization preparing for its own decline.

This value was the subject of one of our most interesting conversations. Covey described it as the key differentiation between successful organizations and those that didn't achieve their potential. The culture of the achieving organization, he noted, is much more likely to include an emphasis on management having a limited number of clear objectives, and employees understanding those few objectives and focusing most of their energies on them, so they could be successfully attained.

Is that how your organization operates? Is that the hallmark of your KDM/DR relationship? Your Organization's Culture should embrace all levels of Execution Commitment (whatever you choose to call it in your organization). That often includes some counterintuitive steps, such as taking action to get rid of systems and processes that time and experience have shown to be ineffective, or adapting new approaches that have been tested in other industries.

CORE VALUE #2: RESPECTFUL CONFLICT RESOLUTION

Conflict of some kind is inevitable in any organization setting, which is why a productive workplace culture is dependent on resolving conflicts respectfully.

I place heavy emphasis on the cultural value of resolving conflict respectfully, especially when it arises (as it inevitably does) between a KDM and a DR. Their ability to use and model effective conflict resolution techniques is important to the productive working culture of the organization as a whole.

Without meaningful efforts from both sides to resolve the most difficult conflicts, the KDM may not invest the necessary time and effort in the relationship with his or her DR—and the DR will not have the trust necessary to give full effort towards achieving goals set by the KDM. The two of you must model effective conflict resolution for the rest of the organization, including (but not limited to) those people who report directly to you.

Successful conflict resolution depends on good will, patience, and the assumption of good intent on both sides. Make sure there are plenty of all three elements on your side!

Very often, conflict resolution problems arise because the KDM and the DR do not take the time to understand each other's true motives. Consider the following true story. Dianne, a DR, mentioned in a group Alignment session that her boss, Carlos, was "paranoid" as he was always asking whether one of the other DRs was doing something against his direction. Conflicts about the "short leash" he kept her, and other executives, on were common. Dianne's moment of empowerment came when she stopped complaining to others about this problem and took action to improve the situation. She realized as long as she "had her boss's back", she could make it clear to Carlos that things were being handled. Carlos had, at times, treated her with suspicion. Concerned he was being undermined, he had kept the reins very tight indeed. The reins loosened, however, as Dianne learned to do the things necessary to make Carlos understand she totally supported him—even if she disagreed with him.

The moral here: you don't have to "brown-nose" for your KDM to realize you have his or her back. You do, however, need to make it clear that no matter how you feel about the KDM's decisions, you are not going to get involved in organization politics that undermine him or her. Then you have to keep that commitment! Direct Reports who "get" this point typically have far fewer conflict resolution problems with the KDM than those who don't "get" it. When the relationship is based on mutual respect, and mutual commitment, then differing perspectives and points of view become much easier to address together.

Sometimes, even with plenty of good will and patience, effective conflict resolution may require the involvement of a neutral third party from outside your organization. If a neutral third party is needed or desired, try to identify someone who understands your organization well enough to facilitate discussions based upon the organization realities of your particular organization.

As in any productive relationship, you and your KDM should learn (and care about) what sets the other person off. Another way of describing conflict resolution, and one I prefer, is "resolution of unaligned behavior triggers." Whatever you choose to call it, aim to find a way to "build it into the DNA" of your relationship with your KDM, and, eventually, your organization.

> **A commitment to mutual respect within the KDM/DR relationship is the foundation upon which all positive cultural experiences and expectations within the rest of the organization are built.**

CORE VALUE #3: TIMELINESS

This value is all about priorities

Some KDMs are entrepreneurs who are "all about the idea." They come up with a great idea, and an individual or team in their organization starts running with it. The individual or team commits to a deadline and starts working towards achieving the goal of the idea. The next thing they know, their KDM is onto the next idea—and the individual/team is told by the KDM to work on something else! This contributes significantly, in many privately owned organizations, to creating a culture where deadlines are meaningless. There is a need to have disciplined Alignment on the part of the KDMs and the DRs to stick to one set of established priorities before moving to the next.

There is a certain amount of overlap here with Core Value #1, and that's as it should be. Here, the emphasis is on respecting (or, in extreme cases, renegotiating) schedule commitments, which is a value that some perfectionists find difficult to embrace. With many entrepreneurs, the value of timeliness is one of **getting it done in a way that achieves goals and honors time commitments, rather than waiting until everything is perfect**. One of the Organization's Cultural values of Facebook is the timeliness required by Mark Zuckerberg throughout his organization, stated as "Done is Better than Perfect." When deadlines are given, and time commitments made, they are expected to be completed on time.

The value by which employees understand that committed-to deadlines cannot simply fall through the cracks is one that, I believe, is built into any and every successful organization. I believe a culture that supports and rewards committed timelines helps employees organize their time and set their priorities. Meeting deadlines gives a sense of satisfaction. An organization that tolerates a team or individual's consistent inability to meet time commitments is an organization that won't maximize its opportunity for success.

When any employee has a clear personal pattern of missing deadlines, the pattern shows that employee either doesn't take his or her job seriously, or doesn't care about the unprofessional image being created.

> **The organization's culture of accountability to make and fulfill time commitments should start within the KDM/DR relationship, and it should go both ways.**

Part of the mutual responsibility for creating effective timelines is for each side to be very clear as to what is expected, and when. For example, a commitment from a DR who promises to having a certain project "ready sometime next week" is not as specific as a commitment that the project will be "ready to e-mail to customer X by 9:00 am Wednesday." There should be clarity on these specifics.

The elements of your organization's culture regarding deadlines should include the opportunity for Alignment between the person committing to the deadline (for our purposes, this is typically the DR) and the person receiving the deadline (typically the KDM). There needs to be a discussion about the real-world viability of the deadline being proposed. Many conflicts between KDMs and DRs arise because of the DR's inability or unwillingness to push back against an unrealistic deadline proposed by the KDM. But that ability to push back—tactfully, of course—is essential. And the DR, by the same token, must be ready, willing, and able to have similarly realistic discussions with his or her own direct reports about the attainability of specific goals under specific timelines. Here again, whatever dynamic plays out between the KDM and the DR is likely to play out between the DR and his or her direct reports.

It reflects poorly on an employee who accepts a deadline that he or she knows cannot be completed on time. It is the responsibility of the employee to suggest, and be able to commit to, deadlines that he or she feels confident about keeping. In many cases, the proper way of responding is to say "no" if you know you simply don't have the time or resources to complete a project to the desired level of quality. Usually, your KDM will respect this response far more than a "commitment" to a project you know you can't finish on time.

There are times DRs have to use the art of "pushing back" against a KDM-imposed deadline request that does not intersect with the reality of their own working worlds. Good DRs know that many, perhaps most, timelines proposed by KDMs are potentially unrealistic. They also know that, unless there is a true crisis involved, the timeline they agree to should include a certain cushion to allow for unexpected factors that may occur.

When I refer to a timeline, I'm not just referring to a date the completed project will be ready. A timeline should include dates for completion of intermediate steps that need to be satisfactorily completed to achieve the complete objective in a timely way.

Mike, the founder and KDM at an online retailer, wanted to create a culture that supported and rewarded open communication between the person who is accountable for the project and all others who need to know how things are progressing along the way. He scheduled weekly status meetings with George, his VP of Marketing, so that George could update Mike on how the organization's promotional plans were unfolding and explain the latest factors affecting the timely fulfillment of the annual plan. Mike's motto for these meetings served as an important cultural landmark for the relationship, and the organization as a whole: "No blame, just the facts."

If unexpected roadblocks emerge, the person accountable for the project needs to inform the others of the roadblocks. Often, plans can be changed so the roadblocks don't impact the timely and successful completion of the project. This dynamic begins with the timeline-related discussions between the KDM and the DR. Remember: making committed-to deadlines applies to KDMs and DRs alike. If either has a pattern of not keeping commitment deadlines, the organization's culture will be affected in an adverse way.

Every once in a while, I run into someone who resists the notion that timeliness really is one of the most important values, and a value that needs to be built into the "DNA" of a successful organization. Whenever I find myself in that kind of discussion, I make these two points:

Usually, no one is upset when a person trying to make a deadline asks for help ... but *everyone* is upset if the person who has committed to a deadline repeatedly misses deadlines. With the kind of workplace value I am advocating, asking for *and giving* help, when appropriate, is part and parcel of the cultural "package." It is okay to ask for help. That must be part of "how we do things here." This is actually a much better situation than the one in which many people work; where the person who faces a challenge in meeting a deadline feels bad about asking for help and consequently doesn't do so until it's too late (or doesn't ask at all).

Whenever a deadline is missed and there are no repercussions, it reinforces an attitude within the organization of, "Well, if *that person* can miss a deadline and no one cares, why should I care about meeting *my* deadlines?" This attitude builds productivity roadblocks for the organization as a whole ... and eventually keeps everyone from achieving at the highest level!

Build a culture where the person committing to the timeline will either accomplish what they say they will by the promised date, or ask for help. Start with the KDM/DR relationship!

CORE VALUE #4: CONTINUING EDUCATION AND PERSONAL DEVELOPMENT

A commitment to ongoing personal development—which I also call "people development"—has a huge impact on the organization's potential.

You want a productive workplace culture that is Aligned with, and supports, the goal of developing all employees to their highest potential where they have a maximum level of organization impact. If your organization hasn't yet embraced this value, you can kick-start the process by committing some portion of your time, perhaps a few hours a week, to an online training program that is relevant to both your personal career path and the competitiveness of your enterprise. We are blessed to live in a time when it is extremely easy to find such on-line programs (for a summary of the many free courses offered online by Harvard University, for instance, you can visit http://www.harvard.edu/faqs/free-courses).

Making "people development" an ongoing, everyday reality in the workplace is a value shared by virtually all highly successful organizations. If your KDM has not embraced this value explicitly, my advice is that you make the first investment of time, attention, or other resources, then, during a one-on-one meeting with your KDM, share what you have done to expand your knowledge. Before the meeting ends, ask for your KDM's guidance in identifying additional ways for you to develop and grow, so you can have a more significant impact on the organization's growth.

Low commitment to Core Value #4, yields lower performance and poor retention of the employees you want to keep. Such a culture drives away high performers, who invariably choose to pursue other employment options whenever they have the opportunity.

Make sure your KDM knows that a positive working culture will help your organization create a major competitive edge—by recruiting and retaining high performers. Sharing Julio's story, which appears below, may help.

At an organization -networking event, I happened to meet Julio—a qualified, highly experienced DR who had recently quit from a government division where he had worked for nearly a decade. The reasons he gave for quitting all tied in with the division's culture that had no interest in supporting him in his goal to broaden his personal and

> **Employee efficiency and organization success are profoundly affected by an organization's commitment to continuing education and personal development.**

professional horizons. Unfortunately, the pattern of the organization's lack of support for his personal development was clearly established in his mind. He told me he had raised the issue many times with his KDM, who simply refused to address it, saying the organization had no business making such investments. Finally, Julio decided it was time to move on. The dollar value of the many years of experience that walked out the door with him is impossible to quantify precisely, but I suspect it easily exceeded two or three million dollars.

In such cases, the problem of "high turnover among executives and managers" is actually the result of a lack of commitment to the core value of continuing education and personal development. That oversight carries potentially serious, negative implications for the organization. Your job as DR may be to make the first critical investment of time and attention in your personal development, so that your KDM can follow your good example! (Reading this book, by the way, is an excellent start.)

CORE VALUE #5: INTEGRITY

Your word is precious—remembering this simple fact is critical to honoring the fifth core cultural value.

You don't say things you don't mean. You don't mislead people intentionally. You don't make commitments unless you fully intend to keep them. You don't play games with other people's expectations of you. To put it another way, your words, your best values, and your actions are in full Alignment.

I saw a television reality show where two actors pulled a practical joke on a person who didn't realize he was being filmed (I'll call the gentleman who was the target of this joke, Ryan). Actor A pretended to be a survey taker. In return for Ryan's answers to some seemingly innocuous questions, such as where he went to high school, where he attended college, and what his last few jobs had been, Ryan received a gift certificate for a nearby store, which he was urged to spend promptly.

When he emerged from the store, Ryan was met by Actor B—who had, of course, carefully reviewed all the information collected by Actor A. Actor B, who had never met Ryan before in his life, pretended to be a member of Ryan's graduating high school class. Did Ryan remember him, he wondered?

Ryan said he did (he couldn't have, of course. This was a lie, perhaps one designed to get Ryan out of an awkward social situation).

Was Ryan still working at such-and-such an advertising agency?

Ryan said he wasn't (that part was true).

Would Ryan be willing to help his old high-school buddy?

Ryan, who seemed eager to exit the conversation, said he would if he could.

The Actor then fed Ryan a story: he was trying to break into the same industry Ryan had once worked in: advertising. He had just come from a job interview that hadn't gone well. Would Ryan be willing to call the personnel office right now and say that they had worked together, and that he, the Actor, would make a great hire?

Ryan not only agreed to give this total stranger a glowing personal recommendation that was totally untrue—he used the Actor's cell phone and made the call on the spot, with a big smile on his face! Here we have a person who showed evidence of having absolutely zero integrity, caught on film for all the world to see. I wonder what Ryan's current employer thought of his performance when it showed up on TV. I wonder what his family thought. I wonder what his life partner thought.

What started the whole cycle? A "little" lie about a "social" matter: whether Ryan remembered someone from ten years ago.

If your word means nothing in "little" situations, how much will it be worth in "big" situations?

If you don't know something, say you don't know!

If you feel, after having read about this practical joke, that you wouldn't choose to trust Ryan with your life, your reputation, or your last twenty bucks, you know why it's so very important to live in Alignment with the value of integrity. You are asking your KDM to trust you with the future of the organization. Your KDM needs daily evidence of your relentless effort to live by this value of integrity, and so does everyone else in your life. You need daily evidence that you're living in Alignment with integrity.

> **Always tell the truth; then you don't have to remember anything.**
> **—Mark Twain**

Will you slip up sometimes? Probably. You're human. But when you do slip up, you'll apologize where appropriate and do your best to make amends to those you've let down. If that's not the standard you're willing to hold yourself to, you should not expect your KDM to take your commitments seriously.

When you give your word, mean what you say. When you commit to something, make sure you keep your commitment, or, failing that, circle back to the person you made the commitment to and explain why you can't keep your commitment.

Bob, a KDM in a manufacturing nonprofit organization, told me a culture had evolved in his organization that he described as an "I never make mistakes" attitude. The nonprofit organization consistently achieved results that fell well short of Bob's goals for the organization.

Bob decided to eliminate the "I never make mistakes" attitude within his organization by issuing a written Culture Statement for his organization. The statement included a sentence that made it clear that employees were expected to admit their mistakes and not make excuses. This is an important aspect of integrity.

Bob then evangelized and protected this culture through his own direct actions with his DRs, who eventually moved beyond the "I never make mistakes" attitude. This one critical cultural change transformed his organization and dramatically improved its performance.

THE MORAL: if you make a mistake, own up to it! This is part of integrity.

Those are the five core values that should be part of your relationship with your KDM, and part of your organization's productive workplace culture. If you can make a personal commitment to live by these values this month, you will quickly see an improvement in the "micro-culture" of your interactions with your boss. Your homework (below) will help you and your KDM extend those positive changes to the "macro-culture" of the larger enterprise. Keep in mind, you can either support or undermine the stated values of your organization with the way you address the following:

- Decision making
- Daily work practices
- Terminology/language
- Rituals (such as a weekly meeting, celebration period, or "morning huddle")
- Symbols
- Anecdotes, stories, and other cultural narratives
- Interactions with other employees, including fellow Direct Reports

YOUR HOMEWORK: PART ONE

Start by discussing and getting your KDM's direct feedback on the value of Execution Commitment, which you learned about in this chapter. Explain that from this point forward, you intend to hold yourself to this value. Ask for "gentle reminders" if you should happen to lose sight of this value.

NOTE: if you have completed the first part of your homework, above, AND you report to the KDM in the organization, continue with the next part of the homework (remember: the KDM is the person who has ultimate personal responsibility for the success or failure of the organization's operations).

YOUR HOMEWORK, PART TWO

Suggest to your KDM that you work together to create a list of "hiring values," based on "what's working now" in your organization. This list of values will help those with hiring and employee assessment responsibilities to identify prospective employees who have the strongest capacity to make a high-impact contribution to your organization. Consider starting with the five values outlined in this chapter. Alternatively, you might each silently think of a person who best exemplifies "what this organization is all about," and then list the qualities you associate with that person. In addition to the values already discussed in this chapter, the qualities on your list might include:

- Welcomes Change
- Empowerment
- Engagement
- Teamwork/Cross Functional Cooperation
- Service that Produces Loyal Customers
- Innovation as a Way of Life
- Corporate and Personal Responsibility
- The following questions should be considered when you and your KDM are comparing lists and discussing the desired "hiring values."
- Is there a value relating to honesty that we want to express?
- Is there a value relating to work ethics?
- Is there a value relating to respect?
- Is there a value relating to talking about people behind their backs?
- Is there a value relating to employee empowerment, i.e. getting employee weigh-in on certain matters, rather than just buy-in/obedience?
- Is there a value relating to employee development/training/continuing education?
- Is there a value relating to timeliness and meeting deadlines/commitments?
- Is there a value relating to respectful conflict resolution?
- Is engagement—honest, open, constructive discussion—something you value from employees?
- How do you value teamwork or cross-functional cooperation among your employees?
- What services to customers and clients are valued, and how are they valued?

- Is change/innovation as a way of life something you desire to see as a guiding value for the organization?

The written cultural statement you work together to develop should include the Core Values outlining: how employees are to be treated; the way employees are expected to interact with customers, clients, and others who are important to the organization; the KDM's most important expectations; and, most important of all, this document should reflect the most positive expression of the KDM's workplace personality.

CHAPTER 8

Align on The Organization's Vision

EXECUTIVE SUMMARY FOR THE KEY DECISION MAKER

Your long-term vision for the organization, over the next five to ten years, should be the foundation for all of the organization's plans. It should bring **about Alignment** by clarifying for your **Direct Report (DR)** exactly where everyone in the organization should be focusing effort and attention. It should also motivate your DR (and everyone else) to see the organization reach your desired destination.

If your organization doesn't have such a document, then it is time to create it. Your DR's assignment is simple: to use the information in this chapter to help you develop a compelling written **Vision Statement for your organization.** By taking time to do this, you will make it easier for others in the organization to support your vision, and harder for projects that don't fit into that vision to get off the ground.

When your DR approaches you about this, discuss the subject in appropriate depth, and let your DR take notes. This process, which entails only a modest time investment on your part, can begin with something as simple as a decision to go out together for a working lunch. The Organization's Vision Statement process will soon pick up momentum of its own. It will benefit both you and your organization in a powerful way once the Organization's Vision Statement becomes a cultural "touch point" for the enterprise as a whole.

CLARIFYING THE ORGANIZATION'S VISION

During an Alignment training session, Bob, a CFO DR, shared with the other DRs his experience of meeting with his KDM, Mia, to discuss the long-term vision of the organization (this factor of Alignment had been discussed in the previous month's meeting). Bob wanted to be sure he was in line with Mia's vision for the organization.

Mia owned six successful retail hardware stores in one major metropolitan area. She had launched her organization from a single dreary location in a desolate strip mall fifteen years ago; now all six of her locations were in prime spots and producing handsome results, despite pressures from the big chains.

Mia responded to Bob by sharing, for the first time, that her dream was, over the next five to ten years, to expand the organization slowly into a ten-to-twelve store chain, with all the stores being within a two-hour drive from her home.

Bob explained to us that, prior to having this vision for his organization discussion with his KDM, he and his fellow DRs were working under the assumption that the organization's future would be that of a region-wide chain, not one that served a single metropolitan area. Only after having a meeting with Mia did he understand the plans he and his fellow DRs were considering conflicted with Mia's personal vision of the organization becoming a chain of local stores.

The discrepancy led to some interesting discussions. Bob and a couple of his fellow DRs had a follow-up meeting with Mia. During that meeting, they pointed out to Mia that she would be able to enjoy annual seven-figure distributions in personal income if the region-wide chain organization's vision were to be reached. Mia, however, did not show any enthusiasm for the possibility of earning more than a million dollars a year—if it involved her organization doing a region-wide expansion.

Mia explained to her DRs that the effort necessary to grow her retail organization into a regional chain was simply not worth it to her, because her personal commitment of time for reaching that goal would need to be enormous. She also shared her belief that such grand plans would require substantial financial risk on her part, risk she had no intention of taking on.

Thanks to good two-way communication and the strong level of trust that existed between her and her DRs, Mia was able to develop a compensation program that fulfilled her own goals for growth, and at the same time motivated her DRs to operate at a level of great synergy and Alignment with her vision. It's worth noting, though, that this compensation plan took several discussions to work out.

Bob learned from this experience that open and respectful communication between the organization's KDM and the DRs was essential to establishing Alignment with Mia's true—and previously unstated—vision for the organization. His next job was clear: to help Mia get the Organization's Vision down in black and white.

THE ORGANIZATION'S VISION STATEMENT MUST BE WHAT THE KDM WANTS!

The organization you work for is a catalyst for your KDM to reach his/her personal dreams. It is the power source that propels your KDM towards reaching his/her personal vision of success and happiness. The core purpose of the Organization's Vision Statement, and the organization as a whole, is thus quite simple: to satisfy the owner's dreams.

No Organization's Vision Statement is viable unless it reflects what the KDM actually wants.

A common mistake among DRs is to assume that the KDM must want money. If an organization is privately owned, and if the owner is like most organization owners, there are many other aspects besides financial results that will affect your KDM's vision for the organization.

Organization image or recognition may be as important for one KDM as generating increased wealth is for someone else. The questions shared below will help your KDM, and you, learn what your KDM really wants from the organization—and it may not be what you think.

Set aside time with your KDM to work through the checklist of questions that appear below (many DRs choose to review these questions during a "working lunch" with the KDM). Note: This discussion is part of the homework for this chapter.

THE ORGANIZATION'S VISION STATEMENT: "WHY BOTHER?"

Where there is no vision, the people perish—Proverbs 29:18

Some KDMs will ask: "Why should I take the time to support and guide the creation of a written Vision Statement for my organization?"

The best answer sounds like this: organizations that know where they want to go achieve better outcomes than those that suffer from lack of direction from the top. **There is always a high cost to be paid for not having a written Vision Statement for an organization.**

One professional service organization, which provides services related to reducing energy costs for their clients, learned this in a costly manner. The owner of the organization had in his mind, but not in a written statement, a clear long-term vision of his organization becoming a leading provider of energy cost-reduction services to clients throughout North America. The organization underachieved on this goal because a written Vision Statement for the organization was not created and circulated. If it had been, the organization could have avoided a costly blunder rooted in a DR's lack of clarity regarding the desired organization destination. That blunder involved a major research and development budget, requested and approved by a VP of the organization, for a real-estate tax reduction system. Monies used to develop this service were not in line with the owner's vision for the organization, which centered on energy savings, not tax savings. This project diverted, and in fact wasted, several hundred thousand organization dollars and countless hours of employee time.

The project, which was never emotionally supported by the owner of the organization, turned out to be a total failure. Even if it had been successfully developed, it still would not have delivered the highest possible impact, simply because the project did not lead to achieving the KDM's vision.

Following my recommendation, this organization's written Vision Statement was developed and shared, one that clearly expressed the owner's desired destination for the organization. It is no accident that this organization, once it had a written Vision Statement in place, better focused the efforts of its DRs. Its financial results improved dramatically.

You may wish to share this true story with your KDM—tactfully of course, and at an appropriate point in the conversation.

The main point to bear in mind during the discussion with your KDM is that, without an organization's written Vision Statement, everyone in the organization is operating at a disadvantage: you, your KDM, your fellow DRs, and, indeed, the enterprise as a whole. There may be actions, there may be energy, there may be movement and noise—but to what end? If you don't have a written Vision Statement for your organization, you can't possibly answer that question. You're a little like one of those kids at a birthday party; blindfolded, spun around and instructed to pin the tail on the donkey. On your own, you have no idea whether or not you are headed in the right direction. That's no way to run a career—and no way to run an organization, either.

THE VISION STATEMENT, THE MISSION STATEMENT

Some organizations publish an extremely concise "mission statement" for their clients, customers and suppliers. This is usually found by excerpting certain key words and phrases from the organization's written Vision Statement. This type of Mission Statement supports the Vision Statement—by definition—since it comes from the Vision Statement. It often identifies the organization's purpose or primary reason for existence. The Organization Mission Statement can also serve as a concise message to remind organization employees about a particularly important factor that relates to the long-term destination of the organization.

Google's Mission Statement is a good example. It reads as follows: Google's mission is to organize the world's information and make it universally accessible and useful. Our organization has packed a lot into a relatively young life.

TRUST AND MUTUAL UNDERSTANDING

As you have no doubt gathered by now, this chapter is all about identifying the specifics of the KDM's long-term vision for the firm. It is also, however, crucially, about trust and mutual understanding.

Your relationship with your KDM must be strong enough to sustain this (sensitive) discussion. Note that Mia's experience, which I described earlier, was initiated by Bob, one of her trusted DRs. The resulting discussions clarified her vision of the organization for them. What's just as important to understand, though, is that this experience deepened the already strong level of trust and mutual understanding that existed between Mia and her most important executives. It kept them moving in the right direction—together.

In many cases, this process will require a discussion be initiated about a future the KDM has not yet articulated. Sometimes, as in Mia's case, KDMs withhold discussions about their vision of the organization's future because, for whatever reason, they don't feel comfortable discussing that vision and need help and support to do so. In other cases, KDMs are simply unclear about what they want to see happen next. Some KDMs are so caught up in running the organization that they haven't taken the time or energy to think about the future vision, even if they had one at the organization's inception.

Your job now is to initiate a trust-driven-with-vision discussion with your own KDM like the one Bob initiated with Mia.

One of the things you'll learn very quickly as you undertake this critical task is that the level of trust between two individuals does not stand still. Trust between two people either increases or diminishes over time. Your responsibility is to make sure the level of trust between you and the KDM is increasing over time—not diminishing.

Here are five simple things you can do to build and reinforce trust with your KDM:

- Avoid "hidden agendas." Express what you want to accomplish and why.
- Be open and sincere. If you feel something—satisfaction, uncertainty, frustration—find a way to express it that is appropriate to the relationship and the situation.
- Maintain a non-judgmental atmosphere. Focus on the action—not the person.
- Have goal-oriented discussions. These are discussions that return in a constructive way to this question: "What are we trying to accomplish here?"
- Avoid overemotional responses. Keep it professional; remember; this relationship is not the place for you to get your emotional needs met.

Making these five guidelines recurring realities in your relationship with your KDM is your first and most important assignment. If you are not moving in the right direction in terms of mutual trust with your KDM, you will find it very hard to carry out the rest of the assignments in this chapter. Seemingly "little things" can have a disproportionately large impact on your ability to fulfill the goals laid out here if they affect your KDM's ability to rely on you, trust you implicitly, and appreciate your good intent.

For your KDM, sharing the true dimensions of the vision that will guide the organization may be the ultimate "sensitive organization discussion," one that is only possible when your KDM is certain you can be trusted implicitly. That level of implicit trust was necessary for Mia and her DRs, and it will be necessary for your KDM and you, too. If there is any area where you need to clean house, regain the implicit trust of your KDM, or perhaps earn it for the first time: do that now.

THE TARGET

The KDM's long-term vision for the organization is the target at which everyone should be aiming. Everything a KDM, a DR, and all other staff do should be in Alignment with the KDM's desired vision of the organization five to ten years in the future.

The organization's use of resources should be focused on achieving those factors critical to achieving the KDM's vision for the organization.

You cannot hit the target if you don't know what it is. If the DRs have a lack of clarity and Alignment with the organization's long-term vision, the organization is not likely to achieve its highest potential level of success.

Lack of clarity and Alignment with the organization's long-term vision is also the cause of great frustration for both KDMs and DRs. The apparent sources of this frustration may appear to be things like lost opportunities, reduced market share, poor "investment" decisions affecting the deployment of available resources, and/or the unexpected departure of key employees. The actual source of all the frustration, however, is nearly always the same: a lack of clarity about the KDM's vision.

As a DR, you cannot help develop the right strategies, the right organization plans, or even the right department projects unless you have an in-depth understanding of the KDM's long-term vision for the organization.

> **The point cannot be overemphasized: sustainable, high-impact results from you (or any DR) require a comprehensive understanding of the KDM's long-term vision.**

TWO KEY ELEMENTS

There are two key elements that combine to make up the long-term vision of the organization. The first element relating to the long-term vision of the organization, are the factors shared in the organization's written Vision Statement. These factors are shared with all organization employees and may be shared with the world by being shown on the organization Website.

The second element, which I call the **Pocket Vision**, involves privileged subjects the KDM wants to see as part of the future of the organization that are not included in the written the Organization's Vision Statement. These are situations where the KDM elects to keep certain facts, plans, and personal conclusions "in his or her pocket." This second element, as you might imagine, is a good deal more complex than the first one.

You will be developing the first of these two vision elements, the Organization's Vision Statement, in your homework for this chapter, side-by-side with your KDM. The second element, the Pocket Vision, is more likely to be an ongoing personal discussion about the organization's (and the KDM's) best interests—a discussion that plays out over time. This discussion must have as its foundation the bedrock of trust you and your KDM establish and/or expand—in part, by working collaboratively on things like the Organization's Vision Statement.

As the DR, you should fully understand and support the Organization's Vision long before you start considering what needs to be done to turn the KDM's vision into reality. If you don't understand the vision, or don't buy into it, you can't expect to implement it very well!

VISION ELEMENT #1: THE ORGANIZATION'S VISION STATEMENT (AN OVERVIEW)

With respect to the first key element—the organization's written Vision Statement—the good news is that it is not difficult to create.

This document requires a few comprehensive discussions between you and your KDM about how best to summarize those parts of your KDM's dreams for the organization that should be communicated to organization employees (and, perhaps, to the outside world).

The most important by-product of creating and circulating this document is that every employee of the organization, including the DRs, can then work to get the organization to the destination identified by your KDM. This is an advantage you should be prepared to highlight consistently, in a tactful but persistent way, during the development process.

If your organization does not have a written Vision Statement, you will find, in this chapter, a clear protocol for creating one. This protocol features specific questions that, once answered, will make creating an initial draft of the organization's written Vision Statement a relatively easy thing for you and your KDM to do. Of course, the content must be driven by your KDM's vision for the organization, not yours—although it is quite common for there to be significant areas of overlap.

If your organization already has a Vision Statement, the questions you will find later in this chapter will help you and your KDM to evaluate and update that document.

DIRECT REPORTS BELONG IN THE CONVERSATION!

In a perfect world, it would always be the KDM who emerged as the driving force to create (or update) the document that clarifies his or her desired vision for the long-term future of the organization. In the real world, this is not always the case.

As a DR, it may well be up to you to discuss with your KDM the need to create your enterprise's written Vision Statement and to communicate it. But regardless of who is the driving force, it is best if the finished statement incorporates input from you and the other DRs in the organization.

Input from DRs on the contents of the organization's written Vision Statement may be granted on a permission basis from the KDM. A DR has no right to alter the organization's written Vision Statement without this permission.

The very best Vision Statements by organizations come about with input from engaged DRs who not only "cheerlead" the process of formalizing the vision, but also share feedback and insights about the way the Organization's Vision Statement is communicated, and how well it matches up with their own personal goals. They also offer their unique perspectives on the vision's realism and attainability.

If your KDM allows you to give input, do so by engaging tactfully to help the KDM create a Vision Statement for your organization that you believe in as deeply as they do.

REMEMBER WHOSE VISION THIS IS!

IMPORTANT: You and your fellow DRs may well be asked to help refine the language of the Organization's Vision Statement, but you do not have the right to set the vision for the organization. It is the KDM who determines if he or she is open to your views about the organization's vision, and it is the KDM who finally decides and leads the organization to the destination set out in the Organization's Vision Statement.

SET THE TIMELINE

The creation (or revision) of a written Vision Statement for an organization will require introspective thinking on the part of the KDM. This is not likely to happen overnight, but the process does not need to drag on indefinitely. To the contrary, one of your most important responsibilities is to create a timeline for making sure the first draft is generated in a timely manner. Having identified the timeline, you should then tactfully, persistently engage to move the process forward.

AN OVERLOOKED OPPORTUNITY

Typically, very few KDMs of small and midsize organizations have given much thought to having any kind of written Vision Statement, let alone one addressing the KDM's deepest beliefs and desires about where the organization should be five or ten years. When I talk to groups of small and midsize organization owners, I often ask those with written Vision Statements for their organizations to raise their hands. It is rare that a hand is ever raised!

Unfortunately, these organizations are more likely to underachieve when compared to what they could be accomplishing with all hands using their paddles to get to the same destination. These organizations, without a written Vision Statement, lack strategic direction. In addition, there is often conflict among organization strategies because some are out of Alignment with the KDM's desired destination.

If your KDM has not yet developed a written Vision Statement for your organization, and is hesitant to do so, it is your duty to advocate on behalf of this document. The right time to create it is now.

THE ORGANIZATION'S VISION STATEMENT: A CHECKLIST

The KDM should closely consider the following "pure organization" factors as they apply to the organization. As part of your Organization's Vision Statement conversation, encourage your KDM to describe how important each factor listed below is to the future of the organization. Take notes. Write brief summaries of your KDM's answers to each of the questions on this checklist.

Product and Service Factors
- What principal products/services would you like your organization to offer in the future?
- Which of your current products/services are part of what you want your organization to offer five to ten years in the future?
- What organization activities or fields should your organization discontinue?
- What do you expect to be significantly different about your organization activity in the future?
- What organization activity or field do you want to expand into? (e.g. for an organization providing carpentry services: to expand into general contractor work).

Quality Factors

- What product and/or service quality factors are integral to your vision for the organization in terms of customer perceptions? (e.g. to be the market leader in product quality; to deliver outstanding customer satisfaction).
- What level of quality do you want your products to have?
- What activities do you want your organization to perform better than its competitors?

Economic Factors

- What economic or financial results are integral to your vision for the organization? (e.g. to operate on a sound financial basis of successful growth).
- What level of productivity do you want from your organization?
- What amount of additional financial investment, if any, are you willing to make in the organization?

Cultural and Values Factors

- Why does your organization exist beyond what it provides for you and your family? (e.g. a belief that it is important to provide life-changing services to the organization-owner community).
- What principles, beliefs and values are essential to your vision of the organization? (e.g. employee honesty and integrity; an open, friendly, and non-political workplace).
- What core social values, beliefs and principles are integral to your vision of the organization? (e.g. to contribute to the local community).
- Do you want your organization to be involved in specific charitable activities?
- Do you want your organization to have a specific positive environmental impact?

Customer and Client Factors

- Who would you like as your future principal customers, clients or users?

Geographic Factors

- In which geographic areas do you want your organization to have a physical presence, such as location of infrastructure or headquarters?
- In what geographic areas would you like your organization to operate or sell?

Principal Outlets and Distribution Channels Factors

- What principal outlets/distribution channels would you like your organization to use in the future? (e.g. virtual community).

Organization Management Factors

- What is your desired management approach or philosophy?
- What is your philosophy for financial, learning, and career growth opportunities for employees?

Organization Position, Image or Recognition Factors

- Do you want others in the industry to see your organization as innovative and risk-taking?
- What level of leadership recognition in industry/profession/community do you want to have?
- What success size or position in your industry do you want your organization to hold? (e.g. do you want to be the leading service provider or largest retail chain of similar type stores in your community).

THE BIG PICTURE

The organization's written Vision Statement should be focused on the "big picture." It is not a laundry list of all factors that might conceivably affect the organization, and it should, ideally, not exceed 100 words. It should not mention specific sales and result figures, but may use terms such as "largest" or "most" or "leading" rather than any specific quantification (there is, of course, a place for numerical goals when specific organization plans are developed, but this document is not it).

The Organization's Vision Statement should focus on the long term in regards to products/services, quality commitments, strategic positioning, and geographic reach, whether that reach is local, national, or international. It should include the "broad strokes" that suggest a desired long-term size for the organization (such as being the biggest in a particular organization field, or being among the leading providers of a certain service.)

Many organizations have Vision Statements that reflect the KDM's desire for the organization to service specific types of customers/clients, or for employees to enjoy a certain level of compensation or challenge. Once again, these should be broadly stated goals, not numerical targets.

"EVERGREEN" ELEMENTS OF THE VISION

The KDM's vision for the organization may include elements that have not yet been achieved, as well as elements that have been achieved for which continued success is desirable.

Consider, for instance, one nonprofit organization that manufactures health equipment. The founder wanted his nonprofit to be known for its high level of quality control and to manufacture products for both government and non-government use. He incorporated both points into his organization's written

Vision Statement at the start of his nonprofit organization, several decades ago. His nonprofit achieved these objectives in the 1940s! The organization, now in its third generation of family management, still has these two points in its organization's written Vision Statement.

These are "evergreen" elements of the vision. Fulfilling the quality control and the government/non-government objectives does not mean these points should be removed from the Organization's Vision Statement, or that they can be ignored.

DIRECT REPORT FEEDBACK ON THE INITIAL DRAFT

You may want to consider asking your KDM to make changes to the Organization's Vision Statement that are suggested by you and/or other DRs, but only if these recommended changes match the expressed desires the KDM has for the organization.

Once you have reviewed your KDM's initial draft of the Organization's Vision Statement, ask yourself: which parts of it are not realistically attainable? Also, consider whether the KDM may be overlooking some part of the bigger picture. Tactfully share your views on these points with your KDM.

This approach of openness, even with regard to difficult issues, will help both of you develop and maintain a high level of Alignment, dedication and trust.

Bear in mind that younger DRs may be more aggressive in terms of what they'd like to see happen in the long-term, and in terms of organization growth, than older DRs. These young DRs may need to take some time to sort things through with KDMs who are likely to think, "I've been through the tough part; the organization can grow a little slower now. Let's distribute more of the success to me now instead of keeping the money in the organization in order to speed up the growth." When two perspectives as differing as these aren't communicated and worked through, DRs may come to feel bitter or even decide to quit. Here, as elsewhere, a pattern of open, nonjudgmental two-way communication is essential.

Without a clear Alignment with the Organization's Vision Statement, DRs may be rowing their oars in a different direction than the KDM, and perhaps even in different directions from each other. DRs who don't understand, accept and support the Organization's Vision Statement can even become destructive and undermine the attitudes of management and the core practices of the organization. This does not always happen on purpose, but sometimes counterproductive actions that "just happen to happen" include episodes of bitterness, and even outright vindictiveness. That's not where you want to land.

Make sure your KDM knows that, without Alignment, dangerously mixed messages about how to interpret the Organization's Vision Statement may come from different (well-intentioned) DRs. Employees will likely become confused as to the direction of the organization and will not agree on where the focus of resources should be. Different departments may follow instructions from different people, each of whom have sharply conflicting agendas for the organization.

No KDM wants that. It's best to get any differences about the Organization's Vision Statement out in the open and try to resolve them directly, through one-on-one or group discussion.

Here is an Organization's Vision Statement from a fabricating organization that participated in the AlignUp training program. Notice how concise it is!

- Create quality products that are produced on time and are affordable.
- Train our personnel so that they sell our services with honesty and knowledge.
- Use high quality materials that can be bought at reasonable prices.
- Employ a loyal workforce that is enlightened and passionate about the benefits of our services and motivated to help customers receive those benefits.
- Operate on a sound financial basis.

IMPART A SENSE OF PURPOSE

A good Vision Statement for an organization will go far in keeping employees engaged and excited about the future. It will provide a sense of purpose for all employees—beginning with you, the DR. If you don't feel that sense of purpose, no one who reports to you will feel it either!

To inspire positive emotional engagement from employees, you must help your KDM ensure the organization's vision is both challenging and grounded in reality. This kind of motivating vision brings about a stimulating work environment.

Last but not least, you and the other DRs should help the KDM refine the language of the Organization's Vision Statement so it appeals to the employees in an emotional way and is not only remembered, but embraced passionately.

An organization's well-written Vision Statement should result in the entire organization being in Alignment with the owner's dreams for the organization. "In Alignment" means the Organization's Vision Statement helps to generate commitment from every employee whose participation is needed to realize the KDM's dream for the organization.

A high-impact DR should not only be in full Alignment with the Organization's Vision Statement, but also should help to ensure that others are, as well. This brings us to our next point.

THE ORGANIZATION'S VISION STATEMENT: EVANGELIZE IT!

Just having an organization's written Vision Statement is not enough. It must be properly communicated throughout the organization. The Organization's

Vision Statement helps keep the organization in Alignment only if it is properly communicated and employees understand and buy into the dreams.

There are some who feel the shared vision needs to be arousing and inspirational. Yet there are many organizations with very effective shared visions who emotionally engage and motivate their employees enough that the employees want to achieve the same long-term desires without necessarily being emotionally excited. What matters is not whether people are screaming and shouting with joy, but whether their actions are in Alignment with the vision.

This is an important point for both KDMs and the DRs who work to implement the vision. Both must accept that employees make decisions and take actions, day in and day out, which either do or do not lead towards the KDM's vision for the organization. Which is happening more often right now?

Neither of you can expect to lead your organization's employees to the desired destination without their understanding and buy-in to the Organization's Vision Statement. You should ask yourself this question, an important one for DRs: has the Vision Statement been so well communicated that everyone in the enterprise is now in Alignment with the KDM's vision for the organization? How do you know for certain the Organization's Vision has been successfully communicated throughout the organization? Also, if it is communicated, how do you know there has been buy-in and belief in the vision?

Many organizations have set up programs where executives ask employees, at any level of the organization, to recite the Organization's Vision Statement. If they recite what is essentially correct (although not necessarily word for word), there may be a modest reward, such as a gift certificate for twenty-five dollars.

Yet knowing the words, and understanding and believing in the meaning of the words, are different things. One procedure many organizations' leaders undertake after hearing the recital of the vision statement, is to spend ten to fifteen minutes discussing their meaning: why, specifically, the Organization's Vision Statement is important to these employees, and how it should influence what they do. Every DR—beginning with you—should be able to do this!

If all your organization's employees, from top to bottom, can't identify at least the essence of the organization's written Vision Statement, that means your KDM, you, and your fellow DRs are not effectively communicating the Organization's Vision (by the way, this is the case at most small and midsize organizations).

WHEN TO UPDATE THE ORGANIZATION'S VISION STATEMENT?

Organization's written Vision Statements shouldn't change frequently, but there are times when they must be revised.

Even if your organization already has a written Vision Statement, it should be reviewed periodically and updated as circumstances change. Note that a vision statement is not like a goal that, once achieved, is eliminated from your plan so you can focus on something else. The vision statement should include some elements that are already being achieved.

> **All the actions of all the employees must always be in alignment with the Organization's Vision Statement!**

One thing that never changes is the reality that things change. For instance, changes can take place in the health of the KDM. There can be economic changes, or opportunities the KDM couldn't have visualized in the preceding years. There can also be competitive factors, such as technology introductions. All of these may be signals it is time for the Organization's Vision Statement to be updated. Of course, such changes should be considered carefully and implemented only after extensive discussions between the KDM and his/her Direct Reports.

Here's an example of a revision to an Organization's Vision Statement that had to happen. During an economic crisis, the Organization's Vision Statement for Miller Constructions changed substantially. The Vision previously included the desire to operate within a 300-mile region. The economic crisis of 2008-2009, however, had severely hurt the entire construction industry. As a result, the organization's written Vision Statement was changed to emphasize operations within the organization's metropolitan area, which was a much smaller area in which to focus marketing efforts. This wasn't simply a short-term change. This organization also went back and changed its long-term goal of operating regionally to focus instead on marketing effectively in a smaller area.

Here's a similar case. A manufacturing government division we worked with had included within its Vision Statement a passage about "becoming" a division whose daily operations reflected a high level of quality control. Years later, having achieved that level of performance, the Organization's Vision Statement was tweaked so the statement referenced "maintaining" a high level of quality control.

Let's look now at the second—and the more complex—of the two vision elements: the Pocket Vision.

VISION ELEMENT #2: THE POCKET VISION (AN OVERVIEW)

As I mentioned earlier, gaining clarity on the KDM's Pocket Vision is likely to be an ongoing project for you, since it involves privileged, and perhaps sensitive, information that does not show up in the Organization's Vision Statement. Often, this is information the KDM has consciously chosen not to reveal. In other words: if you are a DR, it is quite possible you don't know what you don't know about the organization's vision!

Pocket Vision factors are likely to include such things as the KDM's personal expectations from the organization (financial and otherwise), and the specific performance goals related to the organization's financial and material achievements. They are factors not shared with the world at large, but that nevertheless affect how the KDM sees the organization evolving for the next five to ten years. Issues such as the type of role the KDM wants to take on in the future, the balance he or she establishes between work life and personal life, the psychological rewards he or she expects from the organization, and even factors relating to semi or full retirement—all of these would qualify as Pocket Vision factors.

And this is where things can get complicated. It is quite common for there to be Pocket Vision components of an organization's vision the KDM has no intention of sharing with the DRs, or anyone else—at least for the time being. The most common examples of this are situations where the KDM has created financially related plans for the organization, or even exit plans, that he or she believes could have a negative impact on morale if revealed.

Your aim here is not to find a way to persuade your KDM to "come clean" about each and every private decision that has ever been made, or contemplated, concerning the organization. Rather, you want to be sure you are headed in the right direction in terms of the personal trust that exists between you and the KDM. That way, when the time comes to create new plans that will affect you, the KDM feels comfortable sharing relevant information with you—including, perhaps, some sensitive information you may not previously have been privy to.

> **Whenever the level of trust between you and the KDM is expanding, you can expect the quality of information you receive to expand, as well.**

Think back, once again, to Mia's example. Her DRs did not approach her with an ultimatum, demanding to be brought up date on the specifics of her personal financial goals. They asked for her time, her attention, and her feedback on their ideas for the future of the organization. As part of the trusting discussion that emerged, Mia chose to share her Pocket Vision—or, at least, a significant factor affecting it.

Recognize and accept it may be hard for the KDM to share some of the Pocket Vision Factors, and that many of them will remain hidden to you. There are times, of course, when it is perfectly appropriate to ask what is behind a KDM's decision. But asking does not always guarantee a clear answer!

The risk for the KDM who conceals important Pocket Factors can be substantial. If a DR does not understand Pocket Vision Factors relating to the KDM's long-term vision for the organization, then it is not really possible for that DR to have high-level Alignment with that KDM. It would be the same as asking a person to meet you at a particular destination ... while not sharing that destination.

Without knowledge of relevant Pocket Factors, DRs are much more likely to make decisions that are not Aligned with the KDM's vision for the organization. And the negative impact is not limited to DRs' decisions. Gaps in Alignment between a KDM and a DR caused by not sharing Pocket Factors can negatively affect the organization as a whole.

THE POCKET VISION: A CAUTIONARY TALE

Jim, the owner of a chain of personal computer repair shops, wondered how much he should share with his DRs about his Pocket Vision to sell the family-owned organization to outsiders.

Jim planned to sell the organization to outsiders five to ten years in the future. He intentionally did not share this vision with his DRs, most of whom were family members, because he was afraid that doing so would result in losing top talent. So Jim kept this information "in the pocket" to keep his organization from losing good people.

Withholding Pocket Factors that have a direct impact on the DRs' security, however, is a dangerous path to walk. You can't keep your plans to sell hidden forever. The day came when the truth had to be revealed, because someone outside the organization knew of Jim's interest in selling and happened to mention it to one of Jim's DRs. A crisis followed.

To his DRs, it seemed clear that Jim had jeopardized their long-term job security. There was serious anger and mistrust. The DRs felt they had been misled. Even after Jim explained he had changed his mind about selling to outsiders—which he had—the trust level never returned. The organization's capacity to perform at an optimum level had been damaged. In this situation, the level of trust and openness between Jim and his DRs was not high enough to avoid a major trauma for everyone. In fact, the lack of trust reflected some underlying problems in family communication that could have been avoided, I think, if all sides had been committed to implementing the core principles of the AlignUp training program. Unfortunately, this was not the case.

OPENNESS IS NEEDED FOR HIGH-LEVEL ALIGNMENT

If a KDM continually turns down certain budget requests because they conflict with unshared Pocket Factors, the DR requesting the budget allocation will probably be frustrated and confused. However, if you, as the DR, are aware of the Pocket Factor of wanting to sell the organization in five years, you would understand why the organization might not be making large investments in infrastructure or equipment. You might even make suggestions for plans to significantly improve the results of the organization within the time frame, which could affect the price of the organization. But if you don't know what's going on, you can't do any of those things.

Of course, it is the right of a KDM to decide whether or not to share Pocket Factors with his or her DRs. However, it is best for the KDM to be as open as possible with those who are supposed to turn his or her vision into reality. In a perfect world, DRs would be able to discuss and fully understand all aspects of the KDM's Pocket Vision. However, in the world we live in, that doesn't always happen.

A MAJOR CHALLENGE

Pocket Vision Factors are among the most potentially challenging parts of Aligning the executive team on the KDM's vision. Not knowing about factors that will directly or indirectly affect you can damage the two-way trust needed for Alignment between you and your KDM. It will also affect the ability to achieve your KDM's personal dreams for the organization.

At the end of the day, all you can really do as the DR is a) work to create enough trust in the relationship to ensure the KDM feels safe sharing sensitive information with you, and b) share your own personal hope that Pocket Factors driving decisions directly affecting you will be discussed openly.

Sometimes this open discussion happens. Sometimes it doesn't. When it does, there is potential for fully engaged, high-level Alignment with the KDM's vision for the organization's future. When it doesn't (as in Jim's case), the possibility of damaged relationships and lost potential is significant. If you listen carefully enough to informal conversations among DRs at organizations like Jim's, you can often hear distraught DRs saying things like, "Wow, I had no idea about that...."

THE POCKET VISION: PROTECT YOURSELF!

Without a clear understanding of where your KDM really wants the organization to be in the future, neither of you are likely to develop major organization plans that will give the straightest path to your KDM's destination.

If your KDM is open to sharing (for instance) the balance he or she would like to strike long-term between his/her organization life and non-organization life, as well as the areas of the organization on which they would like to spend their time, that will help you to make better strategic decisions.

You can see now, I think, why it is important for the KDM and DR to establish an ongoing dialogue based on trust and mutual respect. Regular "heart-to-heart" discussions are probably the best way to protect yourself, and the organization as a whole.

FOCUS ON THE KDM'S BEST INTERESTS

Even if you suspect certain Pocket Factors are not shared with you as a DR, you should still work hard to confirm that efforts and focus are consistent with the KDM's stated dreams for the organization. No other approach will allow you to expand the level of trust that exists in the relationship.

> **Look for ways to engage person-to-person with the KDM about how best to achieve his or her vision.**

Make it clear your goal is to see to it that the KDM's best interests are identified and respected.

WHEN YOU SUSPECT THERE ARE "POCKET FACTOR" ISSUES

As you work toward building and maintaining Alignment with your KDM, be watchful for recurring patterns that may cause a lack of Alignment: there could be an unknown Pocket Factor in play. In a tactful and respectful manner, during a one-on-one meeting, find an appropriate way to ask your KDM whether there is something you are unaware of that is contributing to the lack of Alignment.

If you are fortunate enough to have a strong reservoir of trust, and a good relationship based on two-way communication, your KDM will feel comfortable sharing his or her Pocket Factor with you. The two of you can then take care of things together, and jointly move toward the goal of supporting the organization's vision.

Even if your KDM is unable or unwilling to share his or her Pocket Factor, all may not be lost. Open communication about the existence of the Pocket Factor, even without the details, can be the first step towards a plan to bring you and your KDM back into Alignment. Consider saying something like: "I understand I don't, and can't, know all of the factors, so what is our next step for accomplishing X?" A question along these lines, posed with respect and good intent, can start the process of getting you back into Alignment.

The following true stories describe common types of Pocket Factor issues that have caused conflict and the potential for a lack of Alignment between KDMs and DRs. I offer them here on the theory that, the more information you have about these kinds of situations, the more constructive your response to your own situation is likely to be.

THE POCKET VISION: EXIT STRATEGIES

Barbie, a KDM, had a dream. She wanted to retire within ten years with enough money to live at a specific minimum level of financial comfort. Her vision relied on the after-tax proceeds of the sale of her organization. Upon retirement, she planned to pursue her love of painting, travel the world and "spend more time with my grandkids." She had kept her plan to sell the organization "in her pocket" because she didn't want Tim and Mike, her two DRs, to worry about job security and possibly start looking for new work.

Over a five-year period, Barbie turned down many requests from her DRs for major organization investments, such as equipment, while she positioned the organization for sale. Her DRs, not knowing the reason their requests were constantly denied, became resentful and angry. Barbie eventually entered into a contract to sell her organization, unbeknownst to her DRs, subject to due diligence. At that time, she informed Tim and Mike of her plan to sell the organization. She explained that they now needed to fully cooperate with the buyer during the due diligence period before the sale was complete and told them she had made a commitment to the potential buyer that any sale was contingent upon multi-year employment contracts for the two executives.

Even with this information, Barbie told me that Tim and Mike were bitter and felt betrayed; they thought they should have been given a chance to buy the organization. "They couldn't discuss anything civilly with the potential buyer when the buyer was doing due diligence," she recalled. Ultimately, the sale did not go through.

Additionally, the relationships she had built with her two most trusted executives, over three decades, had been destroyed because of what they saw as Barbie's deceit in keeping her plans to sell the organization secret—plans they felt had a direct impact on them. And just as their relationships never recovered, the organization suffered in a permanent way. Ultimately this lack of Alignment, allowed to develop over time, resulted in Barbie not realizing her own personal vision.

Your KDM may have a similar desire to either cut back to a semi-retired state, or even sell the organization. Your goal (if you suspect this to be the case) is to find a subtle way to send the message that being open with key executives about the various possible scenarios for the exit will be best for the relationships, and the organization. This kind of sensitive approach usually has the positive effect of inspiring employees to work together to achieve the exit strategy of the owner.

Exit strategies are particularly important to discuss in family-owned organizations. Regardless of what kind of organization you work in, you can help your KDM deal with this complex responsibility by showing appropriate support for his or her long-term goals, listening well, and committing yourself, in both the short and long term, to the task of helping create incentives that keep everyone working in the same direction.

THE POCKET VISION: PERSONAL FINANCIAL ISSUES

Sarah, who owned an IT support organization, had expanded from a single office to open a location in a second city. Both offices were doing well. She met with her executive vice president and chief information officer, the DRs who made up her top management team, to discuss her desire for her organization to have new offices in a number of major cities in the USA within five to ten years.

Sarah then explained her Pocket Vision, which she had not disclosed for quite some time. She did not want to make any personal guarantees of organization loans or leases, because (as she explained it): "I don't want to go to bed at night worrying about financial risks, and potentially losing what I have, from guaranteeing loans for the organization, if, for any reason, the organization can't make payments on the new loans. I just don't need any more than I have, and I don't want to worry about losing everything if the plan fails." Sarah's EVP said he would try to get expansion financing without her personal guarantee of the loans.

The EVP developed a written strategic plan for the organization. It involved financing the substantial capital investment over three years for fixed assets and working capital needed to open the new offices.

Unfortunately, the banks that were willing to make the expansion loans for Sarah's organization all required that Sarah personally guarantee the loans.

As a result, the expansion plans had to be revised. But this was for the best, because Sarah was able to create a viable plan for less aggressive growth, a plan her DRs could buy into that did not conflict with her Pocket Vision.

THE POCKET VISION: MOVING MANUFACTURING OPERATION OUT OF THE COUNTRY

I've known quite a few organization owners who decided to keep private a Pocket Vision of moving their manufacturing operations out of the country to reduce costs. Most of the time, this Pocket Vision is never shared with DRs until the very day the change takes place. As you might imagine, most employees involved in the manufacturing division of an organization would be dubious about sticking around if they were aware their jobs would not be there at some point in the reasonably near future!

Of course, sharing this information with certain discreet DRs can make the denial of certain requests more comprehensible than they might have otherwise been. For example, the KDM of one manufacturing division intended to move the manufacturing division to Brazil. Therefore, the KDM denied all requests for new equipment since he knew the whole division would be closed down in the next three years. The KDM was oddly evasive when asked to explain why he was denying new equipment requests; this response caused a lot of frustration for some of his DRs.

Sharing relevant information with even just one or two key DRs could have helped ease the frustration significantly. Unfortunately, all the DRs and employees were informed of the move of the manufacturing division only after the decision was finalized. This resulted in a major morale problem on the part of the executive team responsible for overseeing the transition. This collapse of organizational communication undermined the sense of security that had previously defined the organization. The DRs—and indeed all of the employees—were now keenly aware the KDM was capable of keeping major decisions about the organization to himself.

KDMS MAY BE OPEN TO REVISING POCKET FACTORS

Only infrequently will a DR be able to help change the thinking relating to the pocket factors, but it can happen. When it does, it is usually to the benefit of both the KDM and DR.

Here's a case in point. Joan was the owner of a consulting nonprofit organization. She shared her vision of slow, conservative growth for the nonprofit with her DRs and asked for their comments. She was met with a silence she hadn't expected. When Shawn and Leslie did speak, Joan was quite surprised at what she heard. It turned out that Joan had a vision for low risk and much slower growth then either of the DRs had envisioned for the nonprofit. They told her as much!

Joan responded as follows: "Look, I'd love for there to be higher growth, but in order for us to really increase the growth, I'm afraid I'm going to have to work a lot harder and assume a lot more financial risk. I'm just not willing to do that." Shawn and Leslie were silent again, and there was another awkward moment.

This discussion led to a major "Aha!" moment for the two DRs.

For years, Shawn and Leslie had been confused as to why Joan had so often vetoed their ideas for growing the organization. They had even harbored an underlying (and growing) sense of anger, due, in part, to the unsettling impression that Joan unintentionally left them with: that she found their ideas for growth to be too weak to even consider implementing.

Within just a few weeks of this discussion, both DRs came to Joan to discuss the implications of her long term vision for the nonprofit organization. They were concerned about their growth opportunities because Joan was no longer focused with aggressiveness on the goal of increasing sales.

Joan decided to deal with the situation head-on and agreed on a compromise that involved significantly greater growth—but not recklessly aggressive growth.

Imagine what might have happened had Joan and her DRs not engaged in open discussions about what had been her Pocket Factor!

Here's another example of the same dynamic in action. As president and part owner of Tipton, I was a DR who reported to the majority owner of the organization—my KDM. I saw the potential of taking the organization public at a time when this was not part of his vision for the organization.

I presented my idea to him with a confidential memo showing what I felt were all the positives it could bring to the organization, and him personally, if we could achieve this objective. Initially he was opposed to the idea. However, over a period of months, and after numerous discussions, he came to recognize that the 'pros' of taking the organization public far outweighed any 'cons.' Note I did everything I could to influence his vision for the organization, but that vision had to be his for it to work!

When it comes to Pocket Factors, the practical reality you are looking to discuss with the KDM is this: **a lack of openness about the KDM's intentions is likely to endanger the trust of the very employees whose help and cooperation will be needed to turn the dreams into reality.** The time it takes to repair that level of damage to trust can set the organization back by years!

KEY POINT SUMMARY

- It is essential you initiate a trust-driven vision discussion with your KDM and help him or her develop (or revise) an Organization's Vision Statement.
- This Organization's Vision Statement must accurately reflect the KDM's dreams and aspirations.
- DR's may, with permission from the KDM, offer feedback and proposed revisions to the Organization's Vision Statement.
- DRs should buy into the Organization's Vision Statement and evangelize on the KDM's behalf throughout the enterprise. Some organizations publish an extremely concise "mission statement" for their clients, customers, and suppliers. This is usually found by excerpting certain key words and phrases from the organization's written Vision Statement.
- Organization's written Vision Statements shouldn't change frequently, but there are times when they must be revised. Pocket Vision factors are those privileged subjects the KDM wants to keep to him/herself even though they are seen as part of the future of the organization. Pocket Vision factors are not included in the organization's written Vision Statement. These are situations where the KDM elects to keep certain facts, plans, and personal conclusions "in his or her pocket."
- Even if you suspect certain Pocket Factors are not shared with you as a DR, you should still work hard to confirm that efforts and focus are consistent with the KDM's stated dreams for the organization.
- When in doubt, focus on the best interests of the organization.
- Whenever the level of trust between you and the KDM is expanding, you can expect the quality of the information you receive to expand.

DIRECT REPORT HOMEWORK ASSIGNMENT #1: WRITING AND REVIEWING YOUR ORGANIZATION'S VISION STATEMENT

If your organization does not have a written Vision Statement, meet with your KDM to discuss the value of having one. Follow this up by working with your KDM to get his/her answers to the above questions, which can ultimately lead to a first draft of a written Vision Statement for your organization.

If your organization has a written Vision Statement, review with your KDM the checklist of questions above, to revise and update the statement to make it more effective. Once the organization's written Vision Statement satisfies your KDM, it should be shared with all the DRs who report to the KDM, followed by a meeting in which the DRs offer the KDM their personal experiences, insights, and advice about how to make the statement read more effectively. In addition, a strategy should be discussed as to how best communicate the organization's written Vision Statement to all employees, so that all employees "get the vision" the KDM desires.

The chances of bringing about an effective written Vision Statement for your organization increases greatly if you and your top KDM can address each of the questions in the checklist provided earlier in this chapter. This moves the information from the mind of the top KDM into a first draft of the Organization's Vision Statement. Encourage your KDM to prioritize the factors based upon their importance to him or her. Volunteer to write out, and report back with, a version of the Organization's Vision Statement the KDM can choose to share with other DRs. This statement should succinctly state what the organization will do in the future, how the organization will do it, and why the organization will do it.

The organization's written vision statement should not exceed 100 words. When in doubt, lean toward the bullet point approach. Wordy visions complicate the process and cause people to lose focus.

DIRECT REPORT HOMEWORK ASSIGNMENT #2: COMMUNICATING AND CONFIRMING UNDERSTANDING OF THE ORGANIZATION'S VISION

- Develop and share your thoughts on a strategy for communicating the organization's written Vision Statement throughout the entire organization.
- Develop a strategy for confirming that employees at all levels understand and buy into the organization's written Vision Statement.
- Share these strategies with your top KDM and come to Alignment on what the "evangelization" strategy will be.

CHAPTER 9

Align on Roles and Responsibilities

EXECUTIVE SUMMARY FOR THE KEY DECISION-MAKER

When a **Direct Report** makes it easier for his or her **Key Decision-Maker** to work on the organization, rather than in the organization, that DR becomes a major strategic asset for the KDM, and the enterprise as a whole.

This chapter outlines six clear "win/win" outcomes your DR can deliver that make it easier for the organization to fulfill your vision. In this chapter, your DR will read about all six win-win outcomes then choose three for one-on-one discussion with you.

These action items will enable the DR to become a substantially higher-impact contributor in a very short period of time—and also free up more of your time to work on the organization.

The full list of six win-win outcomes covered in this chapter is as follows:

1. Understand the KDM's personal vision for his or her own work role.
2. Identify "duty gaps"—responsibilities that you can fulfill so as to free up the KDM's time.
3. Help the KDM create his/her job description.
4. Help the KDM turn the knowledge in his/her head into standardized, written protocols and processes.
5. Help the KDM measure results from the organization's capital investments.
6. Offer the KDM honest feedback.

COMMITMENT TO A HIGH-IMPACT ROLE

Due to the relatively flat organization charts of most organizations, most executives who work in small or medium-size organizations typically report directly to the KDM, the final level of authority within a private organization. I call such executives Direct Reports (DRs). The AlignUp™ training was specifically created for this level of executive.

Most DRs do not fully appreciate the direct impact they can have upon the effectiveness of their KDM, and the success of their own organization. The AlignUp™ training is designed to jump-start the processes that make KDMs dramatically more effective in running and growing the enterprise, and make DRs more likely to assume high-impact roles within that organization. All of those processes depend on a single process: Alignment.

> **If you are a DR, accept personal responsibility— right now, today— for bringing about improvements in your organization, regardless of your job title.**

That process can start right here, right now! It begins with accountability.

Accountability is an essential early step for improving the productive relationship between you (the DR) and your superior (the KDM). Start by being accountable for reading all six of the win/win outcomes described in this chapter, knowing you will eventually pick THREE to share and discuss with your KDM.

This chapter requires a personal commitment from you to create a high-impact role for yourself within the organization. Follow its steps and do the homework assignment at the end—it is essential if you expect to bring about real transformation in your career, or your organization. What you are about to learn has enabled many DRs to become substantially higher-impact contributors in a very short period of time.

THE KEY DECISION MAKER (KDM)

If your KDM is the owner or founder, then your KDM usually wears many hats concurrently and is involved in tactical work that consumes most, or all, of the work day. This is not good for the organization, the KDM, or anyone else in the enterprise.

What is often overlooked is this state of affairs represents not only a significant organizational challenge—but also a major opportunity for both your KDM and you, as the DR. This chapter shows you how to seize that opportunity.

THE DIRECT REPORT (DR)

There are (at least) six ways a DR can quickly make himself or herself more valuable as a strategic asset to the organization and the KDM and become a higher-impact contributor within the organization. These six clear "win/win" outcomes make Alignment easier for both sides. The six outcomes are:

1. Understand your KDM's personal vision for his or her own work role.
2. Identify "duty gaps"—responsibilities that you can fulfill so as to free up your KDM's time. (This is typically the best point of entry for a DR seeking access to the high-impact, high-growth "fast track.")
3. Help your KDM create his/her job description.
4. Help your KDM turn the knowledge in his/her head into standardized, written protocols and processes.
5. Help your KDM measure results from the organization's capital investments.
6. Offer your KDM honest feedback.

This chapter gives you rapid access to all six of these high-impact opportunities. Some will doubtless seem more appropriate to you than others. Remember, at the end of the chapter you will be asked to take action on these ideas by discussing with your KDM which of the three will be most helpful in supporting him or her.

MAKING "WIN/WIN" OUTCOMES A REALITY

In this chapter, you'll find ideas that make a "win/win" outcome possible in each of these areas, for both your KDM and yourself (the DR). In many of the situations that will be discussed, you will need to engage tactfully and assertively as "prime mover" for change. This is a non-negotiable part of the AlignUp™ methodology. It may or may not be easy for you at first, but it is a muscle you can, and will, learn to strengthen.

Engaging yourself tactfully but assertively can begin with something as simple as scheduling a face-to-face meeting with your KDM. Your job now, however, is to concentrate on defining the needed outcomes. Then you can have the discussion needed to review them, confirm your KDM's buy-in, and confirm your shared commitment to action.

WIN/WIN OUTCOME #1: UNDERSTAND YOUR KDM'S LONG-TERM DESIRED WORK ROLE

It is extremely important that you encourage your KDM to share with you his/her long-term desired work role.

Once you do this, you will better understand the areas where you can meet the most critical organizational needs. If your KDM does not have clarity on his/her long-term desired work role, then your job is to encourage your KDM to identify what it is and share it with you.

> **Ask your KDM whether he/she is doing what they envisaged when they started the organization.**

Ask your KDM to briefly, and clearly, share with you the specific areas of responsibility that he or she would like to carry in the organization, as well as the roles others should play. This takes time and thought, so a private meeting or a lunch date may be the best environment for the discussion. When I am working on this point with organization owners, I ask them to think back to when they started their organization and recall how they envisioned their lives would be—are they doing what they imagined they would be when they started, or bought, the organization?

One division manager, whom I will call Carl, found his passion for work waning as his division grew. When asked what he had previously been passionate about at work, he said he loved the technical side of the division. He did not enjoy the administrative and management side, which he felt consumed far too much of his time. Carl rekindled his passion and made the best use of his expertise by making himself the CEO and CTO (chief technical officer). Note; he kept the title of CEO, but gave his COO most of the day-to-day responsibility of running the division. His COO is, in fact, a better-qualified person to lead the administrative side of the division. Carl now enjoys what he does at work, and he flies in the clouds when he comes up with technical innovations that contribute to his division's success.

The most important considerations for any KDM's work focus should reflect the KDM's passion, aptitude and expertise. Many KDMs are unhappily doing work for which they have little or no passion.

Your KDM should specify both the long-term time involvement he/she wants in the organization and the amount of time he/she desires to be away from work. When a KDM is working ten to fifteen hours a day—as many do—it is easy to fall into the trap of saying that at some point in the future there will be time to take care of family matters, finish that novel, or do whatever else shows up on the "bucket list."

As a general rule, though, that time never materializes—unless it is built into a plan. Tactfully point out to your KDM that working extremely long hours on a continuous basis often results in an overload that is irresponsible to the organization, because it results in bad organization decisions. It will take both time and discipline on the part of your KDM to create the balance necessary to enjoy certain things now. You can help support that balance by identifying areas of responsibility that you can take off your KDM's plate.

As organization owner KDMs get nearer to retirement, or semi-retirement, age, they may find the work ethic instilled during their upbringing prevents them from taking time away from work. I have often heard organization owners say, "If I take days off, or come in late, my employees will resent my work ethic or reduce their own work ethic." It often takes a conscious effort on the part of the DR to help their KDM to not feel guilty about taking time to enjoy life outside the organization. By getting your KDM to share their personal vision of their long term reduced work role, you can help your KDM push through the guilt and accept that taking time off is one of the rewards of having taken the risk of owning an organization.

TAKEAWAYS: WIN-WIN OUTCOME #1

- Begin the discussion with your KDM about his/her long-term desired work role.
- Work with your KDM to develop his/her written Personal Vision Statement for what they would like to be doing work-wise, long-term. (See the discussion above.)

WIN/WIN OUTCOME #2: TACTFULLY IDENTIFY "DUTY GAPS"

You will become a much higher-impact contributor to your organization if you learn how to fill the inevitable "duty gaps" that arise within your KDM's optional responsibilities.

What's a duty gap? It's a specific area where your KDM is not doing something as well as it could be done as the result of being spread too thin! It's very common for a KDM who is great at leading a small organization to "hit the wall" as the organization gets significantly bigger. By taking on some of the functional duties within your KDM's "optional" duties, you will be giving your KDM more time to spend on the organization's big picture. Remember, there are certain areas of responsibility your KDM cannot delegate, and thus cannot free up time in, such as setting the organization vision.

Look for ways to take over certain functional areas or projects from your KDM in the "optional" areas you've identified together. Help your KDM reprioritize his or her optional duties by taking over the specific projects that are currently directed by your KDM but don't need to be.

For instance, if your KDM is strong with protocol/processes, but less strong on the creative side, you could consider helping your KDM by sharing your "out-of-the-box" creative ideas.

This area is one that KDMs are likely to easily see as important to the growth of the organization. Many (though not all) successful KDMs will quickly "get" the importance of this appeal from the DR and will be open at least to discussing it.

Ultimately, of course, the decision about whether or not to delegate a given task to you lies not in your hands, but in the hands of your KDM. Some KDMs—and perhaps yours is one—are quite comfortable delegating tasks when they are convinced the tasks are likely to be completed by the KDM at a minimum level of competence. I would challenge you to at least try to identify those tasks that you feel certain you can complete at least as well as your KDM, or perhaps even better. Why? To help you make the case confidently to the KDM that you can make an exceptional contribution in a timely fashion.

I realize, of course, there are likely to be areas where you and your KDM may disagree on whether you can do something as well as, or better than, he or she. This is where tact and patience come in. The practical reality is that you may have to "work your way up the ladder" in terms of changing KDM perceptions about what is, and isn't, appropriate to delegate to you. And you may learn there are certain tasks your KDM simply will not delegate. Move on. Find something new you can take off the KDM's plate.

> **Establishing clear benchmarks the KDM can use to measure your ability to fulfill these responsibilities will make your KDM more comfortable with delegating tasks.**

If the organization has experienced any growth at all, the founder has already learned some core lessons: he or she does not do everything well and does not have time to do everything. Those things he or she does not do well, or does not have time to do, must be delegated to others. The question is not whether responsibilities should be delegated, but which ones, to whom, and why.

When dealing with a KDM who may be challenged by the task of delegating responsibilities, emphasize the point that delegation is the key to achieving balance in his/her work/personal life. Work together to find those areas the KDM is most confident that you, the DR, can handle.

Be tactfully persistent about making the case for taking the right tasks "off your KDM's plate." An example might be to say, "John, you've mentioned to me that you find it a big pain to deal with managing the sales staff. I've been studying some of the techniques and systems for managing salespeople, and I'd like to take that off your back."

When advocating for personal accountability for the fulfillment of a carefully chosen, mutually agreed-upon responsibility, it is essential you also receive the authority within the organization to take effective action on all the goals that relate to that responsibility. In most cases, it will be necessary for your KDM to communicate directly with employees and clients potentially affected by the change in responsibilities. The goal is to bring about a clear public understanding that specific functions in the organization are now your job, and that you have full responsibility and authority for those matters.

There must also be a private understanding between your KDM and you, the DR, that you may well make occasional, minor mistakes while fulfilling the new responsibility. The KDM must agree to step back and see what happens for an agreed-upon period—say, thirty days—and then evaluate the results based on benchmarks both sides understand and accept ahead of time.

I emphasize advocating for both responsibility and authority, because failure to Align ahead of time on both these issues is where the delegation process often goes off track. I have seen far too many high-performing executives leave their organizations because their KDMs gave them responsibility over areas without giving them commensurate authority. This reflects a failure to establish what a good salesperson would call an "up-front contract" about what is to be accomplished, when, and how.

It is simply too frustrating, and in some cases humiliating, to work in an environment where you have responsibility but not authority. In almost every one of these situations I've observed, the DRs could have (and, I believe, should have) brought about needed authority, if they had been assertive and clear about this need. If the KDM is truly committed to bringing about Alignment, he has the responsibility to grant you the authority you need to do the job.

TAKEAWAYS: WIN/WIN OUTCOME #2

- Ask yourself, which of your KDM's current responsibilities could be managed competently (at least) by you. Spend some personal time examining this question, and come up with at least one area you would feel comfortable accepting responsibility for.
- Look for unfilled gaps. Many KDMs aren't highly structured and don't have the kind of discipline every outstanding organization needs. If your KDM is not highly structured, or is not strong on self-discipline, ask yourself how you can fill these needs for your KDM.
- Discuss this idea with your KDM. Maybe it will fly, maybe it won't. Regardless, begin the conversation. Ask what you can do to help your KDM succeed, what you can "take off his or her plate." This conversation should include a review of your current written job description as a DR.
- Be prepared to make the "organization case" for why you can competently take over the task from your KDM: that it frees up time for your KDM to do what he/she does best.
- Once a responsibility has been assigned, make sure you have both authority and responsibility to do the job well.
- Ask your KDM how the particular job responsibility fits into the priority of things the organization does. Make an effort to understand how these job responsibilities link to the organization vision.
- IMPORTANT: if your KDM agrees to delegate certain additional

responsibilities to you (a common result), get a commitment from him/her to spend time teaching you the particulars of the job you are taking on.

- If your KDM feels he/she cannot add to your responsibilities, ask what needs to take place for that view to change.

What If the KDM Says "No"?

> **Be emotionally prepared to handle the possibility of your KDM rejecting your request for additional responsibility.**

If the KDM says no and you feel strongly that the request you are making is in the best interests of the organization, you will need to decide for yourself whether or not it makes sense to press the point in the short term with your KDM (very often, it does not). It may be best to move on to another potential win/win outcome.

WIN/WIN OUTCOME #3: HELP YOUR KDM CREATE HIS/HER JOB DESCRIPTION

If you, as DR, don't have a written job description, you will need to get one done fast before attempting to bring about this outcome. There are many good websites that can give you a running start. Creating and/or revising a job description for yourself, with input from your KDM, will help lead you naturally into a discussion of whether your KDM should create a written job description for him/herself. Once your KDM has a written job description, it will be much easier for you to find areas where you can assist.

Help your KDM understand that his or her success depends on knowing, and taking full advantage of, his or her own skill-set (some KDMs know this, intuitively or otherwise; others, I suspect a solid majority, do not). Knowing and taking advantage of one's own skill-set starts with a written job description. So ask: does your KDM have one? If not, offer to help your KDM develop a written job description for his or her own position.

Like many parts of the aspiring DR's job, this job-description creation requires tact and diplomacy. Part of your challenge is to find out what the real job description is for the KDM to whom you report.

Builder or Navigator?

Someone can be very good at building a boat, and may even know where the boat is supposed to go. This doesn't mean, though, that the boat builder has the ability to navigate the boat through stormy waters in a way that ensures it stays on course.

There are many entrepreneurs who have the ability to build an organization, but when it comes to a point where additional management or executive-level people are needed, reality emerges. The founder, or entrepreneur, is clear on the destination, but isn't all that good at navigation. The wise entrepreneur recognizes this and understands the importance of DRs who have the ability to help lead the organization so it stays on course. But even those wise entrepreneurs sometimes neglect the important step of identifying the things they currently do that they don't want to spend all day doing. By addressing the larger topic of "what you want your job description to be," you can spark an important discussion about personal and organizational priorities.

Help your KDM find ways to stop struggling with the common problem of wearing many different organization "hats." In order to help your KDM do this, you should offer to help create his/her "ideal" job description and (this part is crucial) a measurement system for monitoring the organization as a whole.

As I say, this discussion often gets rolling with a topic most KDMs are happy to address (and often can't avoid): the feeling they are wearing too many hats. In many cases, a tactical decision to wear many hats was once a non-negotiable concession necessary for the organization to survive, thrive, and get where it is today. Too often, however, the KDM who is personally responsible for too much ends up keeping the organization from realizing its full potential. These discussions can help clarify the areas where you can take on additional responsibilities (see #2) in both the short and long terms.

When I asked one organization owner/CEO what his COO did, he said his COO was the "chief fun officer" for the organization. This seemingly flippant "joke" title was actually the result of a careful re-evaluation of the CEO's job description and personal responsibilities. The CEO was an engineer who was brilliant at designing, troubleshooting, and inventing—but he was not an inspirational-type leader. The COO had only two departments reporting to him—sales and marketing—but he knew how to run those two critically important teams. The COO also knew how to make working at the organization an enjoyable experience for everyone. This arrangement was the result of a clearly thought-out job description that established what the CEO was, and wasn't, comfortable trying to accomplish each day.

The job description you come up with should allow your KDM to play to his or her strengths and do things that he or she enjoys. In organizations that I've owned or served as CEO, I keep control and responsibility in the marketing area. The reason for this is that I have a proven record of capability in marketing, and I love doing it. Another CEO I know has almost no involvement in the marketing of his organization, and, instead, focuses on sales because that is his strength.

Remember: The KDM is in charge of managing the business of the organization, regardless of his or her title. This person is responsible for keeping the organization moving toward his/her vision destination. While the responsibilities of the KDM are likely to change as the organization grows, at no point should the

KDM ever give up responsibility for creating the vision for the organization and making sure all goals and strategies of the organization are moving toward that vision. Additionally, there are other responsibilities a KDM must retain and not delegate: providing and supporting creativity, establishing culture (through his or her actions), and building the senior management team, for instance.

Most KDMs don't get optimum results from their DRs, simply because they don't understand exactly what their own job is supposed to be! Further confusing the matter is that in small and medium-size organizations, particularly family organizations, titles often do not match actual responsibilities. If the person you report to does not have the authority to reverse any decision relating to managing the business of the organization, your boss is not the KDM, regardless of his or her title.

You can use this "job description" discussion to help your KDM carve out more time to think long term, work on the high level parts of plans (as opposed to the tactical involvement) and, in general, focus more time and attention on those things your KDM must do. Ideally, your KDM keeps those responsibilities at which he or she excels. Responsibilities that are delegated should (in a perfect world) be optional responsibilities that the DRs can do as well as, or better, than their KDM.

The optional responsibilities your KDM retains should be based upon who he/she is—what he/she is good at, and what he/she has the greatest passion for. You won't find two organizations, even in the same industry, where the KDM duties are the same (other than those that can't be delegated).

BEYOND THE "ONE-PERSON BAND"

You become a higher-impact contributor in your organization whenever you can help move your KDM away from being a "one-person band" and toward being a conductor of the orchestra of DRs. The conductor may be responsible for all the sounds harmonizing, but does not create any of the sounds.

The KDM in an organization with a core of capable managers should be spending a significant amount of time every week involved with the strategic planning process. The larger the organization, the greater the amount of time the KDM should be spending on strategic matters. Your impact and value as DR will rise as you do more and more to help make sure this actually happens!

Milt, who had just sold his organization for tens of millions of dollars, shared with me how he had relinquished responsibility for most functional areas to his Executive Vice President years before he sold the organization. He turned over all responsibility and authority for every functional area in his organization to his Executive Vice President, except the four things he passionately loved to do: setting the grand vision, selling big accounts, negotiating deals, and presenting. He retained the title of CEO, but as I hope I've made very clear by now, you must never confuse title with responsibility in a privately owned organization.

The EVP, by being proactive and volunteering to manage most functional areas of the organization, helped to bring about this transition, which had a dramatic positive impact on the organization.

Interestingly, after Milt retired, he found he was so good at presenting before groups, and loved doing it so much, that he was able to create a professional comedy routine that took this skill of his onstage. I caught his act one night. He was very good!

During one memorable Alignment session, Ben, a DR who was the manager for an IT division, completed exercises in which he identified what he thought was a weakness of the CEO he reported to. Ben explained that Ted, his CEO, was "a great guy and very creative," but he also shared stories that suggested the CEO was a disaster when it came to requiring or following systems, protocols, processes, and measurements—all of which, he felt strongly, were essential in order for the IT division to be well run.

One of the DRs from another division, who was attending the session, asked Ben whether he had ever talked to Ted about allowing the Director of IT to report to him, rather than to the CEO. The manager responded that he had no background in IT. I pointed out that Ben's behavioral style survey results, which had been shared with the training class, showed his own natural behavioral style was consistent with what he had determined was needed in the IT division, and that Ted, his CEO, apparently lacked.

As part of the homework assignment before his next session, Ben met with Ted to discuss Ben's interest in having the IT Director report to him. Ted was delighted with the idea.

After Ben had attended all the training sessions, I led a concluding session with just him and Ted. The purpose of the session was to discuss the positive impact that had occurred from changes suggested, and what additional changes could be made. Ted, the CEO, believed the single biggest benefit from the Alignment training was the decision to change the IT Director's reporting relationship. This had freed up his time by eliminating the hours he had previously spent on matters with IT, allowing him to spend more time working on division strategy. It also reduced his stress levels, because he was no longer struggling to (as he put it) "bounce so many balls."

TAKEAWAYS: WIN/WIN OUTCOME #3

- Start the "job description" discussion. Be prepared to do so from the point of view of the KDM who has "too many hats to wear."
- Before meeting with your KDM about the job description topic, take a look at any one of the many different job descriptions available on the Internet for CEOs and COOs of a small or mid-sized organization. You may even want to walk into the meeting with printouts of one or more examples of these types of job descriptions.

- Gain clarity on what duties your KDM feels most strongly about retaining.
- Get creative. There is no rule for what your KDM's job should be, other than certain responsibilities of a KDM that cannot be delegated.

Beware of Titles

- Focus less on your KDM's title and more on your KDM's responsibilities. Only then can you determine your own strategy for proactively becoming the highest-impact DR you are capable of becoming.
- "Being inspirational" does not have to be in your KDM's job description. Some of the most successful organizations have KDMs who are not particularly inspiring, yet they expect their organization to have an atmosphere where the people enjoy their work and are challenged to grow. Very often, these KDMs are not the 'rah rah' types. If the KDM you report to is not particularly inspiring, this is an area where you may be able to fill an important gap.
- Look in the mirror first. Before you even think about taking over optional responsibilities for your KDM, you need to understand your own areas of strength and natural behavior, and those of your KDM.
- Have a "duty gap" discussion with your KDM. Here's a good point of entry: what does he/she "have to" do but dreads doing?
- Decide what needs to be delegated in your own world. To become a high-impact DR, you need discipline to look at what responsibility boxes you should assume from your KDM. At the same time, this means you will have to identify roles that need to be taken off your plate. Training may need to be provided to those being assigned the roles you will no longer do.
- Understand your organization's (and your KDM's) current growth and development stage.

Timing Is Everything

If your organization is small, there's probably a sharply limited amount of resources, and your organization owner is likely to be in charge of some responsibilities he or she isn't particularly good at fulfilling. This is natural and appropriate. Your KDM is likely to be involved in translating organization strategies into functional action plans, and is also responsible for everything else, including addressing any day-to-day changes that need to be made, whether or not those changes are critical to the organization's survival.

So for example: while an organization is small, the organization owner will typically be directly involved with organization development. There may be no other salesperson, or certainly not one who can be trusted with the key accounts. As the organization grows, your KDM may still sometimes, wear his/

her "sales hat." Is that really the best role? Or would the KDM and the organization be better served by his/her decision to step back and coordinate the sales staff or manage the sales manager?

As the organization grows, and has greater resources available to hire managers, it's essential your KDM delegate functions such as HR, finance, technology, or operations—especially those functions the KDM dreads doing—if the organization is to keep growing. Your KDM will still keep track of these functions, but at a higher level, with managers directly responsible for them. This will also lessen the need for your KDM to be involved in creating the action plans, and will allow him/her to focus more on identifying and making sure the right changes are made in the most critical areas.

With greater resources, there should be discussions about using part-time workers, contract help, and perhaps even virtual/remote staff. Volunteering to oversee such changes is one area where a qualified DR can have a significant impact on organizational success. Very often, these personnel changes are low-investment, high-return decisions that remove time-intensive tasks from the to-do list and free up the KDM—and other staff—to focus on higher-value activities.

Such shifts can be major career opportunities, but you must know where the organization is in its growth cycle, and what changes will best serve both the KDM and the organization!

WIN/WIN OUTCOME #4: HELP YOUR KDM TURN HIS/HER KNOWLEDGE INTO STANDARDIZED, WRITTEN PROTOCOLS AND PROCESSES

Very often, the KDM has, with the best of intentions, built his or her organization executive team in an environment where much essential information is still "in the KDM's head." The KDM hasn't created the operations manuals, systems, protocols, and processes needed to take the organization on the road toward its destination: the fulfillment of the KDM's vision. As a result, crises and growth stalls are common.

If you notice that people in your organization are operating without essential systems or documentation, you may be able to become a higher-impact contributor by helping your KDM transfer the knowledge in his or her head into written standardized protocols and processes. This is essential for all tasks that must be repeated. If you are certain creating protocols and processes is part of your skill set, you should make a point of offering your KDM new ways to develop this knowledge into standardized routines that others can follow.

At Tipton, my co-owner, who was the founder of the organization, once told me the best thing he ever did in organization was to decide that if he wanted to take the organization from a relatively small organization to one with hundreds of employees, he would have to employ someone who could bring to the organization the strategic thinking, processes, protocols, and systems that were needed. When he and I first met, we had a very clear discussion on my responsibility for continuing the "process revolution" he had initiated, bringing about strategic leadership, and creating the team needed to achieve the vision we both shared.

A word of warning is in order here: some people are skilled at creating and implementing systems and protocols for teams and individuals to follow. These systems, once they're formalized, work when the KDM is not there to supervise matters. Other people definitely are not skilled at setting up such systems. Many visionary entrepreneurs fall into the second category, and desperately need help in this area. You must, however, be absolutely certain you fall into the first category before you attempt to offer help in this area.

I strongly urge you to closely examine your own career successes and failures before you present yourself as a "processes and protocols expert" on either a small or large scale. You don't want to make a bad situation worse! If neither you nor your KDM is good at developing good process documentation, you could benefit from working with someone else, or at least put together a check-list on how to create a good process document. There are certain guidelines that are considered best practice, such as having key bullet items in certain areas rather than using a lot of text.

The RASCI Chart

One great, easy-to-use, process document tool is the RASCI chart, available at http://www.osu.edu/eminence/assets/files/RASCI_Charts.pdf. This is a simple chart showing who in the organization is Responsible, who has Approval, who provides Support, who provides Counsel, and who should be Informed for a given initiative. This chart can be a great "first step" in process development since it ensures not only that key tasks are documented, but also notes the involved parties for each step.

TAKEAWAYS: WIN/WIN OUTCOME #4

1. Start the "processes and protocols" discussion. Be prepared to do so tactfully from one of these two perspectives:
2. Be prepared to launch this discussion with the KDM who has "everything in his/her head." Make the case that the organization has hit an obstacle to growth that will not be overcome until there is a change in the organization's reliance on your KDM to offer information and instructions. What happens (for instance) when your KDM is ill?
3. Be prepared to launch this discussion with the KDM who is tired of "putting out fires" that result from unclear, out-of-date, or nonexistent procedures. If the processes were clearer, and the conflicts and crises

were fewer, how much time and energy would your KDM have to devote to strategic issues?

WIN/WIN OUTCOME #5: HELP YOUR KDM DEVELOP WAYS TO MEASURE RESULTS

No matter what kind of organization you work for, strategically important, new measurements can be developed in many areas your KDM has not yet considered. For example, many organizations use the number of visits to the organization website as measurements that help determine the validity of capital allocation decisions related to marketing and promotion. If your organization isn't using that metric, it should.

The KDM in any privately owned organization is personally responsible for managing the organization's capital. That means determining what resources are available versus what resources are necessary to achieve the goals that will fulfill the organization vision. This is another of those important responsibilities that cannot be delegated. What this means, in practical terms, is the KDM is ultimately responsible for approving all budgets and funding all projects involving major expenditure.

Even if your KDM is not a "financial person," he or she is still responsible for making critical budgeting and funding-related decisions. This is a difficult situation for many KDMs, and one where a "financial" DR can make a huge positive impact.

It's a simple reality of organization life that department heads will always vie for a greater and greater portion of the organization's resources. Rarely, if ever, will a department ask that its budget be reduced. Not all requests for funds, however, are equally defensible as investments in the organization!

Which budget allocations represent the best investments? Often, the KDM has no idea. You can help your KDM deal with this difficult challenge by showing him or her ways to more accurately measure the results of the organization's resource allocations. Helping your KDM develop clear metrics for evaluating these decisions makes your KDM more effective, and you more valuable.

Assuming you have access to the right data and possess the relevant skillset, you can help the KDM devise financial measures appropriate to the organization, including traditional measures such as return on assets for a capital-intensive organization. You can also help your KDM invent more organization-specific measures, such as return on training dollars for an organization that places a high strategic value on state-of-the-art training for its employees.

Hard Numbers

In most privately owned organizations, KDMs get much less information than they should about the wisdom of their capital allocation decisions. It is not uncommon for small and mid-sized organizations to have no tracking mechanism for evaluating the financial impact of these decisions.

You may be able to help change this situation for the better by designing and tracking financial measures that help get your KDM better information. By monitoring several such measures, your KDM will learn how to link his/her budget decisions to hard numbers that link to specific outcomes, rather than soft, non-measurable, less relevant factors (like the intensity of the appeals of their subordinates).

TAKEAWAYS: WIN/WIN OUTCOME #5

- Begin the "measure capital results" discussion with your KDM. Ask how he or she evaluates the real-world effectiveness of specific capital investments.
- Propose a numbers-driven analysis as an aid to decision-making.
- Volunteer to do the number-crunching your KDM does not have the time or inclination to do.
- Consider beginning your analysis with a simple traditional measure such as return on assets, broken down by department or team and evaluated regularly over time, say, monthly or quarterly. Some interesting trends identifying greater and lesser results by department will soon emerge.
- Consider beginning by making use of the simple return on assets calculator you can find online at http://www.calculatorpro.com/return-on-assets-calculator/
- If you are not a "numbers person," do not take on this responsibility!

WIN/WIN OPTION #6: OFFER YOUR KDM HONEST FEEDBACK

Another way to create a greater positive impact to your KDM is to give honest, relevant feedback about his or her performance, or the performance of the organization. By doing this, you can help your KDM gain perspective and rise above the seemingly never-ending series of "fires" he or she takes responsibility for putting out. Yet, it is important to recognize this path is a potentially dangerous one for even the most well-intentioned DR. It requires a strong relationship marked by trust and personal rapport between the KDM and the DR.

Some KDMs are able to grow their organizations to a certain size because of their ability to provide certain services, or because they've developed a certain product or service. These KDMs may not be as good at seeing the potential in such things as improving relationships with vendors, improving customer service standards, or identifying new products or services. They may face challenges in communicating with, or motivating, key people in the organization.

They may have trouble managing salespeople. These are areas where you may be able to bring higher-impact value to your organization by speaking tactfully and frankly about the functions you see in your KDM's personal approach to your organization at which your KDM may not be great.

Obviously, this is a potentially sensitive area. As a DR, how do you let your KDM know that he or she is making poor decisions, or communicating poorly? Even when a KDM asks directly for honest feedback, there is always the fear your non-flattering feedback may hurt your position, and future, in the organization. One way to negate the fear of reprisal is to suggest the organization adopt a confidential, online, 360-degree feedback process (you can learn more about one such system at https://www.echospan.com/360_degree_feedback.asp). Of course, adopting such a system does not guarantee your KDM will act on the feedback!

By the way, A KDM's failure to "understand" what needs to take place in a specific, functional area of the organization is not really all that surprising. No KDM is an expert in all functional areas of an organization, and (unless the organization is a very small one) the KDM should not be expected to have mastery of all the details that relate to a given organization situation. Once an organization gets to the point of having twenty or more employees, the KDM who "knows the details" better than the DR is a KDM who is facing serious problems. Either the KDM has the wrong management team in place, or he or she is spending too much time at the wrong levels of the organization.

Some KDMs have a tendency to ignore feedback they don't want to hear. Your challenge in these situations will be to find creative, nonthreatening ways to get your KDM to truly listen to what you have to say—this is part of your ongoing responsibility as DR to tactfully and assertively engage with your KDM.

Your goal should always be to find ways to use feedback that allow you to be an initiator of constructive change—not just change for the sake of change. Let's consider three possible methods for constructive feedback interaction with your KDM.

1. When pointing out issues that connect to the KDM's shortcomings, first and foremost, accept you cannot force your KDM to address shortcomings by any means that may be considered disrespectful or threatening to his/her image. The feedback you offer must be shared in private, delivered sensitively and compassionately, and must focus on improving the way the KDM does some things.

2. Approaching these discussions with a great deal of humility is also important. If you, as DR, can acknowledge some of your weaknesses during this discussion, that will make it easier for your KDM to accept your input. Nothing will be accomplished unless you can first persuade your KDM you are giving the feedback with his or her best interests in mind.

3. A KDM in a privately owned organization is not accountable to anyone. This means he or she may need some practice listening to, and acting on, constructive feedback.

The KDM's ability to process and respond to constructive feedback has a huge impact on the growth rate of the organization. At many of the organizations I've worked, there were DRs with real strength in a given functional area, and a corresponding willingness to offer feedback relevant to organization challenges within their own field of expertise. Some of these organizations experienced growth rates that took them to 100 times their initial size! By the same token, without honest feedback from qualified DRs, many KDMs have been lulled into a sense of complacency. They accept mediocrity because they never identified what was possible and achievable for their organization. These organizations are usually marked by much more modest growth.

> **When offering feedback, don't make it personal**

When offering feedback, focus on a specific, narrowly defined functional area—not on the person. Even with this precaution, however, you are likely to hear, in response, some thoughts from the KDM about areas where you could stand to make improvements. Hearing the KDM's honest feedback may be an initial shock to the system, but you must not let it become an excuse to "get personal." If you're caught off guard, don't react. Stop and think about what you've heard. Consider saying something like, "This is news to me; I guess I need some time to think about this." Do not counterattack; do not instantly dispute what the KDM has shared with you.

The second category of feedback involves sharing your concerns in private about the performance of one or more of your fellow DRs who reports to your KDM. This, too, should be done carefully, and with a focus on behaviors, not people.

The third category of feedback involves suggestions for improvements in the organization operations that do not fall into the first two categories. The best time to present this feedback may be at Executive Team Meetings. This gives you recognition for the feedback and a forum for discussing the merits of the feedback.

In all three situations, you must carefully gauge your KDM's responses to your initial suggestions—proceed slowly and with the utmost caution based on what you see and hear. There is no advantage to anyone if you offer "advice" to your KDM that will be perceived as hostility, betrayal, or political gamesmanship.

TAKEAWAYS: WIN/WIN OUTCOME #6

- Think twice before offering any kind of frank feedback about what you perceive to be your KDM's personal "blind spots." First of all, you may be mistaken. Second, even if you are correct, sharing your perspective will not serve either you or the KDM—unless you have first established strong levels of trust and personal rapport within the relationship.
- Be sensitive to the fact that it isn't easy being a KDM in a privately owned small or mid-sized organization. When things don't go as expected, your KDM may have a tendency to deal with these challenges in a very direct way because he/she just wants it done right.
- Be sensitive to the reality there is likely to be no day-to-day accountability for your KDM's actions. Your challenge is to find a way to help your KDM become more self-accountable.
- Help your KDM see, and be in agreement with, the organization's competitive advantages. Maintaining or defending this competitive edge is often a good point of entry to "honest feedback" discussions.
- Ask your KDM whether he/she is open to using a 360-degree feedback process that might indicate other areas you and/or other DRs could help the KDM by taking items off his or her "to-do list." Remember: every time you take items off your KDM's to-do list, you're allowing that KDM to be more effective and focus more of his or her time and attention on other issues that will make a big difference to the team or organization.
- If you understand your KDM's vision for the organization, it will be much easier to offer suggestions on how you can make constructive changes to the things you do that will lead to the vision being achieved.
- You can also focus on feedback about those aspects of your organization that are not performing at desired, reasonably achievable levels. What areas need improvement? What areas, if improved, have the potential to "move the needle"? When you have identified these areas, focus on the most critical ones and look for measurable performance data that can help make your case. Collect plenty of information before you make your pitch to help bring about improvements in this under-performing area.

YOUR HOMEWORK ASSIGNMENT

Before you move on to the next chapter, identify three Takeaway lists from this chapter that you think make sense for you to adopt in support of your KDM. Once you have done that, meet with your KDM and ask for his or her guidance in using one, two, or all three of these lists to take work off his or her plate. If the answer is "no," ask your KDM for guidance on how you can become better prepared or prove yourself as capable of taking personal responsibility for at least one of these potential "win/win" areas.

CHAPTER 10

Align on Critical Success Factors

EXECUTIVE SUMMARY FOR THE KEY DECISION MAKER (KDM)

Have you ever had the experience of uncovering a major investment of your organization's resources ... an investment of which you were unaware ... and realizing the project had nothing to do with achieving your long-term vision for the organization?

Most **Key Decision Makers (KDMs)** we work with are far more familiar with this kind of experience than they'd like to be! I call it a "Who Authorized This?" moment. It's no fun for anyone.

In this important chapter, your **Direct Report (DR)** will ask you to take the lead in conducting a special kind of team-driven enterprise assessment and analysis session. This session will give you the opportunity for a close evaluation of your organization, an evaluation dedicated to identifying the **Critical Success Factors (CSFs)** that support your personal vision for the organization. This face-to-face session will require your leadership, as well as the input of the key DRs in your organization. It is designed to keep the "Who Authorized This?" experience from ever happening again.

This Critical Success Factor assessment should only involve you and your DRs. Conducting this assessment sooner rather than later will require a modest investment of you and your DRs' time, especially when compared to the high-impact rewards your organization will experience. This is an investment that really can protect your organization from future "Who Authorized This?" moments.

Schedule the time to identify your organization Critical Success Factors when your DR approaches you about this.

THREE THINGS YOU CAN COUNT ON

They say you can only count on two things in life: death and taxes. Actually, that's wrong.

There are three things you can count on in life. There's death. There are taxes. And the third thing you can count on: unless the KDM and all the DRs are absolutely clear about what is and isn't critical to the successful achievement of the **Organization Vision**, you can count on someone, somewhere in the organization, spending precious time, effort, and organization resources on projects that don't support that Vision.

Agreement on your Organization's CSFs is essential if you wish to avoid this problem. With that agreement, you and your KDM can determine how best to focus your organization's resources on the task everyone should be devoted to: propelling the organization forward in pursuit of the Organization Vision.

ALIGN ON CSFS!

Alignment on your organization's CSFs is extremely important. It provides two things:

- The solid platform upon which you and other organization executives can build plans that involve the coordinated efforts of multiple departments.
- The CSFs also provide you with the clarity necessary to design individual project plans for yourself and all those who report to you. Not only will these plans clarify what you and your team should be doing—they will also make it clear what you definitely should not be doing.

As a DR, you can help bring about this kind of Alignment by discussing with your KDM and fellow DRs the need for regular **Strategic Leadership Team** meetings —the first of which should be scheduled as soon as practicable. This meeting should be attended only by KDMs and DRs (although others may occasionally be called in to give updates or provide background information). One of the early sessions should follow this three-step process:

Step 1:   An Organization **Diagnostic** of your organization
Step 2:   **A Strengths, Weakness, Opportunities and Threats (SWOT)** assessment of your organization
Step 3:   The creation of a mutually-agreed-upon, written **Critical Success Factor Statement** for the organization

In this chapter, we'll look at all three of these steps. Taken together, they will uncover the CSFs that *must* be executed in order for your organization to achieve its true level of potential. The analysis you and your KDM will conduct during this Retreat is not "extra work," but an organizational test your enterprise must pass if it is to fulfill the KDM's vision. *Not* **identifying your CSFs is what actually creates extra work for everyone.**

What follows in this chapter is the three-step agenda for the Strategic Leadership Team Retreat that your KDM must lead. It will probably make the most sense for this event to be scheduled for a weekend in the near future. Regardless of when or how the event is scheduled, however, it is your job to tactfully, persistently engage with the KDM until the Strategic Leadership Team Retreat takes place.

STEP 1: ORGANIZATION DIAGNOSTIC FOR THE ORGANIZATION

As the first order of business in the retreat, the **Strategic Leadership Team** needs to consider the key areas of the organization that should be assessed for performance results. This means conducting an organization diagnostic.

There are many ways to do this. To begin with, I suggest the simplest way: You each separately complete the Organization Diagnostic Questionnaire that follows, then compare and discuss your individual ratings. Using this approach, you will be able to evaluate your beliefs about the organization's performance against the perceptions of your fellow DRs and the KDM.

This discussion will help the group explore the larger issue of how best to achieve the highest possible level of Alignment in each of the ten areas laid out in the questionnaire. These exchanges, if conducted openly and with good intent, will bring important insights to the surface and perhaps even change some long-held assumptions. Of course, your KDM must have the last word concerning the appropriate next steps.

I can't overemphasize the importance of interaction and frank give-and-take during these discussions. The exercise is meaningless without that!

One more suggestion: Think twice before awarding tens or zeros as you complete the Organization Diagnostic Questionnaire. These extreme numbers mean the organization could not possibly be doing any worse, or could any better. That's rarely true!

ORGANIZATION DIAGNOSTIC QUESTIONNAIRE

Planning

1. The organization holds effective strategic planning sessions.

   (strongly disagree) 0 1 2 3 4 5 6 7 8 9 10 (strongly agree)

2. A clear organization vision has been established.

   (strongly disagree) 0 1 2 3 4 5 6 7 8 9 10 (strongly agree)

Employee Development

3. The organization effectively motivates employees to achieve goals.

     (strongly disagree) 0 1 2 3 4 5 6 7 8 9 10 (strongly agree)

4. Most people who work here feel fulfilled.

     (strongly disagree) 0 1 2 3 4 5 6 7 8 9 10 (strongly agree)

Marketing

5. The organization marketing is effective.

     (strongly disagree) 0 1 2 3 4 5 6 7 8 9 10 (strongly agree)

6. There is an understandable marketing process.

     (strongly disagree) 0 1 2 3 4 5 6 7 8 9 10 (strongly agree)

Sales

7. The organization trains its salespeople well.

     (strongly disagree) 0 1 2 3 4 5 6 7 8 9 10 (strongly agree)

8. The organization has a well-documented and well-communicated selling process.

     (strongly disagree) 0 1 2 3 4 5 6 7 8 9 10 (strongly agree)

Internal Communications

9. All employees of the organization are updated on the performance and future of the organization.

     (strongly disagree) 0 1 2 3 4 5 6 7 8 9 10 (strongly agree)

10. Managers find it easy to get the information they need to complete key tasks.

     (strongly disagree) 0 1 2 3 4 5 6 7 8 9 10 (strongly agree)

Customer Service

11. Employees service both internal and external customers well.

     (strongly disagree) 0 1 2 3 4 5 6 7 8 9 10 (strongly agree)

12. The organization evaluates the service it delivers from the customer's perspective.

     (strongly disagree) 0 1 2 3 4 5 6 7 8 9 10 (strongly agree)

Operations

13. The organization has developed and is following effective internal procedures to operate the organization.

    (strongly disagree) 0 1 2 3 4 5 6 7 8 9 10 (strongly agree)

14. Internal procedures are so clearly communicated in writing that the organization operates effectively.

    (strongly disagree) 0 1 2 3 4 5 6 7 8 9 10 (strongly agree)

Information Technology

15. Critical organization data is secure against disaster.

    (strongly disagree) 0 1 2 3 4 5 6 7 8 9 10 (strongly agree)

16. Managers have easy access to critical organization data.

    (strongly disagree) 0 1 2 3 4 5 6 7 8 9 10 (strongly agree)

17. Most manual information processes have been automated.

    (strongly disagree) 0 1 2 3 4 5 6 7 8 9 10 (strongly agree)

Corporate Finances

18. The organization has an effective process for developing and communicating internal financial information to those who use it to guide decision-making.

    (strongly disagree) 0 1 2 3 4 5 6 7 8 9 10 (strongly agree)

19. The organization's capital resources are allocated effectively.

    (strongly disagree) 0 1 2 3 4 5 6 7 8 9 10 (strongly agree)

Human Resources Procedures

20. The organization recruits employees effectively.

    (strongly disagree) 0 1 2 3 4 5 6 7 8 9 10 (strongly agree)

21. The organization does a good job of retaining key people.

    (strongly disagree) 0 1 2 3 4 5 6 7 8 9 10 (strongly agree)

22. The organization follows required procedures to insure against legal actions from employees, former employees, and potential employees.

    (strongly disagree) 0 1 2 3 4 5 6 7 8 9 10 (strongly agree)

23. Exit interviews are conducted and their feedback is shared effectively.

    (strongly disagree) 0 1 2 3 4 5 6 7 8 9 10 (strongly agree)

What I've just given you is a first step. Of course, not all of the ten categories I have shared here are likely to be of equal importance to your organization. That's why I recommend your team take the additional step of assigning "weights" for each category based on that category's importance to your organization. In this additional step, each of the ten organization categories should be assigned a rating from 1 to a maximum of 25 points—25 points being the highest priority and the most that can be given for any category. Another category on the list might have a priority of only 5. **Important: the sum of priorities for all categories must total 100 to provide for a meaningful analysis.** So now you can begin another discussion: What are the highest priorities?

> The whole purpose of doing an organization assessment for the organization is so you, your KDM, and the team of DRs can gain essential insights by assessing the organization from a comprehensive, analytical perspective.

In answering that question, you should try to find measurable, relevant, industry-specific statistics for each of these categories and, in a measurable manner, compare how your organization stacks up to the competition. Most people who have completed this process tell me this kind of industry-specific comparison is much easier to obtain than they'd imagined, thanks to Google and the information provided by various trade associations. Find the data you need to make meaningful comparisons! You will be glad you did.

Discuss the numbers before you finalize them. Comparing the initial ratings of your KDM to your ratings and to the ratings of the other DRs is usually a very revealing process. Remember, the KDM gets the last word.

Once your team has completed this Organization Diagnostic for your organization, you will be ready for the second step: the SWOT Analysis.

STEP TWO: YOUR ORGANIZATION SWOT STATEMENTS

With step one complete, it is time to look at how you, as a DR, can help your organization understand and reach Alignment on a process known as a **SWOT analysis**. SWOT stands for Strengths, Weaknesses, Opportunities, and Threats.

To complete this second step, the Strategic Leadership Team needs to closely consider the results of the Organization Diagnostic conducted in Step 1. The Organization Diagnostic provides a path toward developing an internal assessment—a look at where the organization is right now. This internal assessment gives rise to identifying the Strengths and Weaknesses. It does not, however, provide a strong pathway to identifying Opportunities and Threats. That's because there are often external factors that give rise to Opportunities and Threats not flushed out by the internal assessment.

SWOT FACTORS

In the SWOT exercise I'm about to describe, the team may underestimate the impact of external factors that point toward evidence of Opportunities and Threats. The team should consider all external factors that might have a bearing on the future of the organization. Remember: Opportunities and Threats are generally uncontrollable by an organization's leaders, whereas Strengths and Weaknesses, ascertained from the internal assessment you just completed, are generally more predictable and controllable.

Important external factors to consider in creating your list of Opportunities and Threats include: Economy, Legal, Government/Legislation, Technology, Competition, and Served Market.

Now you're ready to evaluate a new list—one that is as important as the one that drove your Organization Diagnostic. Each one of the following functional organization areas should be assessed carefully then described as a Strength, a Weakness, an Opportunity, or a Threat. The functional areas are:

- Planning
- Employee Development
- Marketing
- Sales
- Internal Communications
- Customer Service
- Operations
- Information Technology
- Corporate Finances
- Human Resources Procedures

In addition to the ten functional categories listed above, which apply to all organizations, you may also want to consider a SWOT analysis for other organization areas that need to be separately considered because of the specific activity in which your organization engages.

The following are examples of functional areas that relate to other organization activities that may be important to your organization:

- Bid for Work/Projects
- Distribution
- Family Organization Dynamics
- Manufacturing
- Not-for-Profit
- Exports to Overseas Markets
- Retail

You, your KDM, and fellow DRs may come up with additional areas important to your organization that should be added to the list. If they stimulate your SWOT thinking and make it easier to identify and evaluate your organization

SWOTs, they probably belong on the list. In the end, there is no one "right answer" to the critical question of which topics should be discussed and evaluated as part of your SWOT analysis. There is only your team's vigorous discussion of this topic. Fortunately, that is enough.

Once your Strategic Leadership Team has identified the relevant functional areas, each member should, individually, assign every functional category one of five letters:

- (S) if he or she believes that item to be a potential STRENGTH
- (W) if he or she believes that item to be a potential WEAKNESS
- (O) if he or she believes that item to be a potential OPPORTUNITY
- (T) if he or she believes that item to be a potential THREAT
- (N) if he or she believes that item is NOT IMPORTANT TO DISCUSS RIGHT NOW.

Don't press too hard for "final answers" at the beginning of this process. You are simply looking for early consensus on these issues; you can always change the list if the consensus changes later (this kind of change is quite likely because the members of the Strategic Leadership Team will develop a keener sense of what the four SWOT elements actually are, and how they differ, as the discussion moves forward). For now, you are only looking to generate initial instincts on what does and doesn't belong in what category.

Some factors may qualify as both an Opportunity and a Threat. One example of this could be a breakthrough in technology that could be utilized by a competitor. If your organization is able to become a quick and competent adopter of the new technology, this can be viewed as an Opportunity. If, on the other hand, your organization is not capable of quickly and competently adopting the new technology and only plans to follow if forced to then it may be viewed as a Threat.

In developing each of your Organization's SWOT statements, each member of the Strategic Leadership Team should separately identify between three and five Strengths, Weaknesses, Opportunities, and Threats that have the potential for the greatest impact on the organization's future.

REACHING ALIGNMENT ON SWOT STATEMENTS REQUIRES OPEN AND HONEST DISCUSSION

Once each member of the Strategic Leadership Team has created his/her top 3-5 Strengths, Weaknesses, Opportunities and Threats, these statements should be read aloud at a Strategic Leadership Team Meeting.

Your team needs to discuss each of the various views about SWOT areas presented by each member. After discussion, you should come to collective agreement on which of the items in each of the four SWOT areas are the most important to attaining your Organization Vision Statement, with the KDM having the final say. Some people may feel strongly that a given topic represents an important point for discussion, while others may disagree. The rule of thumb here is usually to look for ways to include topics, rather than look for reasons to exclude them. When in doubt, put it on the list.

Your team's final SWOT Statement should have three to five points collectively deemed to have the greatest potential for significant impact on your organization. Below, you will find some additional insights on reaching that (often difficult) final consensus for each element.

BUILDING THE ORGANIZATION STRENGTHS (S) STATEMENT

Keep your fears to yourself, but share your courage with others.— Robert Louis Stevenson

Organization Strengths are what your organization finds easiest to leverage successfully when seeking to gain additional business, results, or market share. They are your organization's "strong suits."

These Strengths must be deployed to the greatest possible extent if you want to maximize the chances of the organization reaching the KDM's vision for the organization's future. Of course, if you hope to deploy these Strengths, you must first know what they are! So the first part of the conversation must be about creating consensus about what your firm's strong suits really are.

Your organization Strengths have different degrees of potential ability to impact your organization. Make sure the group chooses only Strengths that have the potential to bring about a major impact in helping your organization reach the future the KDM desires.

Now look at your SWOT list of ten functional categories and other organization areas that your Strategic Leadership Team has identified as applicable for your type of organization and assign an "S" if you think it is an area of Strength.

Take your time with these questions. Create thoughtful written answers to each. Compare your answers. Writing down your views on Strengths will help you and your KDM prepare for the next task: creating a first draft of your Organization Strengths Statement that everyone on the Strategic Leadership Team can buy into and support. Note: make sure the list is limited to a maximum of five strengths only.

Here is an example of one department's Organization Strengths Statement:

> **Remember:**
> **Your formal written Organization Strengths Statement should reference only the Organization Strengths that have the highest potential for making your organization succeed in attaining the KDM's vision!**

ORGANIZATION STRENGTHS STATEMENT: ABC DEPARTMENT

- Experienced management and manufacturing personnel
- Well-documented Manufacturing System
- Patents on certain products and parts
- Building for manufacturing has room for a great amount of growth

BUILDING THE ORGANIZATION WEAKNESSES (W) STATEMENT

Recognizing a problem doesn't always bring a solution, but until we recognize that problem, there can be no solution. —James Baldwin

Your Organization Weaknesses are the flip-side of your Organization Strengths. They're the components that could keep you from attaining your KDM's vision as soon or as completely as you'd like. Relying on Organization Weaknesses that you mistakenly believe to be strengths may even take your organization down for the count!

Even the most successful organizations have weaknesses. Being honest about identifying Organization Weaknesses can be very challenging, because it requires an honest look at possible deficiencies that may reflect on you, your KDM, and your fellow DRs. Many weaknesses are acknowledged, but not understood in their true dimensions.

When facilitating a discussion about identifying possible Organization Weaknesses, focus first on those Weaknesses that can have big-picture impact. Your goal should be to spend most of the group's time discussing the weaknesses most likely to keep the organization from reaching the destination described in the Organization Vision Statement.

Looking at your Organization's Weaknesses isn't always enjoyable. You may not like hearing about the realities of weaknesses that fall within your responsibilities as a DR, particularly if those weaknesses have been causing your organization to underachieve. None of us likes talking about our personal flaws.

By the same token, it can be awkward trying to look closely at weaknesses that fall under the responsibilities of your KDM or other DRs. Even so, it's important the conclusions reached by the group reflect major Organization Weaknesses that most of the Strategic Leadership Team actually see and experience. You must not build this evaluation around only what you are willing to talk about because you don't want to upset someone with whom you work. The idea is to focus tactfully but honestly on what you see as a weakness, without playing the 'blame game' or assigning fault to particular individuals. An example would be identifying marketing as a weakness without taking potshots at the director of marketing.

WHAT IF THE ORGANIZATION WEAKNESS IS WITHIN THE DIRECT RESPONSIBILITY OF THE KDM?

Chip, a KDM, had the dream of doubling the size of his chemical department within five years. It didn't happen.

According to Kevin, Chip's Strategic Leadership Vice President, the department had a major weakness standing in the way of the desired growth pace. He felt the weakness was Chip's inability to lead the organization strategically. Kevin expressed his belief the chemical department failed to grow the way it was otherwise capable of growing because Chip consistently got caught up in handling day-to-day matters and didn't stay focused on developing and implementing strategy.

Kevin's challenge was how to honestly address the need to help his KDM in strategically leading the department without risking reprisal. After an AlignUp training session that focused on getting Alignment on organization **Critical Success Factors (CSFs)**, Kevin met with me and explained his view. He thought Chip was "brilliant" in areas related to technical product innovations, but despite Chip's astonishing ability to solve specific project problems, he was weaker at tasks requiring "process focus," such as strategic planning. Kevin added that he believed Chip was an ineffective leader because of his continued involvement in day-to-day matters, which led to decisions that often seemed to lack strategic direction.

I asked Kevin if he had ever approached Chip about these problems. "Oh I've tried," Kevin sighed, "but it's hard to tell your boss how ineffectively he operates."

When the Strategic Leadership Team, that included all the DRs reporting to Chip, met to identify and become Aligned on the department's CSFs, they were able to identify, as a group, that one of the most important Organization Weaknesses was strategic leadership. Kevin and a few other DRs shared their concern with Chip that Chip's habitual focus on day-to-day matters was a significant Organization Weakness that was keeping his organization from growing to the level he wanted.

Chip listened carefully and even took some notes. A consensus emerged—something had to change. Offsetting this weakness became a central element of one of the CSFs identified in that meeting. Making this weakness into a strength became an initiative on which the entire team, including Chip, agreed.

Let's consider the opposite type of reaction by a KDM. When a KDM reacts negatively to perceived criticisms about their weakness from one or more of their DRs, the DRs need to react in a practical manner. It's time to back off, unless there is a belief the weakness is so extreme that it will lead the organization down a failing path.

Now look at your SWOT list of ten functional categories and other organization areas your Strategic Leadership Team has identified as applicable for your type of organization, and assign a "W" if you think it is an area of Weakness.

Your thinking process should reflect this concern: "If we don't correct such-and-such a weakness, it will most likely result in our vision not being achieved."

All team members need to be open to the task of examining previously unexamined, or under-examined, weaknesses. After you review the written assessments completed by each team member for your Organization Weaknesses, collectively select the weaknesses that have the greatest potential negative impact on your organization's ability to attain its Organization Vision. Select no more than five of these factors and build your written Organization Weaknesses Statement around those elements.

> **Important: Don't try to explain or justify any of the weaknesses you identify!**

THE FOLLOWING IS AN EXAMPLE OF ONE ORGANIZATION'S WEAKNESSES STATEMENT:

Sales department weaknesses include: top domestic person diverted to international sales; poor sales training and sales training materials; no sales manager; lack of sales methodology; website sales wording and messaging is weak.

Marketing department weaknesses include: poor marketing materials; less brand awareness than competitors; too dependent upon outside marketing firm.

Manufacturing weaknesses include: poor quality control; poor project management and execution of new product development; lack of capable manufacturing supervisor backups; weak employee culture in manufacturing plant.

Poor competitive analysis process to ensure we remain competitive and know how to position against the competition.

Building the Organization Opportunities (O) Statement

> *Life, for the living, is a gift of opportunity, an exercise of the will to choose.—T.F. Hodge*

An opportunity is a situation that offers the realistic prospect of meaningful, measurable progress toward the goal of fulfilling the KDM's Organization Vision.

Your organization may miss out on its best chance for greater success if you, your KDM and fellow DRs do not clearly identify the most promising opportunities for your organization. The challenge is to agree on the realistically attainable opportunities, rather than the "blue sky" opportunities, which sound great but may not be achievable.

Identifying the best opportunities for your organization means conducting a reality check of sorts. There are some opportunities your organization simply may not have the infrastructure or the capital to have any real likelihood of achieving. There are others that may not seem quite as flashy, but have a much higher potential of being converted from a dream into reality.

Not all opportunities are created equal. Your team should identify only those few (up to five) that are both attainable and capable of delivering a major positive impact on your organization. Too often organizations make the mistake of spending resources on achieving goals that either do not meet their objectives or have only minor impact upon the organization's strategic objectives.

> **Listen to other members of the team: the right organization opportunities may not always be obvious to you but may be "right in front of the nose" of a fellow team member.**

GET EXCITED ABOUT OPPORTUNITY!

Maria, a DR in an organization specializing in metal parts fabrication, requested a team meeting to complete SWOT statements. As the written evaluations of Opportunities were being read out, her KDM shared his thoughts, for the first time, about opening an entirely new department—fabricating parts for the aircraft industry. This initiative, he explained, could use many of the same skill-sets and much of the machinery already existing in the organization.

The KDM's idea met with a unanimously high level of excitement from his team and resulted in the organization hiring an executive with deep experience in manufacturing aircraft parts, including certification and sales. The team eventually agreed to implement a course-changing plan that capitalized on a previously unexamined opportunity. This course-changing plan—which ended up having a major positive impact on the organization—started with recognizing an opportunity!

The written SWOT statements you create in this area should be succinct. Consider using the following Organization Opportunity as a model:

Expand into other cities, with small offices having one to two employees, each supported by the main office.

Now look at your SWOT list of ten functional categories and other organization areas your Strategic Leadership Team has identified as applicable for your type of organization and assign an "O" if you think it is an area of Opportunity.

Keep focused on your Organization Vision Statement while answering the questions. You should only list opportunities reasonably achievable within thirty-six months.

Here are examples of Opportunities listed in the Organization Opportunities

Statement of one organization:

Increase results generated from current clients by delivering ancillary services (so called "back-end services") to current clients.

Open up a division for exporting services.

Expand into new territories by buying organizations that currently provide the same services as our core services.

Watch Out for the Naysayers!

"That will never work!"

It's quite common to hear some variation on this response when you read the group's written evaluations of opportunities. Help your KDM look beyond the instinctive responses of naysayers by unemotionally examining all the possible reasons a particular opportunity offers your organization a potential advantage.

Have a discussion that engages the whole team. Don't prejudge any opportunity.

Now look at your SWOT list of ten functional categories (and any other organization areas your Strategic Leadership Team has identified as applicable for your type of organization), and assign a "T" if you think it is an area of threat.

BUILDING THE ORGANIZATION THREATS (T) STATEMENT

A threat to your organization is something that can have a significant negative impact on your organization and is outside your control.

For example, you have no control over a global recession. Advancements in technology, the changing social consciousness of the nation, a sudden and unanticipated medical emergency, and many other circumstances can suddenly turn a formerly non-existent or benign factor into a looming disaster. Even though you can't stop such things from happening, you can prepare for them in a way that minimizes the potential damage to your organization.

New threats to your organization can appear at any time, which is one more reason annual SWOT meetings with the top KDM and the DRs must take place.

Identifying these threats to the organization may not be anyone's idea of fun, but it is necessary. When you recognize a new threat, you can exercise a greater measure of control over the situation by making more informed choices. Perhaps you will opt to upgrade your organization with armor that will do a better job of protecting you against the threat; or perhaps you can make strategically sound changes in the course your organization is traveling so as to eliminate risks you face from a factor outside your organization's control. None of that can happen, however, unless you evaluate the risks.

Failure to have an "early detection system" for any threats can negatively affect your organization's long-term health. Reaching Alignment with your KDM and your fellow DRs, by being part of the supportive team that writes the Organization Threats Statement, is the key to early detection.

Here's an example of one organization's Threats Statement:

Competition offers lower online prices because they do not use a high commission dealer network.

Possible new Government regulations for manufacturing.

Only nine years left on patents.

STEP THREE: CRITICAL SUCCESS FACTORS

Organization SWOT Statements Make It Easy To Identify Organization CSFs

Your final written Organization SWOT Statements should be edited until they reflect concise answers to these broad questions:

- What strength do we need to capitalize on?
- What weakness do we need to shore up?
- What opportunity do we need to take advantage of?
- What threat do we need to protect ourselves from that will have the greatest impact on our ability to achieve our vision?

One government department's SWOT Statement identified as an Opportunity that the department's existing equipment was under-utilized. The group felt the organization could triple production without having to invest in additional equipment or building space. After looking at the government department's SWOT Statements, it became clear to the DR that the department needed to significantly lower its manufacturing costs per unit in order for the products to be priced more competitively. She recommended to the team that one of the department's CSFs be to develop additional lines that could be manufactured without any new equipment cost.

Every organization is faced with certain factors critical to its success—CSFs. Identifying your organization's CSFs is the "payoff" for all the organization diagnostic and SWOT analysis work you do up to this point.

Your organization's resources should be focused on achieving that which is most critical to the vision of long-term success for the organization. Getting Alignment on the best use of organization resources from every member of the Strategic Leadership Team first

> **Your organization's CSFs should be conceptual and non-measurable. They are unique to your organization.**

requires identifying the organization CSFs, which must show your KDM, you, and your fellow DRs, where individual and collective time, energy, and financial resources of the organization should be invested.

Once your team has completed the first two steps, it should not take long for you to create your organization's Critical Success Factor Statement. Look at the four SWOT statements and ask which points identified in the Organization SWOT Statement are the most important factors—the factors that could "make or break" your ability to make the KDM's vision for the organization a reality. Satisfying those CSFs is essential to your organization's success!

THE REAL "X FACTOR"

Start this team process with your KDM and other DR team members, each of you filling in the blank for "X" in this statement:

"If X does not take place, the long-term dreams for the organization will not be achieved."

Keep your written answer to the "X" question simple and conceptual. Do not tell stories or cite statistics.

For example, one nonprofit organization owner, upon reviewing his written Weaknesses Statement, identified "X" as follows: "If the nonprofit doesn't proactively address top management's lack of commitment to systems, processes, and protocols, the Nonprofit Vision will not be achieved."

As each person's suggested CSF is put on a screen or flip chart, the team needs to challenge each CSF suggestion by considering the importance to the organization and whether your organization has the ability to achieve the CSF. For example, you may identify a CSF to take on a new product line. This CSF may have the potential to generate great results, but it may be unachievable because it requires human or financial capabilities beyond your organization's current capacity.

Review your Organization SWOT Statements closely to help determine if a proposed CSF is realistically achievable. The information in the Organization SWOT Statement should lead you to identify such factors as; the need for improved marketing, the development of a new unique product, sales, improved distribution efficiency, and other issues critical to the success of your organization. Sometimes the result is not to eliminate the CSF suggestion, but rather to change or modify it in a way that makes it more attainable.

Key CSF Points

- Profit alone cannot be a CSF. Profit is as much a part of a for-profit organization as the act of breathing is to human survival. For most of us, breathing is not a major life goal.
- CSF's do not contain timelines.
- Your organization may have as few as one CSF—and as many as five.

- The number of CSFs your enterprise can successfully address depends upon your organization's financial strength and your human resources infrastructure.

CSF Realities of Privately Owned Organizations

The smaller the organization, the more likely the most important factors critical to the success of the organization will be highly dependent on the efforts of the owner (probably your KDM). As an organization grows, its infrastructure grows, and the organization's CSFs are no longer quite as dependent on the owner. The team for one organization we worked with identified the most critical factor for the success of their organization as "the ability of the owner to spend more time on things that could have 'big picture' impact upon the success of his organization." This is a typical CSF for a smaller, privately held organization.

Ask yourself whether there is a critical factor like this related to your KDM organization owner; one that needs to be addressed before his or her long-term vision for the organization's future can become a reality. If there is such as factor, write it down as one of your recommendations for your Organization Critical Success Factors Statement.

EXAMPLES OF ORGANIZATION CSFS

The following examples show you how to distinctly identify organization Critical Success Factors.

- We need a low-priced entry-level product with fewer features to compete more effectively.
- We must increase customer loyalty by creating "devoted fans".
- We need to sell regionally rather than just locally to achieve our desired growth.
- We need to make much greater use of the current capacity of our manufacturing equipment in order to reduce per unit manufacturing costs.
- In order to stay competitive, our website must provide efficient, easy-to-use ordering by our customers.

MORE EXAMPLES OF CSFS

James, a DR, brought up with the Strategic Leadership Team his concern about the potential of a key employee leaving when there was no one else in the organization whose skill-set fit the person's role. In response to this, a CSF agreed on by the team was, "We must have written operations manuals and personnel responsibilities to cover key employee vacancies."

Tim, another DR, shared with his team his concern about the organization's sales distribution not having an Internet component while faced with threats from web-based competition. The organization, which had been successful for several decades selling clothes and other items by catalog, started to face intense competition when the Internet created the ability for potential buyers to buy similar products at reduced prices. He pointed out that, "The Organization cannot eliminate the new web-based competition," and asked, "How are we going to react to it?"

Indeed, the threat couldn't be eliminated, but early awareness of it resulted in the team agreeing to a CSF involving the creation of its own web presence. The organization soon offered its entire inventory via the web and before long was able to compete very effectively.

Boyd, a DR, discussed with his KDM his concern over one customer being responsible for more than twenty percent of his organization's sales volume. He saw a clear and present danger to the organization if the customer decided to go to a competitor. Boyd suggested that becoming less dependent on its primary customer (who refused to sign a long-term contract) be identified and agreed upon as an organization Critical Success Factor. It was—and the sales picture improved in short order.

CREATING YOUR WRITTEN ORGANIZATION CSF STATEMENT

Remember your goal here is to identify the four or five highest-impact factors. Each member of the team needs to share his/her thoughts on three to five potential CSFs for the organization. The recommendations from each of the team members should be put up on a screen or flipchart and discussed. When there is agreement on up to five CSFs that are most important for the organization, they should be written down as the Organization Critical Success Factors Statement.

THE DRIVING CRITICAL SUCCESS FACTOR (DCSF)

Once the team has completed the Organization Critical Success Factor Statement, it is time for the team to discuss, and agree on, the answer to the following critical question: which of your CSFs is most essential to your organization's success?

This CSF is the one most needed for your organization to excel, and, in some cases, it may be what is needed to survive. This is the factor that holds the potential greatest economic benefit for your organization.

Key Point: Too many small and mid-size organizations mistakenly misallocate organization resources by pursuing CSFs that, if achieved, will have too little impact on their organization compared to what would take place if a more impactful CSF was achieved.

The CSF your team mutually agrees upon as the most essential CSF will become your organization's Driving Critical Success Factor (DCSF). This DCSF will be the CSF on which the greatest share of organization resources must be focused.

EXAMPLES OF DRIVING CRITICAL SUCCESS FACTORS

Here are some examples of what a manufacturing organization's Strategic Leadership Team might agree upon to be the organization's DCSF (remember the organization would select only one of these to be the DCSF):

1. To make greater use of expensive manufacturing equipment that is owned but underutilized, so manufacturing can be done without increasing fixed equipment costs and, in turn, create greater success
2. Increase per store unit results
3. Expand into another country
4. Add an additional product line
5. Develop and provide online training and webcast training for dealers so they can do a better job of selling our products

KEY POINTS

1. Schedule a Strategic Leadership Team Retreat. This should include the KDM and all DRs.
2. During the Strategic Leadership Team Retreat, the KDM has the last word, but consensus and vigorous, open discussion are essential.
3. Conduct an Organization Diagnostic as part of the Strategic Leadership Team Retreat.
4. Conduct a SWOT Analysis as part of the Strategic Leadership Team Retreat.
5. Identify between one and five Critical Success Factors (CSFs) as part of the Strategic Leadership Team Retreat.
6. Choose the organization CSF that is the most important for your organization. This most-important CSF is your Driving Critical Success Factor (DCSF), which will be the foundation for your first organization wide plan.
7. It is essential your KDM allocate the necessary human and financial resources to make sure this DCSF is satisfied!

YOUR HOMEWORK

1. Tactfully, persistently engage with the KDM until a Strategic Leadership Team Retreat is scheduled. This Retreat should include the KDM, who will lead the meeting, you, and any other DRs the KDM wishes to include.

2. Discuss this chapter's key points with your KDM and use it as the agenda for the Executive Team Retreat.
3. As a team, complete the Organization Diagnostic for your organization, following the steps laid out in this chapter.
4. As a team, create the organization's written SWOT Statements, following the steps laid out in this chapter.
5. As a team, write an Aligned Critical Success Factor list that reflects the views of all the members of the Strategic Leadership Team and gives the KDM the last word.

CHAPTER 11

Align on Strategic Direction Initiatives

EXECUTIVE SUMMARY FOR THE KEY DECISION MAKER (KDM)

The surest way I know to get lost on a hike is to hike into unfamiliar terrain without first looking at a map. Similarly, you need a map to reach your dreams for your organization or you stand a good chance of getting lost and failing to achieve what you want. Far too many organizations are underachieving because their organizations' leaders are operating without a map.

For your organization to achieve its highest impact, you and your Direct Report (DR)* need to have, and be Aligned on, a limited number of Organization Strategic Plans, each with a clear Goal that serves as your destination, and each with a clear strategy for how to get there. These Organization Strategic Plans cannot be improvised; they need to be mapped out in a documented manner, whether on paper or in computer files. Your DRs assignment in this chapter is to help you begin the process of mapping them out. This process is painless when undertaken in the step-by-step manner outlined here and will save you and your organization countless days, hours, and weeks of time down the line. When your DR approaches you about this, allocate the modest time investment necessary to fulfill the assignment at the end of this chapter. It will be among the soundest investments either of you have ever made.

THE ORGANIZATION STRATEGIC PLAN: WHY BOTHER?

Why bother with any of the steps laid out in this chapter? Let me share a story that illustrates the answer.

For a definition of Direct Report and other capitalized terms, see the Glossary (Appendix C).

Brenda, a DR going through Alignment training, mentioned to me during one of our sessions that her department's prices for the specialized video equipment and software it sold were significantly higher than those of the competition. She also said she would be willing to bet that her department's cost of manufacturing was higher than the competition's. During discussions related to a goal-setting exercise, I asked Brenda to create a goal she could show to Mike, her boss; a goal that would get him excited enough to not only sign off on, but to ensure its adoption throughout the organization. Here's what she came up with:

"Our department must find a way to lower prices to match the reduced prices of the competition; this lower pricing strategy requires us to cut our cost of production."

She proposed this Goal for an Organization Strategic Plan to Mike at their very next meeting. Mike enthusiastically agreed with the plan, and immediately began "evangelizing" it to the rest of the team. Brenda did her share of evangelizing too. The result: a decrease in both prices and cost of production by an average of 15% within just eighteen months.

This compelling goal—impossible not to understand or remember—took a lot of work, but also resulted in the first price reduction in the department's four decade history. It stopped the department's downward spiraling cycle of sales. And it marked Brenda's transition from "DR" to **"High-Performing DR."**

Of course, Mike, Brenda and her fellow DRs all had to be in Alignment for this plan to work because the plan involved a number of bold and assertive moves, including a large investment in newer, more technologically efficient equipment and more effective use of department personnel. When taking bold actions that require calculated risks, such as this one, it is essential that the KDM and DR team all be pulling their oars in the same direction.

ANATOMY OF THE ORGANIZATION STRATEGIC PLAN

- **Organization Goal** satisfies a **Critical Success Factor**
- **Organization Goal + Strategies** to achieve that Goal = **Strategic Direction Initiative**
- **Tactics** are the steps to complete the **Project/Action Plans** that satisfy the **Strategies**
- **Strategic Direction Initiative + (Project/Action Plans & Tactics) = Organization Strategic Plan**

MORE ON THE ORGANIZATION STRATEGIC PLAN

Organization Strategic Plans should be limited to those that are critically needed for the success of the organization. These need to be organization-wide plans rather than project or action plans. For an Organization Strategic Plan to have the highest chance of success, it needs to have three things: organization-wide commitment, a clear focus on the Goal, and a clear focus on the associated Strategies that will drive the plan.

To increase the chances of your organization successfully making the transition to a high-impact, results-driven organization, you need Alignment with your KDM and fellow DRs on short-term organization Goals and the Strategies for getting there. Brenda succeeded in this. And so can you.

Eliminate "Idea Of The Week" Leadership Style

Well-defined Organization Strategic Plans, each with a Goal and Strategies, will lead you, your KDM, and your fellow DRs away from the frantic "idea of the week" leadership style (so common at low-impact organizations) and into a more strategic approach to an organization's leadership. A clear Goal for your organization's destination and clear Strategies to get you there will help to head off the frustration, waste of energy, and failure that come from you, your KDM, and other DRs making spur-of-the moment decisions.

Creating effective Organization Strategic Plans, and the Strategies that support them, takes a lot of patience, time, and openness to feedback—sticking to the implementation process takes even more of all three. Because patience is often difficult for many organizations' leaders to achieve, slowing things down until there is Alignment on a plan may, at times, require you to consciously "push back" against your organization executing something when it should be planning. If it is your job to do this—and you will know when it is—then it is imperative you perform it to the best of your ability with tactful, assertive engagement during your interactions with your KDM and your colleagues.

> **Ultimately, the top KDM needs to embrace the final selection of any organization Goal or Strategy for a Organization Strategic Plan to have any chance of succeeding.**

One of the common characteristics of low impact, non-strategic organizations' leaders is they are too eager to move into action right away, the minute they have an Organization Goal in mind. They tend to do this before their Organization Strategic Plans are sufficiently developed; this development, of course, requires substantial interactions with the responsible DRs.

It is not how fast you create your Organization Strategic Plans that is important—but that you do it effectively. Your **Organization Strategic Plan Statements** should be short, concise, and easy-to-follow, thus creating a clear path of where the organization needs to go and what needs to be done to get there.

One of the very best ways to become a higher-impact DR is to help in the development of both the Goal and Strategies of your Organization Strategic Plans.

ALIGNMENT IS THE FOUNDATION

Alignment is the foundation of all top-level organization strategic leadership. If you've ever watched a construction crew work on a multistory building, you know that before the concrete can be poured, the steel reinforcing rods must be set and the forms must be in place. After the pouring, the finishing must be done before the concrete sets. And if you ever saw a construction crew begin preparing and pouring the foundation as an afterthought, after all the work on the upper stories was "complete," you saw a construction crew that needed to find a different line of work. Similarly, your Organization Strategic Plans are only as strong as the foundation of Alignment that serves as their base. Alignment is created when those charged with making the plans successful have a true belief in the viability and importance of the Organization Strategic Plans.

If a building is not secured to a solid foundation, chances are when a storm comes, the structure will be severely damaged. A well-constructed Organization Plan supported by all DRs involved, will, like a well-constructed building, help your organization successfully address any challenges that arise on the way to achieving the Organization Strategic Plans.

REACHING TRUE POTENTIAL

Unless your organization is being run strategically, it's unlikely it will reach its potential. The point cannot be overemphasized: the chances of your Organization Plan achieving optimum levels of success is many, many times greater if the fully supported organization Goals and Strategies are developed for the plan before the first action takes place. For an organization to be run at its highest level of success, Aligned strategic thinking and action from your KDM, you, and your fellow DRs is absolutely imperative.

This high level of Alignment comes about from following a formal planning process that involves your KDM and all the DRs who are needed to make the plan succeed—including, of course, you. The process for Aligning on an Organization Strategic Plan has two basic steps, each of which must play out on an organization-wide level: Goal setting, and identifying the strategies to achieve the Goals.

STEP 1: THE GOAL

The most important thing about goals is having one. – *Geoffry F. Abert*

Goal Setting

KDMs who are strategic leaders typically propose organization-wide goals. If you are blessed with a good leader, he/she will share these Goals with the DRs before launching them on the world at large. However, Goal-setting should not stop there. Your KDM should receive and evaluate feedback that you and your fellow DRs provide about each proposed short-term organization-wide Goal. After everyone has had a chance to reflect on the feedback, there will be discussions, revisions, consensus, and buy-in from the entire DR team. Only then should the KDM communicate the chosen goal, as modified by the feedback, to the organization at large.

Goals should be broadly stated targets such as operational improvement activities, new program initiatives, new market entrees, and so on.

As a DR, you should help your KDM and fellow DRs transfer their thoughts and ideas into written Organization Strategic Plans that will provide the path towards all aspects of the organization's success. Writing a Goal for a Organization Strategic Plan involves taking a conceptual factor that is critical to the success of your organization and adding to it those things that will make it specific and measurable within explicitly stated timelines.

> **The Goal that connects to your Organization Strategic Plan should NOT be focused on day-to-day operational activities.**

Creating this kind of Plan means allowing all DRs the chance to express their views. The objective is to get agreement among you, your KDM, and all the DRs after participating in vigorous discussion of a limited number of potential Goals that connect to the Plan.

IDENTIFY THE MOST IMPORTANT GOAL

Now, after considering all potential Goals, it is time to discuss the Goal that, when achieved, will have the greatest positive impact on the organization. Only after you have done this should you consider the Strategies necessary to achieve this Goal. You need a single most-important Goal for each Organization Strategic Plan. Some KDMs are good at identifying this critical Goal. Others need some help.

ONE PLAN AND ONE GOAL AT A TIME

The smaller your organization, the more important it is to focus on developing and implementing one Organization Strategic Plan at a time. This usually involves getting that Organization Strategic Plan well under way to implementation before adding any additional Organization Strategic Plans.

The first Goal should be the one from your list of potential Goals that will have the greatest effect on satisfying factors critical to your organization's success. You can then create written a Goal Statement.

Your most important Organization Strategic Plan should be built around the single Goal that satisfies the factor most critical to achieving the organization's desired success and it should outline the strategies for achieving that Goal. Achieving this first Goal of the first Organization Strategic Plan becomes the first priority for the organization as a whole.

THE ORGANIZATION GOAL SHOULD BECOME A WELL-MEMORIZED MANTRA

Your most important organization Goal should become a well-memorized mantra known by you, your KDM, and all fellow DRs. This Goal of your most important Organization Strategic Plan should generate the greatest organization-wide focus because it is the most critical to the success of the organization. Every DR should keep the organization Plan at the forefront of their day-to-day thinking so they don't ever lose track of it.

One nonprofit organization developed an Organization Strategic Plan with a Goal relating to "increasing customer satisfaction." The Goal was to "get a minimum of eighty percent satisfied to extremely satisfied rating from our current customer base within three years." They achieved that goal!

Another organization developed a Goal that involved increasing organization sales three fold within three years, through the use of independent sales representatives, while cutting manufacturing costs by ten percent per unit. The organization achieved its goals. Every employee in both of these organizations had to know and be able to recite, if requested, these goals.

Your organization should have a Goal that is just as clear and just as hard to forget!

REALISTICALLY ACHIEVABLE WITHIN A SPECIFIC TIMELINE

Organization Goals must be realistically achievable within a maximum of three years, although they may be reached much earlier. A one-year timeline is likely to be most relevant to smaller organizations.

I set a three-year maximum timeline for organization-wide goals for small and midsize privately owned organizations, because this maximum timeline reflects the realities of these organizations. Long-term five-to-seven year type goal setting typically does NOT work for privately owned small and mid-size organizations because organization owners require more immediate results to maintain their focus. Typically in small and midsize privately owned organizations, goals set five to seven years in the future are never achieved. The organization owner becomes sidetracked with more pressing, immediate concerns, and never commits time and energy to attaining the goal.

Organizations' leaders in small and midsize organizations who set Goals too far in the future are inclined to lose focus on the things they need to do to make those Goals happen. The shorter timeframe of a Goal that takes no more than three years to achieve makes it easier for an owner of a small/midsize organization to focus limited amounts of resources and energy.

The three-year limit is quite different from traditional strategic planning employed by large, publicly owned organizations. Large, publicly owned organizations have the infrastructure and resources to carry out plans that have goals set several years or more into the future.

Also, it is important the Goal you decide upon be reasonably achievable within the time-period identified for achieving it. If it isn't, you will not get the support from those who will be integral in achieving the Goal. For example, you may want a 35% increase in annual sales results by the end of next year, but simply saying this will not make the sales team more likely to attain the Goal. It's possible the sales team will perceive the Goal as unrealistic. You may even see a drop in sales if you do not confirm it is possible for the Goal to be attained within the timeline.

If the goal you propose is not reasonably attainable, you run the risk of not having the support of most KDMs. While an organization's leaders may or may not ever choose to gamble in Las Vegas, when it comes to business, the risks they feel comfortable taking when going after a Goal are often based upon having a certain feeling of control on the outcome. A good KDM will also want to understand the downside impact if the plan for achieving the Goal does not work.

When evaluating if a proposed Organization Plan Goal is realistically achievable, consider things such as your organization's human resources, your equipment capacity, and your organization's financial ability to achieve the Goal.

Don't pick Goals for your Organization Strategic Plans like a poker player who bluffs! In poker, players may hold onto risky cards in hopes of a long-shot, even though there is a good chance of losing. If you want to see positive results for the organization, plan for the most likely hand to be a winner. Overestimating your organization's capabilities by trying to focus on unrealistic Goals can make you a loser.

Before you finalize your Goal, consider whether the positive benefit potentially gained from attaining the Goal is worth the risk, or is the downside of failing to achieve the Goal too high a price to pay?

Measurable with Milestones

Milestones are the compass that lets you know you are "on course." When identifying the Goals you will be recommending, consider the following:

- What is the time-line for attaining the Goal?
- Can you measure your Goal in increments, with the last one being within a thirty-six-month time period?

Organization-wide Goals must be measurable and written in a way that gives you, your KDM, and fellow DRs, a basis on which to gauge achievement. This typically involves milestones of different phases of achievement that need to be attained while moving toward the fully completed goal—again all within three years.

Measurements of results for phases are needed as checkpoints for you to see if the results are tacking on course. This can be as simple as; "Achieve a ten percent increase in annual sales for the first year, a twenty percent increase the second year, and a thirty percent increase compared to this year, by the end of the third year."

The measurements must be of a type that can be easily tracked **by Key Performance Indicators (KPIs)** that can be reviewed on a regularly scheduled basis. For example, one organization compares their monthly new client acquisition to last year's performance from the same month.

A good example involved a six-store retail shoe chain. Chris, the VP of marketing, explained during an Organization Strategic Planning Goal-setting exercise that her division faced the threat of competition from a new international retail chain giant that had announced it was entering their market. She discussed concerns about how the division could successfully compete against the "giant" that was coming to town.

During discussions, she mentioned an idea about finding the products and services to sell in as differentiated and more personable way as possible. She proposed a Goal for a division plan to have all store employees trained within six months to sell new lines of comfort shoes, with store personnel also trained to create custom insoles for the shoes. Terri, her KDM, loved the idea, and the whole team began working on it.

This became the goal of an Organization Strategic Plan. Within six months of setting the goal, the plan was put in effect and the basic organization model of the division had been changed in a way that allowed it to compete successfully with a global player.

Is It The Right Goal?

When identifying the Goals you will be recommending, consider the following:

- Is your Goal specific enough so there is no chance of anyone misinterpreting its meaning?
- Is your Goal clearly measurable?

QUESTIONS TO HELP YOU IDENTIFY GOALS

As you begin to identify your organization Goals, keep in mind it is also important to know where you are before you try to figure out where you want to go. For example, if you want to improve service, do you have a current metric or series of metrics showing what your current service levels are? If not, it is premature for you to define your Goals with specific targets. Instead, a program should first be undertaken to establish baseline metrics that will serve as the basis of improvement.

Below, I share some questions I have categorized by functional areas of organizations, which will help you develop questions needed to identify the first Goal for your organization. Remember, the Goal of your first Organization Strategic Plan is the one most critical to achieving the highest-impact success.

These questions are not intended to be viewed as all-inclusive for identifying your organization Goals, and they may not be important (or even apply at all) to your organization. But they will help you create questions that follow the same type of thinking.

Sales:
- What does your organization need in measurable, improved rates of repeat sales or retention of customers/clients?
- What increase in sales is needed for each of your major product or service classifications?
- What is a reasonable rate of sales increase for the next three years?

Customer Satisfaction:
- What measurable target for customer satisfaction do you need?
- What measurable quality attributes for your product/service is needed?

Operations:
- How much do your operating costs need to adjust for your primary product/service?

Financial Factors:
- What improvement is needed in cash flow?
- What debt-to-equity ratio is needed?
- What is needed to retain current asset and liability ratios?

Only after a Goal is identified for a plan should the Strategic Leadership Team work on creating or helping to create Strategies to achieve the Goal.

STEP 2: STRATEGIES FOR EACH GOAL

A Plan with only a Goal is not much of a plan! Strategies are the conceptual guidance system that brings you to the realization of Goals. Strategies lay out the ideas and resources you will use to achieve your Goal.

Once you have established the Goal you need to achieve to fulfill the Organization Strategic Plan, it is time to identify the Strategies for achieving your Goal.

WRITE DOWN THE STRATEGIES

Before any actions are taken towards achieving an Organization Goal, you need to identify and commit to writing the Strategies necessary to get the results identified in your Goal.

Your organization Strategies should be very strategic and conceptual in nature. They should not be measurable, because they are not meant to be quantified. Strategies are to be conceptual, not detailed or specific. In other words, save the details for your **Action Plans** (which will be discussed more in a moment).

> **The written strategic plan, with a Goal and Strategies, needs to be completed before you, or anyone else, takes any action meant to follow through on the Goal.**

Before you finalize your strategies in support of a Goal, you and your organization's entire Strategic Leadership Team should stop and ask yourselves; "If my organization achieves these Strategies, will the Goal be accomplished?"

If the answer is "Yes," you have identified the right set of Strategies!

It is extremely important your KDM stay involved and "in the loop" at this strategic level. All decisions made in the organization must be based upon strategies chosen by the KDM among the many likely to be suggested by you and your fellow DRs.

To ensure steady progress toward that destination, you and your fellow DRs should be giving constant feedback to the KDM on the starting strategies, and don't be afraid to suggest changes to the strategies as needed.

CHANGES

High-impact DRs constantly look for and suggest ways to update and revise strategies and also make suggestions about alternative strategies. Ultimately, the final selection of any changes to an organization Goal or Strategies must be embraced by the top KDM for the changes to be implemented.

Strategies: Organization Commitment To Allocating Resources

The Organization Strategic Plan Strategies show where the organization should best direct your KDM's time, as well as the time of you and your fellow DRs, and the resources of the organization. Your organization must be committed to allocating the necessary

> **Strategies must be reviewed and revised as circumstances change over time.**

resources to the Strategies needed to accomplish the Goal.

Resources for attaining your most important Goal should be the last area that is cut. Therefore, you must firmly decide on the resources needed for the Strategies to succeed before you finalize them.

The Right Number Of Strategies

Although it is possible to have only one Strategy for attaining your Goal, it is much more likely you will need as many as, but not more than, five Strategies for each Goal. The more Strategies you have, the thinner you will end up spreading you energies and the less focused you will be. One of your challenges will be to limit yourself to a manageable number of Strategies.

Examples Of Strategies

One KDM we worked with, Jill, had a desire to move her consulting organization to a much greater level of success. She set a Goal of reaching $7,000,000 in annual results within three years.

Her first strategy was: "To use my strong training abilities to develop additional salespeople needed to expand organization sales."

The second strategy she developed was: "To reduce organization dependence upon me personally selling organization products."

For her third strategy, Jill proposed: "Selling additional services to our current clients."

She further raised the concern that: "Key accounts may not like new sales people taking over my selling relationships and, as result, may stop giving their purchases to the organization."

As a fourth strategy, Jill responded: "To engage independent representatives to sell the organization's products to out-of-town clients."

These were all excellent examples of Strategies that support the Goal.

YOU NEED GOOD STRATEGIES TO ACHIEVE YOUR GOALS

Let me repeat: for every Organization Strategic Plan Goal, you will need to develop strategies—with the number of strategies being dependent upon the size of your organization. For example, large organizations may be able to effectively handle as many as five strategies for each Organization Goal.

Your KDM has a duty to develop (or at a minimum, sign off on) the organization Strategies necessary to take the organization to the short-term Goal destination in one to (let's say) three years down the road.

This may take some thought. As a group, you may need to discuss what best utilizes your organization strengths, what neutralizes weaknesses, what takes advantage of opportunities, and what best prepares you for addressing threats outside your control.

An in-depth review of such assessments can help you determine key aspects of what should be in the strategies for your Organization Strategic Plans. One strategy for an organization Goal may involve making greater use of the areas in which your organization has strengths. Is there a strength that, if used to a much greater degree, could be helpful to your organization's success in reaching a Goal?

Take note of your organization weaknesses, too, especially those that exist to a greater degree in your organization than they do for your strongest competitors. Ask yourself whether you need strategies to neutralize organization weaknesses for your Organization Strategic Plan to succeed. As my father used to say: "The last thing you want to do is get in a fight in an organization area that is a weakness of your organization, but a strength of your competitor."

Is there an opportunity you have identified that will help make your Strategies more likely to succeed? One manufacturing government department's current equipment was being underutilized. The KDM saw the opportunity to engage sales representatives to increase sales. The Organization Strategic Plan had one strategy involving the engagement of independent sales representatives with the Goal of tripling the department's production within three years, without having to invest in any additional equipment or building space. The increased sales that resulted from the plan brought down the manufacturing cost per unit by 15% in year three!

Is there a threat to your organization you have identified, which, if not addressed or prepared for by your organization, can derail your organization's chances of reaching the success of an organization Goal? Think of Kodak's position in the world as a developer of film and the impact of digital cameras (which do not have film and don't need developing). Not long ago, Kodak filed for Chapter 11 bankruptcy protection.

STRATEGIES THAT REQUIRE CAPABILITIES OUTSIDE YOUR ORGANIZATION RESOURCES

Watch out for Strategies that require capabilities outside your organization resources. Take the time to look realistically at how easily you can bring a capability to your organization. If it's not readily doable, don't make it a Strategy!

One manufacturing organization's Strategic Leadership Team developed a strategy for improving their sales representatives' knowledge by creating a series of eight online training programs—one for each of their eight primary products. This strategy was developed without an awareness of all the different tactics that had to be completed for a project of this magnitude to be delivered in a professional manner. A major problem emerged: No one within the organization was capable of developing the online training! The team was also unaware of the total costs that implementing this strategy would incur. When they shopped around for outside resources to complete this project, they found the costs prohibitive. The whole program had to be shelved after a considerable investment of time and resources.

Strategies Require Creative Thinking

Approach the development of Strategies with as much creativity as you can possibly summon. Creating Strategies is, in many ways, an art. The kind of creativity necessary to master that art is based on past experience and specialized knowledge of your organization, your industry, and your leading competitors. All of these can provide a secure framework when creating Strategies, but instinct and intuition also play an important role in developing "out of the box" Strategies. This type of creative thinking can only occur when you remain open to "breaking" the status quo. It comes from those who are not locked into the common thinking of your industry.

Be prepared for resistance from others who might respond to new strategy ideas by invoking the popular adage, "If it ain't broke, don't fix it." This kind of thinking has stopped many organization owners from developing the kinds of Strategies that move an organization from "good" to "great." D. Wayne Callaway, former President of Frito-Lay, used to challenge his team with a revised version of this statement: "If it ain't broke, fix it ... because if you don't, your competitor will!" This is a potent reminder that is sometimes worth sharing during discussions about creative organization strategies.

The answers you provide to the following questions will help you identify the best Strategies for your Organization Strategic Plans. Note these questions are meant to assist you in thinking through how you approach your Strategies. These questions will not apply equally to every organization owner, and are meant to illustrate the type of questions you should ask yourself as you develop your strategies.

Marketing:

- What is unique or distinct about your organization that can be leveraged to create a Strategy to attain your Goal?
- What are the marketing Strategies used by the leading competitor in your industry from which you can learn or adapt to your organization?
- If you are operating in more than one geographic market, what are the common characteristics of the geographic markets in which you are operating successfully that can be used as a Strategy for further expansion?
- What Strategy for developing your organization's marketing and operational infrastructure is needed to successfully smooth the progress of desired growth?
- What are your market segmentation and niche Strategies?
- What aspects of your pricing Strategy should change?
- Are there market opportunities that offer strong upside potential without an unreasonable risk?
- What strategic alliances should your organization develop?

Sales:

- What Strategies for sales compensation programs need to be changed?
- What Strategy for sales management could increase results?
- What Strategies for sales training may make your sales staff more effective?
- Are there Strategies that will increase customer retention?
- What Strategy might yield increased results from current customers?
- What Strategy might be used to increase referrals from your satisfied customers?
- What additional capabilities or tools do your sales force need?

Product Improvement:

- What Strategy should be used to address any unsuccessful products/services?
- Is there a Strategy for adding products or service features that you can offer to your existing customers or clients?
- Is there a Strategy for adding features to your products that would create greater value for your products compared to your competition?
- Is there a Strategy for improvements that create greater value than your competition offers?

Organizational:

- What Strategies will make the organizational structure of your organization more effective?
- Is there a Strategy for improving the corporate culture involving

improvements, such as cutting down on organization bureaucracy and minimizing organization politics?
- Is there a Strategy that will improve fluidity of communications between departments and from bottom to top?
- Is there a Strategy for improving your management infrastructure?
- Is there a Strategy for improving technology?
- Is there a Strategy for improving employee relations?
- What is your Strategy for eliminating poor performers among your employees?
- Is there a Strategy for employee development that would facilitate organization growth or improvement?

ACTION PLANS, PROJECT PLANS AND TACTICS

To make Organization Strategic Plans succeed, you will need to create Action Plans to carry out the Strategies. In a small or mid-size organization these Action Plans are usually Project Plans assigned to the DR responsible for the functional area most needed for the success of the Action Plan. Typically, the individual DR will personally, or through a subordinate in the DR's functional department, create and complete the Project Plans, including the Tactics needed to carry out the particular Project Plan.

Action Plans are both specific and measurable, and show the point person who is responsible for driving its success. Your Action Plans must show one, and only one, person as the point person who is responsible for driving its success.

Here is an example of a partial Action Plan from one organization's Strategy to develop a sales training program for their sales representatives:

Strategy 1: Create a Product Training program for sales representatives

- By 11/30/12, Donna produce the proof-version for initial 100 binders, with the DVDs and other training material content for the first three training sessions
- Once proof is ready, get quotes for production
- By 10/28/12, Erin produce necessary marketing material: Brochure, email templates, informational presentation, direct mail pieces, etc.
- During the first week in November 2012, sales representatives to start marketing in their territories for registrants for

their first Training class with the first training session to start January 2013.

- Jeff to do Training Program Informational presentation, Dec 11 and 13.
- Erin to coordinate emails and calls starting on 11/27, by contracted organization.
- By 11/01/12, Erin to finalize a marketing strategy to promote the Training program. The strategy may include such things as:
- Email drip campaign with follow-up calls
- Mention in monthly newsletters to customers
- Video to all customers promoting the Training Program
- Live webinar for customers, to answer questions and explain the benefits of the Training program.
- Darren to start Training Program online modules beginning of January 2013.
- Timeline–approximately 3 weeks per module
- By January 15, 2013, Donna to produce the DVDs and all other training material needed for sessions four through six as well (one through three are complete).
- Videos to be recorded 12/14/2012
- Videos back from video editor 1/11/2013

STRATEGIES FOR CARRYING OUT PLANS AND TACTICS

Project Plans, also called Action Plans, and Tactics are needed to make Organization Strategic Plans succeed. In small and midsize organization they are typically managed by the DR who is in charge of the functional area of the organization most involved in the plan. Thus, the director of marketing is usually responsible for creating and implementing a marketing project plan. Project Plans typically require little or no involvement from the entire Strategic Leadership Team of KDM and organization DRs.

HELP YOUR KDM LEAD THE ORGANIZATION MORE STRATEGICALLY

How do you, the DR, launch this process?

In most organizations it is necessary for DRs to begin the Goal and Strategies discussion with their KDMs, either in a one-on-one setting or as part of a team meeting. This discussion typically starts with the DR sharing a written Goal Statement outlining what the organization needs to do short term. Most KDMs will welcome discussions about Goals for the organization even when they have not created such a statement. Of course, they generally reserve the right to make revisions to the Goal Statement; as well they should!

Look for changes in market situations, people, and technological advances that suggest (or require) a revised Strategy from what your organization may have in informal Strategies.

Follow up persistently but tactfully in getting the most important Strategies for the Organization Strategic Plan identified.

KEY POINT REVIEW

A critical part of your job is to help the KDM identify a number of organization-wide goals. These goals;

- Should be critical to the success of the organization
- Should be measurable
- Should be accomplishable within three years or less—prioritize with the KDM and other DRs.
- Then select one Goal to work on. In other words, get buy-in and build Alignment.
- Ask the KDM to communicate the chosen Goal to all employees.
- Help turn the Goal into a simple "mantra" for all to memorize.
- Identify the milestones and timeline for completion.
- First, measure where your starting point is.
- Next, identify conceptual Strategies that support the Goal.
- Write out the Strategies before taking action
- Identify no more than five supporting Strategies
- Identify whether the Strategies require resources or support from outside the organization.
- Of course, you can't do it all on your own. Your KDM must allocate resources to accomplish the plan and must support it publicly and privately.
- Engage with your KDM to revise the Strategies and plan as needed, based on circumstances
- Create Project and Action Plans for each Strategy that follow these guidelines:
- One responsible individual assigned to each Strategy
- Measurable results
- Timeline for completion
- Specific tactics

Your KDM must be engaged at the strategic level throughout the planning process. Ultimately, the plan itself, and the final selection of any organization Goal or Strategies, must be embraced by the top KDM for the plan to be implemented.

HOMEWORK

1. Now it's your turn. Write out up to five important Goals you see for your organization. This is the list of potential Goals that will have the greatest effect, within the next three years, on satisfying the factors you have chosen as critical to your organization's success.

2. Next, pick one of those five Goals to focus on, and be sure that it includes measurements and timelines. Choose the Goal from your list you believe your KDM will consider the most important. The Goal selected should be the one that will have the greatest impact on your organization when achieved. This Goal must be achievable within three years and measurable, with a clear and easy to understand timeline. Be sure to include specific measurements, timelines and accountability, and be ready to explain your reasons for each of these.

3. Now it's time to put your thoughts together about Strategies to achieve the Goal. Write your draft of up to five Strategies for accomplishing the Goal you have identified. Be sure that each of your Strategies is conceptual, but still crystal clear. Avoid measurements and timelines. Each of the Strategies you write must show a clear and easy to understand way to reach the Goal you have identified.

4. Schedule time to meet with your KDM to discuss the suggested organization strategic Goal and Strategies that you are recommending as an Organization Strategic Plan.

CHAPTER 12

Alignment Is Evergreen

EXECUTIVE SUMMARY FOR THE KEY DECISION MAKER (KDM):

This is the final "factor" of the book ... but it is only the beginning of your organization's continuous long-term journey toward Alignment. This chapter helps you master the tools and techniques that ensure Alignment is an ongoing daily priority, a never-ending evergreen commitment throughout your enterprise.

The ultimate factor of Alignment is the willingness to make Alignment an aspirational cultural value. That means it is something people throughout the organization keep trying to perfect, keep improving, keep reviving. If you ever think you have attained Alignment and can safely cross it off the list of "things to do" ... think again!

This chapter should be read in full by both you (the KDM) and the Direct Report(s) (DRs) who have made it this far through the book with you!

An Evergreen Commitment to Alignment is the Ultimate Factor of Alignment.

I consistently see an ongoing level of commitment to Alignment in high-performing organizations. Your organization can be one of those organizations, if you are willing to commit to what I call **Evergreen Alignment**.

Having Evergreen Alignment in your organization requires that the KDM and all the DRs work continuously on all the factors of Alignment you have read about in this book, and that you do so as a present tense priority. This is how you build deep, enduring Alignment—what I call Evergreen Alignment—up and down the enterprise. This level of Alignment takes time, attention, and continuous effort; however, that is certainly justified, assuming you want your enterprise to be a highly successful, high-impact organization!

The key is to maintain your personal and organizational momentum. The better you are at that, the easier it will be to build Evergreen Alignment into your organization. The trick is to remind yourself and others, as often as necessary, that bringing about Evergreen Alignment does not cost time and effort, but rather saves time and effort, and makes everyone's life a lot more enjoyable!

Don't Try to Re-Invent The Wheel!

Evergreen Alignment for your organization is actually relatively easy to achieve and keep—if you follow the three simple steps mentioned here. These three steps have been tested and proven to work with organizations in just about every industry you can think of. Follow them.

EVERGREEN STEP 1: ACCEPT THAT THIS NEVER STOPS

The essential first step to Evergreen Alignment is to acknowledge that there is always still work to be done. This is true no matter how deeply Aligned you consider your organization to be, and it is certainly true as you complete your first passage through this program.

At this point, I hope you have established solid improvement in Alignment on many areas such as roles, vision for the long term future of the organization, culture and so on. Yet even if you have worked with great zeal on each and every one of the factors of Alignment I've shared in previous chapters, there are areas where you and your organization can improve.

Getting an organization into Alignment and keeping it there is a little like being a professional athlete: you have to stay in shape. If you should ever fall out of shape, then you will probably have to work twice as hard to get back to where you want to be. Don't let that happen!

I have seen many organizations make great progress on Alignment until there was a change in leadership or a loss of focus, or both. That's when the meetings stopped, the commitments became murkier, and the progress toward achieving the Organization Vision became fitful and sporadic—until the team eventually found itself in deep trouble. Most of the executives at these organizations imagined they had "gotten" the Alignment principles you have read about here. I wrote this chapter to make it easier for your organization to avoid becoming one of those organizations.

To promote and support true Alignment, both KDMs and DRs need to identify what is currently working in

> **Remember: Alignment is a direction, not a final destination!**

terms of Alignment, and why. Together, you need to continue to do what is working, and recommit to better mastery of the factors of Alignment that are not yet working as well as they could.

The remaining steps will help you to do just that.

EVERGREEN STEP 2: IDENTIFY HOW FAR YOUR ORGANIZATION HAS PROGRESSED IN ALIGNMENT

How can you tell how far your organization has come in terms of Alignment? **Do a simple Alignment Benefit Assessment.**

What specific benefits have accrued, both personally and on the organizational level, as a result of improvements in Alignment? The team should create and document clear answers to this question.

For instance, Myra, a DR, experienced that her CEO got better at holding weekly one-on-one meetings with her. As a result, she and her CEO reported a much clearer sense of what her priorities were, thanks to closer adherence to the guidelines for their one-on-one weekly meetings. This translated to fewer "bottlenecks," fewer delays, better cohesion with the rest of the team, and increased productivity throughout the enterprise.

What kinds of experiences like that can you point to right now? Look at each of the **Alignment Buckets** below and consider how Alignment has progressed in each area. What specific benefits have resulted due to your organization's improved Alignment? Here are some likely outcomes you may have encountered already. Use the following list as an inspiration to make a list of your own, and don't limit yourself to what you see here!

Alignment Area: Commitment

Commitment on Alignment. Possible benefits: Better retention of key DRs; higher productivity; reduced stress for all team members

Alignment Area: Communication

Align on Two-Way Communication: Possible benefits: Less time and energy wasted resolving needless misunderstandings; better conflict resolution; greater cohesion between KDM and DR; clearer understanding of expectations and responsibilities

Align to PAVE Your Way to Success

Possible benefits: Reduced stress; substantially greater productivity; substantially greater motivation to show up at work each day; reduced turnover among key executives.

Align on Plans and Priorities through Weekly One-on-One Meetings

Possible benefits: Reduced overlap of responsibility; better prioritization of plans; greater efficiency; greater likelihood of organization attaining targets that support strategic goals; significantly reduced time and capital investments in projects that do not support strategic goals.

Align with the Team through Strategic Leadership Meetings

Greater team cohesion; greater and deeper understanding of key projects among all members of the executive team; shared experience in resolving specific challenges.

Alignment Area: Culture

Align on Creating Mutual Respect. Possible benefits: Fewer conflicts and misunderstandings among members of the executive team; greater sense of mutual respect and cooperation in the workplace.

Align on Organization Values and Working Environment

Possible benefits: Clearer and more consistent standards for what is and is not acceptable behavior; better and more productive employee performance evaluation sessions; reduced liability from problems arising from negative workplace culture (harassment, Wrongful termination, etc.).

Align on the Organization Vision

Possible benefits: Greater connection of departmental projects with KDM's dreams and aspirations; higher buy-in on these projects and support of them from KDM.

Alignment Area: Collaboration

Align on Roles and Responsibilities for Your Highest-Impact Results. Possible benefits: Reduced stress and significantly reduced workload for KDM; higher retention rates for key executives; increased job satisfaction for KDM and DR; better short-term and long-term decisions from KDM due to reduced stress and fatigue.

Align on Factors Critical to Organization Success

Possible benefits: Substantially greater progress on attaining both short-term and long-term organization goals

Align on Fully Supported Organization Goals and Strategies

Possible benefits: Deeper understanding up and down the organization of critical goals and strategies; greater buy-in throughout the enterprise on key corporate initiatives; greater likelihood of attainment of personal and organizational goals.

EVERGREEN STEP 3: IDENTIFY WHICH FACTORS OF ALIGNMENT ARE NOT YET WORKING AT THE HIGHEST LEVEL ... AND WHY!

This is the big one.

The key to Evergreen Alignment lies in the successful implementation of Step Three. As we have seen, within your organization there are certainly some Alignment areas where there is still significant room for improvement, areas where the Alignment impact that should be happening so far has not happened.

Why?

Posing that question, and being willing to answer it honestly, is the beginning of positive change. Admit when a factor of Alignment isn't working, find out why it isn't working then commit to doing whatever is necessary to correct the problem.

Once you identify and acknowledge the cause for the Alignment problems in your organization, you can develop the appropriate course changes needed to eliminate the misalignment in your organization. Not before! If you don't accept the problem and acknowledge it, you can't start working on it.

WHAT IS HOLDING YOU BACK?

Right now, something is keeping your organization from maximum Alignment. What is it? One way to get to the bottom of things is to look closely at the most common challenges faced by organizations implementing this program for the first time. I call these Alignment Roadblocks. There are many, but write down any that might apply to your situation.

Commitment Roadblocks

It should not come as a surprise that this problem comes first on the list of Roadblocks. A simple lack of commitment is the single most common reason for misalignment in any organization.

Alignment will deteriorate if it is not an ongoing commitment. Focusing on Alignment commitment is not something you do once and cross off your To-Do list. It is something you return to, both as an individual and organization.

Your organization's current Alignment should never be viewed as something static. In fact, the dynamics are constantly shifting, constantly in need of intelligent responses to new situations.

This factor of Alignment involves a commitment to continuously strive for improvement in each of the factors of Alignment I have shared with you in this book. For Alignment to be Evergreen in your organization, it must be something you and your KDM commit to as a way of organization life, both on the personal and organizational level. It is something you will need to remind yourself and others of on a regular basis, and reinforce constantly.

Misalignment is the result of no one working on Alignment. There will be "backsliding" on important factors of Alignment, even after they have worked well in bringing about positive results for your organization, if there is not an ongoing commitment to reinforce Alignment up and down the organization.

We conducted a follow-up training session with Martha, the KDM of a pool cleaning and landscaping organization, and two of her DRs. Martha's team had completed the initial round of Alignment training, but they had not yet made Alignment "how we do things around here."

During the follow-up session, Martha said this to her managers: "I bring you together by having social functions, like going to the ballgame, but you still seem to functioning more and more individually rather than as a team. We no longer have the kind of Alignment we all said we wanted. We're going in the wrong direction. You seem to be overlapping each others' efforts, and sometimes even seem to be working against each other, rather than working as a team."

This is a classic example of a Commitment Roadblock. Social functions between the KDM and managers who report directly to the KDM are great for bonding, but they are just not enough to sustain Alignment as "the way we do things around here." **For a team to stay in Alignment, it takes constant effort by the KDM and from all members of the Strategic Leadership Team.** It takes discipline and constant efforts using all the factors of Alignment on an ongoing basis.

During the team discussions, it came out from the DRs that Martha was, among other things, canceling most of her weekly team and one-on-one meetings. I told Martha that the right step for her now was to go back to holding weekly team meetings and one-on-one meetings, as scheduled, with each and every one of her DRs.

Martha explained that she had cancelled these meetings because she "didn't have time" to make the meetings. Martha's priorities were off. In reality, she didn't have time not to meet with her team! Strengthening her level of commitment to one-on-one and team meetings ended up winning back hours in the day for Martha, because she spent less time "putting out fires."

Victor, the KDM of a manufacturing division, and his four DRs, including his two sons, completed the AlignUp training program. As a result, Victor ran a division that came to have outstanding Alignment. The division was quite successful ... and then something dangerous happened. Time passed.

Victor reached the point where he wanted to retire. Both of Victor's sons had worked in division management positions for over a decade after going through the AlignUp training program. When Victor retired, he felt comfortable handing over control of the division to his sons. They would run it jointly.

Alignment started to deteriorate, first slowly and then rapidly—because the sons, eager to "do things their own way," stopped doing the things that had created great Alignment in their organization. Over the course of two years from the time of Victor's retirement, the division's success plummeted, and then the organization began losing serious money.

It took one of the division DRs to point out, during a weekly Team Meeting, exactly how Alignment in the organization had deteriorated. Victor's sons had lost sight of the importance of the one-on-one meetings that are the core of this process. (Very often, the one-on-one meetings are the first things to go when Alignment slips.) The two sons recommitted to the factors of Alignment that had helped the organization succeed, and they did turn things around. It was, however, a long, hard road back.

Evergreen Alignment takes committed persistence in applying and reinforcing all of the factors of Alignment you have learned about in this book!

> **RECOMMIT!**
> Once you identify the cause for deteriorating Alignment, recommit yourself and your enterprise to a course of action that will re-establish Alignment!

Communication Roadblocks

Second only to lack of commitment, difficulties in communication are the next most common reason for misalignment. The most common challenges in this area are outlined below.

- **Roadblock: KDM Still Operating in "One-Way" Communication Mode**
- **Solution: Align on Two-Way Communication**

Do your organization's DRs still feel there is too much one-way communication between KDM and DRs? Alignment requires two-way communication, particularly when it comes to encouraging DRs to share their ideas. KDMs who lead organizations with deep Alignment do not "close the door" on others who wish to express thoughts and ideas. They know these ideas may ultimately result in better plans, and so they listen carefully. That doesn't mean they agree with everything they hear, of course!

I asked one group of AlignUp trainees (which included both KDMs and DRs) this question: "Imagine that when you come to work tomorrow, you find out your CEO has been in a fatal accident and has legally left the organization to you. What three things would you do differently to make sure the organization was as successful as possible?"

The KDMs smiled, but the DRs looked shocked at the question. That only lasted for a moment, though; once they saw that answering the question was not going to be a huge lapse in etiquette, they quickly became animated and began laying out some truly great ideas. In each case, I made a point of exploring with specific KDMs the ideas their DRs had shared during this exercise. Each of these KDMs agreed to a separate brainstorming session with their DRs to discuss these ideas. Many were implemented!

This is the kind of discussion we want to make a conscious effort to initiate in support of true two-way communication. It's quite important to make a conscious effort on this front, because KDMs who settle into their "default setting" can become so locked into their own views and assumptions that they are just not receptive to creative ideas from the team. All too often, the desired Alignment with DRs is thwarted by the KDM's "default" negative emotional response to potentially great ideas. The good news is that this "default" setting is easier to change than a lot of DRs think.

One great way to overcome this roadblock is for the KDM simply to ask for ideas on how a particular goal can be accomplished then stop talking. Sometimes I have asked this question at meetings and then left the room, letting my own DRs know that they have to hammer out the ideas and get consensus on them among themselves. Some extremely creative ideas have come from this approach.

- **Roadblock: Missed or Poorly Conducted One-on-One Meetings**
- **Solution: Align on Plans and Priorities through Weekly One-on-One Meetings**

Are weekly one-on-one meetings between the KDM and each DR being missed or poorly conducted? **Alignment failure may be traced to a KDM's failure to do weekly one-on-ones, week-in and week-out (yes, this also signals a lack of Commitment; there is often an overlap between the two issues).**

During our twelfth training session with Carter, a KDM, and his DRs, to review the progress that had been made with Alignment and identify areas in which Alignment had not progressed, one of the DRs, Anne, said: "A major problem for me is that I simply don't know my priorities. Most of the time I just don't know what I'm supposed to work on first." She was absolutely right. That was the "why".

Earlier in the same session, Carter had mentioned that Anne's department was a "bottleneck" and had suggested she was someone who kept things from getting completed in a timely way. It was in response to this remark that Anne explained the "bottom line" as she perceived it: her weekly one-on-one meetings with Carter simply weren't happening. "Maybe one out of every five scheduled meetings actually take place," she said. These meetings were being scheduled on the weekly planner, but Carter routinely canceled them. When the meetings did take place, the two of them got so wrapped up on the first few items on the to-do list that Anne would leave the meeting without any clear sense of what she was supposed to do about all the other items on the list.

Carter then said: "I have to be honest. Doing my one-on-one weekly review meetings is a weakness of mine. I get busy and, as a result, most of my weekly one-on-one meetings with my DRs are just not happening."

Acknowledging that was the essential first step, Carter and Anne agreed to follow, to a tee, the protocols for weekly one-on-one meetings. The follow-through they brought to this one commitment is a major reason they were able to turn the Alignment problem around. This led to better communication and dramatically improved efficiency, not just in their own relationship, but throughout the enterprise.

These one-on-one meetings must take place. Not only must the KDM make time for them, the DR must prepare for them properly! It's just as essential that all DRs update their To-Do list in a timely manner prior to each meeting in order to discuss that list with the KDM. The Alignment that will result from that discussion will save immense amounts of time and energy. Without these discussions, it is quite common for DRs to spend time and other resources on activities that are not considered highly important by the KDM.

One reason some KDMs have a problem with doing effective one-on-ones each week is that they have too many DRs. As a result, they don't have time available for optimum one-on-ones with each DR. There should never be more than ten manager level DRs reporting directly to the KDM. It's certainly easier and more effective to limit the number of those management level people who report directly to the KDM to no more than six.

- **Roadblock: Missed or Poorly Conducted Team Meetings**
- **Solution: Align with the Team through Strategic Leadership Meetings**

Are the weekly Team Meetings not taking place, or taking place only inter-mittently? Are the meetings conducted poorly? Are some team members not being open to learning from the experiences of other members?

Each team member must listen to and benefit from the past experiences of the other team members during Team Meetings. The advice received from fellow team members on how they have attempted similar endeavors in the past, and (just as important) what they learned when they failed, can provide great insight.

Of course, during these meetings, you should also take into consideration any past situations you may have experienced that may be analogous to a current challenge. The longer you have been in the business world, the easier it will be to make a judgment on what is and isn't worth sharing, and how you or other members can best respond to specific "challenge" situations.

- **Roadblock: "Verbal Armor"**
- **Solution: Temenos**

Do you have one or more members of the team who are engaging in verbal behavior at weekly team meetings that causes others on the team to don their "verbal armor?"

This is among the easiest roadblocks to overcome. **Review your Temenos agreements!**

Perhaps the KDM, perhaps one of the DRs, has lost sight of (or not yet implemented) the Temenos exercise. I have shared this exercise in Appendix A. The Temenos process, was developed for establishing an environment of trust, may need to be repeated periodically during Team Meetings and reviewed as necessary.

TEAM MEETINGS

Let's look separately now at some of the communication challenges likely to arise at weekly and annual team meetings.

Weekly Team Meetings

Skipping weekly team meetings, as we have seen, is a common roadblock; so is failing to prepare for them; so is holding them without allotting time for team members to give feedback and address problems. The weekly meeting format described in Chapter 4 helps team members learn to hold each other accountable for their commitments and actions in the short term. Long-term personal and organizational commitment to Alignment is just as important, but that requires Annual Team Meetings.

Annual Team Meetings

Annual Team Meetings are mandatory. This is the best time to **review, re-examine, and reassess goals and plans.**

Are your Annual Team Meetings ever skipped? Are they poorly conducted? Is the organization KDM serving as the Facilitator of your Annual Strategic Leadership Team Meetings? All three of these are major roadblocks.

Failure to use a third-party Facilitator at Annual Team Meetings is a particularly common and serious roadblock to getting optimum Alignment benefits from these meetings. I discussed this issue briefly in Chapter 11, but since it is such a potentially serious roadblock to long-term Alignment, I want to share some additional thoughts on the Facilitator's role here.

Sadly, I have witnessed Annual Team Meetings facilitated by the KDM of the organization where the KDM, without realizing it, kept the atmosphere from being truly open and creative. Although there are many CEOs and organization founders I have worked with who are capable of effectively facilitating a weekly meeting, it is quite rare that a KDM can facilitate the Annual Team Meeting effectively. This is because they are too vested emotionally to do the optimum job of facilitating the assessment portions of the annual meetings, which are critical. It is best to have an outside, third-party skilled Facilitator handle this job; a seasoned, experienced Facilitator with strong organization experience who has no direct personal stake in any of the decisions made.

If you elect to engage a third party Facilitator for the meeting, and you should, then another important procedural issue is worth discussing here. The Facilitator needs to meet in private with the KDM for a couple of hours, at least a week before the meeting, to discuss ground rules and learn exactly what priorities the KDM views as important. The Facilitator should also discuss protocols for the meeting and determine both what the KDM really hopes to accomplish from the meeting and what issues are best not discussed.

An example of an issue best not to discuss would be a situation of tension between the KDM and Executive X, where the KDM has decided to let Executive X go, but has not announced this to anyone. Another example might be a "pocket vision factor" that is not shared with the team, such as an intent to sell the organization that the KDM has not yet made public. The Facilitator needs (at the very least) to know where these landmines are, so he or she can avoid stepping on them!

Cultural Roadblocks

These roadblocks to Alignment often go undetected and under-examined. In many cases, this is the result of long-standing, tacit agreements about what may and may not be said or done in front of the KDM. Regardless of past history, these cultural roadblocks must be removed.

- **Roadblock: Lack of Mutual Respect**
- **Solution: Align on Creating Mutual Respect**

Is there a lack of mutual respect among the KDM and Team Members? If so, meaningful Alignment is impossible!

Lack of mutual respect can be one of the more difficult roadblocks to overcome, for two reasons. First, there are likely to be very different perceptions about whether or not a particular action or remark is disrespectful (of course, one need not intend to disrespect someone in order for that person to feel disrespected). Second, where a lack of mutual respect is perceived from the KDM, it is often difficult for the DR to express his or her true feelings about the problem.

The best approach may be to examine and discuss, during a private meeting, the different responses offered in writing by the KDM and the DR to the following brief essay question:

Is there mutual respect in KDM/DR interactions? If so, why? If not, why not?

Of course, each side must be willing to approach this question honestly and tactfully for this essay exercise to deliver positive results. Very often where this roadblock exists, mutual trust has not yet reached the point where an open discussion about mutual respect is possible. This is one of those potentially difficult issues that may need to be addressed with the help of an impartial facilitator.

- **Roadblock: Cultural Mismatch**
- **Solution: Align on Organization Values and Working Environment**

Does your organization have a cultural mismatch under which people proclaim one culture, but follow another?

The phrase "cultural mismatch" describes the common situation where the stated organization culture does not match the actual daily working culture. Of course there are occasional emergencies to be dealt with, and every organization is different. Even with those two significant allowances, however, it is imperative your organization "walk its talk" when it comes to living up to its stated culture. This stated culture must match up with the actual organization culture that employees experience every working day. So for instance, if your stated culture celebrates innovation (and it should), employees should not be made to feel small for making well-intentioned suggestions about how to improve.

Although there are many different views on what constitutes a successful working culture, and although many organizations approach this question differently, it is undeniable that solving Alignment problems must be part of your organization culture! Open the door to new ideas, approaches, and opportunities for improving Alignment ... and make sure it stays open.

- **Roadblock: Blurred Vision**
- **Solution: Align on the Organization Vision**

Do all DRs and all other employees know and understand the current Organization Vision well enough to advocate on its behalf? You have a major Alignment problem if the answer is "No."

Perhaps people are taking actions that are inconsistent with the vision. Perhaps the vision has not yet been identified, or is not yet clearly expressed in an Organization Vision Statement? Perhaps some of the DRs either do not know or do not believe in the KDM's written long-term vision for the organization. Perhaps the KDM has refused to share a "Pocket Vision" for the organization, thus creating a lack of Alignment with the vision. Whatever the challenge is, it must be identified and addressed.

This type of Alignment Roadblock often connects to the failure to have a written Organization Vision Statement in the first place, a Vision Statement that is out of date, or a Vision Statement that has been poorly communicated. Consider such issues as whether there have been, or should be, any change in the Organization Vision. It's possible that there has been a paradigm shift and the Organization Vision needs to be changed, typically as a result of something that has happened during the previous year. That's actually quite rare, but when it does take place it's important for everyone on the team to take part in the discussion. Ideally, the KDM will put forward a revised Vision Statement and ask for comments, after explaining the reasoning behind the change.

More common are situations where the members of the team are unfamiliar with, or unable or unwilling to buy into, an Organization Vision Statement. The reasons for these disconnects may be both complex and easy for a KDM to overlook or ignore, which is why it's wise to periodically review and discuss the Organization Vision Statement in depth at Strategic Leadership Team meetings. A good time for this is once a year, during an in-depth Vision discussion at the Annual Team Meeting.

Collaboration Roadblocks

These roadblocks involve problems on day-to-day interactions where people try to get work done together. They can be overcome only by mutual good intent.

- **Roadblock: KDM Still Operating in "Hands-On" Mode**
- **Solution: Align on Roles and Responsibilities for Your Highest-Impact Results**

Is the KDM still operating mostly in "hands on" mode? Are DRs still underutilizing their known strengths? If so, you have an Alignment problem.

Too often, a KDM and DR start implementing the Alignment program you have read about here with great focus, and then, in some areas, find themselves reverting to previous habits that take them out of Alignment (for instance, the KDM tries to personally solve all problems at every level).

It is not unusual for a KDM to revert to greater "hands on" involvement, particularly during a time of organization challenges. During these times, a KDM may feel things aren't being done as well or as fast as they could be, and may become more "hands-on." Some KDMs, however, "backslide" into a level of non-Aligned, heavily detailed involvement to fix any problem, anywhere in the organizations that they feel "needs" their involvement, with or without an emergency!

Of course, there are times when a KDM simply has to do what is best for the organization at that particular moment. But whenever possible, it is far better for the KDM to serve more in the role of the mentor, and to give the DRs a wider berth to resolve problems on their own. Being personally committed to this interaction goal is extremely important for both the KDM and the DR, and developing self-accountability to achieve that goal is one of the most important benefits of the weekly meetings regimen outlined in this book.

- **Roadblock: Underutilized Strengths**
- **Solution: PAVE Your Way to Success**

Are DRs still in roles that do not maximize use of their competitive edge strengths? DRs should identify their competitive edge strengths and then use them for most of their organization activities. If this is not happening, DRs will not fully buy into the roles they have been assigned!

When people take on too many tasks, or tasks that don't tap into their best abilities, they can easily become distracted and lose the focus necessary to come up with creative ideas and tactics. When there is too much on your plate, there will inevitably be problems that arise from the overwhelming number of matters that demand your immediate attention. This is how the "fires" start.

Both the KDM and the DRs need to identify and make full use of personal competitive edge strengths.

- **Roadblock: Lack of Clarity about the DCSF**
- **Solution: Align on Factors Critical to Organization Success**

Is your organization Alignment Roadblock the result of your organization not clearly identifying the organization CSFs, and, in particular, the DCSF?

Most private organizations, it is true, have not identified any of their Critical Success Factors, and, as a result, cannot clearly identify the most important of these, the Driving Critical Success Factor. However, since the KDM and at least one of the DRs from your enterprise has now been through this program, it should be second nature for you to identify, discuss, and support your organization's DCSF on a daily basis. If this is not the case, you've got a problem! You can begin the process of resolving that problem by reviewing Chapter 10.

- **Roadblock: Planning Paralysis**
- **Solutions: Align on Fully Supported Organization Goals and Strategies**

Are plans in disarray or dispute? Is there a lack of Alignment about what, exactly, the plan should be?

A failure to make necessary changes to the Strategic Plan, or to examine the reasons for disagreement about that plan, may be the problem here. Alternatively, there may be a lack of Alignment because the relevant Goals are not yet specific, measurable, and/or realistically attainable.

During one AlignUp session with a food production department, an Alignment problem concerning the department's Strategic Plan came up. It involved a disagreement among the members of the Strategic Leadership Team about whether a particular Goal should continue to be pursued.

Vince, the KDM who managed the department, had developed with his team a plan for development and rolling out a new cookie product. The product's sales, however, were very disappointing—even after large amounts of marketing money had been devoted to promoting the product.

In spite of this product losing money, another food production department, with much greater distribution capabilities, had expressed an interest in buying the product. One of Vince's DRs, Juan, stated that he was not in Alignment with Vince and some of the other DRs with regard to the Goal of making this product a major success stream for the organization. He felt the department's resources should be used in other areas and that the organization should be negotiating the sale of the assets related to the new cookie product.

After meetings with his full team of DRs and discussions with his outside accountants, Vince approved a Strategic Plan to sell the rights and processes connected to the product. The eventual sale of this one product cut off large losses and provided money toward promoting several other department products that were already successful in the marketplace.

Another organization we worked with had already spent over $800,000 developing a new computer software program and was continuing to pour money into improving the product. The continued cost of product development was harming the organization's cash flow, because no sales of the new program were taking place.

The problem was that Randall, the KDM and president of the organization, who was also the majority stockholder, had conceived the idea for the software program. Even when his DRs explained they all felt the software package was going nowhere and that it would never attain sufficient sales to justify the R and D cost, Randall could not admit his mistake and refused to change the organization Strategic Plan.

Over the objections his DRs expressed at one of the organization's Annual Team Meetings, Randall turned down requests to kill the project and elected to stay with the plan. This decision resulted in even more of the organization's money and human resources being poured into improving the software product. Years later, in a private conversation with me, one of the organization's former DRs expressed his belief that failure to make needed course changes was the cause of the organization's demise.

A sobering story, to be sure. Share it!

Another story is relevant here, one that reminds us that, sometimes, the lack of Alignment isn't connected directly to a Goal, but rather to the timing of achieving the Goal. A window-covering manufacturing division we worked with had a Goal for one on the division Strategic Plans that involved developing an on-line training program for its distributors. The plan called for producing all the on-line programs within two years. During an AlignUp training session with the manager and several of his DRs, Evelyn, one of the DRs brought up her belief that that there was not Alignment on the decision to use division resources for the on-line training programs (which were only half done) because of other pressing needs the division had.

After the session, the KDM met with his team to discuss the matter in depth, and a decision was made to put the training programs on hold. The Goal of the plan was revised: to finish producing the remaining on-line programs only after measurable progress on certain other division objectives had been achieved.

- **Roadblock: "Too Busy"**
- **Solution: Narrow Your Focus**

Make progress in one area at a time. You're not "too busy" to make Alignment a priority.

Anna, a KDM who took this program with her whole executive team, told me during a follow-up session that she "did not have the time" to work on Alignment because she was "just too busy." I asked her to recount, as accurately as she could, how she had spent the previous night. She rather sheepishly admitted she had spent over two hours playing computer games! Anna said she just could not face the commitment of the Alignment activity she had been assigned and had used the computer games as an escape.

In fact, her assignment was not so daunting, and working together, we were able to get her and her organization back on track. Yet the experience reminded me that this kind of response is the reason I broke the Alignment process down into lessons that require you to focus on only one of the Alignment areas each month.

This is a principle you should follow in the weeks and months subsequent to the "completion" of this program (note the quotation marks!). I recognize that many KDMs and DRs become so overwhelmed by the multitude of things they have to do each day that if they are asked to do too much about Alignment, they will avoid doing anything at all. Their time will fly by, with no structured efforts to achieve and maintain Alignment.

The solution is to narrow your focus. You will be far less likely to "freeze" your progress on Alignment if you work on just one lesson at a time for a particular month, whether it is your first or fourth time through the material. This approach will keep you from becoming overwhelmed by the magnitude of the task of addressing everything you know needs to be done.

- **Roadblock: Falling Back into Old, Un-Aligned Habits**
- **Solution: Call ALIGNMENT CHECK!**

Everyone who has made it through this program has a right—and an obligation!—to call "ALIGNMENT CHECK" whenever any situation emerges that shows a person or team is falling back into un-Aligned habits.

Use the checklist below at least once a month, and as needed in specific workplace situations, to keep yourself and your organization on track and moving towards Evergreen Alignment. Whenever you cannot answer a question with the word YES, call an "ALIGNMENT CHECK". Say the words Alignment Check, out loud, with whomever you're working with. Ask for that person's help in bringing the relationship and the organization closer to full Alignment in that particular area.

"ALIGNMENT CHECK" CHECKLIST

If you cannot honestly answer YES to one of the questions below, call "Alignment Check!"

Get the KDM to complete the simple questionnaire below. Then ask each manager who reports directly to that organization owner to answer the same questions ... but SEPARATELY from the organization owner. When all the questionnaires are completed, compare the answers. You should also compare your final results with those that eventuated after completing Chapter 1.

"ALIGNMENT CHECK" QUESTIONNAIRE

1. Do I believe there is an ongoing effort toward continuous improvement of Alignment in this workplace? (YES/NO)
2. Do I feel that my subordinates are in Alignment and are focusing their energies on the factors critical to the success of the organization? (YES/NO)
3. Are ideas from DRs elicited, encouraged, discussed, and—where relevant and appropriate—implemented? (YES/NO)
4. Are there weekly ONE-ON-ONE meetings between the organization's leader and EACH manager who reports to him or her? (YES/NO)
5. Are DRs updating their To-Do lists and project plans for which they're responsible prior to attending a one-on-one weekly meeting with the organization's leader? (YES/NO)
6. In this workplace, do we have and keep mutually understood, mutually acceptable agreements with regard to respectful communication? (YES/NO)
7. Is there a clearly identified Strategic Leadership Team composed of the organization's leader and the managers who report directly to him or her?
8. Are Strategic Leadership Team Meetings taking place every week? (YES/NO)
9. Are Annual Strategic Leadership Team Meetings held once a year, in a locale different from the normal work environment? (YES/NO)
10. Is our stated or desired working culture USUALLY the same as our actual daily working culture? (YES/NO)
11. Does my organization have a culture of working together in an aligned fashion? (YES/NO)
12. Do all my subordinates clearly understand my long term vision for the organization? (YES/NO)
13. Do all members of the Strategic Leadership Team understand and support the Organization's Vision well enough to focus on fulfilling it? (YES/NO)
14. Is the organization's leader consciously avoiding going into "hands on" mode? Note: "Hands on mode" = doing something that one or more DRs can do and should be doing. (YES/NO)
15. Do I personally have a clear sense of what my own Competitive Edge Strengths are ... and use those strengths MOST of the time during the

typical working day? (YES/NO)

16. Can I identify the organization's Critical Success Factors—the factors that, if left unattained, will prevent the organization from attaining its vision? (YES/NO)

17. Is there at least one complete, written Strategic Plan? (YES/NO— answer NO if you don't know.)

If any of the answers do not match up, or if there a single "NO" answer, then you can be sure that the team is out of Alignment in that area!

The Alignment Checklist is a great Evergreen tool, one that everyone on the Strategic Leadership Management Team should use on a regular basis. Everyone must be willing to "Call Alignment"—and respect the input and opinions of anyone else on the team who does.

Another important tool for keeping the factors of Alignment operating on an ongoing Evergreen basis for your organization is for the KDM and DRs to each become join an organization advisory boards or group coaching.

Organization advisory boards help ensure your KDM and all the DRs stay on track for Evergreen Alignment. It's not required that you take this step to create Evergreen Alignment, but I do recommend it highly, because it's so easy to fall back into old non-Aligned habits. It's much easier to make Alignment Evergreen when you know there is someone involved with you month in and month out, someone who will be asking about your Alignment progress and helping you to improve over time.

Your fellow board members, too, can help keep you accountable to a high Alignment standard. They will help you perform honest evaluations of where your organization Alignment stands in relation to each of the checklist items mentioned in this chapter. They can also coach you on how best to take corrective action in those Alignment areas where the KDM and DRs may find themselves slipping.

There is nothing noble in being superior to your fellow man; true no-
bility is being superior to your former self. —Ernest Hemingway

IS YOUR ORGANIZATION ALIGNMENT EVERGREEN?

Evergreen Alignment means that Alignment is not a passing fad, neither for the KDM nor for the DR. It is how each of you choose to live your working lives.

This last and most important factor of Alignment involves making Alignment an ongoing commitment, one involving the KDM and (eventually) every single one of the DRs who collectively make up the Strategic Leadership Team. It is a permanent process with no stopping point.

Are all the factors of Alignment shared in this book part of your permanent working culture? Are they consistently implemented, discussed, revisited, reassessed, and implemented all over again, so that Alignment in your organization has become Evergreen? My aim throughout this book has been to get you to be able to honestly answer that question with a resounding "Yes!"

Allen Fishman

KEY POINT REVIEW

Remember: Acknowledging you still have work to do on Alignment does not mean failure. It means success ... if you are willing to take action on that realization!

HOMEWORK

Alignment Benefits From AlignUp Training

Identify the gains in Alignment that have happened as a result of implementing any or all of the factors of Alignment. In what ways, specifically, has the organization seen improvements in terms of Alignment over the past months? What have the specific benefits been?

Identify the one Alignment Roadblock that represents the most significant challenge to your enterprise. Set aside a full month to review, reinforce and implement the relevant lesson from this book, so you can improve in that area.

Conduct an "Alignment Check" at least once a month, using the check-list provided in this chapter. "Call Alignment" in any area where you cannot honestly answer YES.

APPENDIX A

A Safe Place: Build Trusting
Two-Way Communication
with Temenos

Apowerful, proprietary technique called Temenos can quickly help you create open and trusting two-way communications. I try to use it with all the KDMs and DRs with whom I work.

Temenos is from the ancient Greek word which means sanctuary. Temenos creates a sanctuary—a safe place—for two-way communication. It does so through a series of interactions which lower the natural defenses people raise in response to perceived attacks from others. Once both partners in an exchange lower their defenses, communication can and does improve.

This simple exercise, successfully completed with your chapter partner, is the heart of everything else you will accomplish in The Aligned Workplace. **It is not elective. It is mandatory. DO NOT SKIP IT**.

The Temenos exercise can be conducted with or without a facilitator. It consists of three simple questions posed to both the KDM and the DR. If there is no facilitator, the KDM and the DR can decide between themselves which of them will read the three questions out loud.

The responses must be written as the questions are read, and there should be no judgment as to the rightness or wrongness of these responses. I prefer the responses to these questions be written on a board or large pad that is displayed on an easel so both parties can easily read them. In this situation, it is probably best if the KDM and the DR both write.

The first question asks: **How would you describe what your own protective armor or communication defenses look and sound like?**

The second question asks: **What actions taken by others cause you to don this armor?**

The last question asks: **What benefits will be gained as a result of feeling safe enough to set aside this armor in order to conduct the meeting within a safe and open Temenos environment?**

IMPORTANT: One of the keys to keeping the environment safe for open, two-way communication is the willingness of all participants in this exercise to make a commitment. That commitment, too, is mandatory: In future meetings, each person will refrain from any of the comments or actions identified as causing the other person to don his or her armor.

If you are not both willing to agree to this condition, the Temenos exercise will not deliver positive results for you or your organization.

On the other hand, if you are willing to make this commitment, then the Temenos exercise will result in a significant improvement in the effectiveness of your communication. It's really as simple as that.

If, despite this mutual commitment, an inadvertent violation of the agreement happens, the other person must politely re-establish the agreement with the person who made the violation. Notice that this requires a change in paradigm, one that explicitly encourages the DR to tactfully but persistently engage with the KDM when he or she perceives a violation of the agreement. It might sound like this: "You know, Jim, I hate to say it, but I think you just interrupted me there, and with all respect, that's not what we agreed to."

This approach usually works quite well, and brings about a rapid change in behavior and an improvement in the quality of the communication between the KDM and the DR. **With this change in communication, Alignment is possible, which means anything is possible. Without this change, Alignment is impossible, which means only disempowerment is possible.**

The key moment in the Temenos process comes, not when the agreement is made, but when people hold each other accountable for fulfilling its terms. The Temenos list developed by one organization's planning team noted that using the expression "stupid" to refer to an action or comment by another team member was a major cause for armor to be donned and for open communications to shut down. At the very next meeting, one of the members referred to an idea being expressed as "stupid." Another member immediately politely, tactfully, but persistently pointed out the commitment the group had made not to use the term "stupid." The person who had used the word instantly apologized, and the tense atmosphere relaxed. Over a year later, the owner of the organization commented to me that he was amazed at how quickly the cooperation among his management team had improved from the moment attention was called to this violation of the Temenos contract.

Once you have completed the Temenos exercise, the "ground rules" in your one-on-one and/or team culture should be expanded to include the concept of "calling Temenos." Whenever you "call Temenos," you can express a concern about something you object to that showed up in another person's communication ... but you can do so in a light and almost humorous fashion. "Calling Temenos" with people who have gone through this process with you can be extremely effective, because everyone understands what you mean, and because (when it is done correctly) no confrontation or escalation is involved. People can safely let down their guard.

Temenos Responses: Common "verbal armor" defense mechanisms

- Interrupting
- Sabotaging
- Defensive response
- Deflecting/change subject
- Avoiding or diverting issue
- Yelling
- Over aggressiveness
- Sarcasm; cynical remarks
- Eye rolls
- Sighs

Temenos Responses: Common causes of "verbal armor" defense mechanisms

- Side conversations
- Overly aggressive behavior
- Attempting to control
- Appearance of favoritism
- Withholding facts
- Overly emotional responsiveness
- Not listening
- Grandstanding, overselling/persuading
- Excuses
- Devaluing others' opinions based on years/experience

Temenos Responses: Commonly Cited benefits of reducing "verbal armor"

- Greater participation in team meetings and better contributions during those meetings
- Enhanced teamwork
- Greater productivity
- Better preparation
- Increased creativity

- Better use of time & energy: effectiveness
- Synergistic solutions
- Accountability
- Trust
- Motivating

Very often, there are complex emotional, personal, and social factors to consider here. Temenos builds the trust necessary to help you and the other person address these issues sensitively. One executive I worked with, someone who was a key factor in making many of my plans succeed, was perceived by her co-workers as having a strong air of overconfidence, of being condescending, and of considering herself incapable of error. In one-on-one meetings, I found that even the slightest hint of criticism thrown her way caused her to lose focus and become overly defensive. As soon as she heard me say anything she interpreted as criticism, her facial expression and body language clearly changed to indicate that her focus on what we were discussing had been lost, and that she was instead thinking about how she was going to protect herself against perceived criticism.

Because we had conducted the Temenos process together, we were able to identify part of the problem was my making certain comments that caused her to don her "verbal armor." Together, we had gotten much better at avoiding these polarizing exchanges. In private discussions, though, we were able to determine that, even though these kinds of comments were a problem, they weren't the entire problem.

At one point, I had a lengthy heart-to-heart chat with her about these issues. She said the problem stemmed from her childhood, and that her air of overconfidence was in fact a cover for problems she had with low self-esteem. This explained why she was so sensitive to perceived criticism. I had to decide what communication style would be most effective to use with this executive, so she would not feel threatened and lose her focus. From that point on, whenever I felt she was approaching something in the wrong way, I always tried to begin my communications with her by mentioning something she was doing right (and she did most things right.). Then I would talk to her about the things she was doing that did not satisfy me. I made it a point to criticize her actions, rather than criticizing her as a person. This is an important communication principle for all relationships, but it took on special importance with this particular executive, who was, I must emphasize, an extremely important and valuable member of our team.

After I began using a communications style better tailored to her personality, most of the barriers to our trusting, two-way communications disappeared, and we had a very productive working relationship from that point forward. **The changes we made to establish a pattern of trusting two-way communication simply would not have been possible without the Temenos process.**

I cannot emphasize the point strongly enough: **completion of the Temenos process I have just shared with you is, in my opinion, the single most important benchmark for KDMs and DRs who are seeking to establish Alignment with one another.**

APPENDIX B

Questions All Strategic Leadership Team Members Should Consider Before the Annual Retreat

Planning

- Looking towards the future, what existing factors have the potential to become critical weaknesses? (Be tactful but unapologetically honest.)
- What changes could you make to strengthen the effectiveness and skills of your management team and other personnel? (Such initiative might include outside or online training classes, seminars, or mentoring.)
- Is there a pending regulation or law that could reduce your organization's taxes, improve your organizational efficiency, or open up new markets? (Could you realistically expect to help get that law passed?)
- What strategic alliance/partnering opportunities exist? (Acquaintances may be interested in coming into the organization or becoming a strategic partner.) Do you have a list of referral sources? Do you meet with them regularly and ask them for referrals?
- Are there trends that could negatively affect the nature of the competition you face? (Example: competition from mass merchandisers like Wal-Mart or Home Depot developing stores in areas where you have a retail presence.)
- Is your organization an easy-entry organization for possible new competitors? (Are barriers to entry lower or higher now than they were five years ago? Why?)
- Is your organization exposed to risk in the marketplace because you haven't protected your copyrights, trademarks, and trade secrets?

- Are any of your products and/or services vulnerable to product/service substitution? (Which ones? Why?)
- What advantages does the competition have over you? (Be tactful but unapologetically honest.)
- In what ways are your major competitors vulnerable in regard to any specific products/services you offer? In what ways can you capitalize on their vulnerability?
- Which competitors may be able to under-price you? (How does their organization model differ from yours?)
- Are there products or services currently under development that could be produced at a lower cost or with higher quality than yours? (Example: A competitor has similar products in the works using new materials and/or processes.)

Employee Development

What departments or members of your management team have demonstrated outstanding ability that can best contribute towards building the value of your organization? (Consider factors such as strategic thinking, innovative thinking, technological savvy, team building, customer relations, use of resources, communication, problem solving, mentoring ability, great leadership skills or any other strengths members of your leadership team or departments bring to the table that are very valuable.)

Do the members of your management team have a high level of organization experience when compared to other organizations in your industry?

- Does the sales team utilize a particular sales system? Does a new hire adapt quickly to that system and find it easy to succeed with?

What kind training or personnel development is essential to meet a new, higher standard of required performance? (How will you measure the effectiveness of a given program or initiative?)

MARKETING

What new product, service or process requiring development is needed?

What market area needs expansion?

What improvements in your sales and marketing methods, practices or personnel are needed?

What aspect of your marketing program is the most effective in generating sales leads?

Does your organization have a social media plan? How often is it revised? How well is it executing on that plan in comparison with industry competitors?

What aspects of your marketing team are least effective? (Does the marketing team ever fail to supply a steady stream of leads to the sales team?)

What industry and social trends exist on which your marketing and sales efforts can capitalize? (For instance: how recently have you updated your social media plan?)

What situations exist related to consumer buying trends that could have a positive impact on organization sales? (How could you act on those trends to improve the overall customer experience with your organization?)

Would it be more beneficial if you refocused more of your marketing funds towards existing customers instead of new ones? (Here again, investing in current customers usually delivers a better return.)

Is there a new technology or platform you can use to market your goods or services in a new way? (How well is your social media plan aligned with your marketing and sales plans?)

Are there new or untapped markets that could be entered easily using the organization's current areas of excellence and capabilities? (Look for areas that do not require a complete overhaul of your organization plan!) Are there activities your organization is currently undertaking that should be discontinued?"

Is the market for your primary product/services contracting? (By how much?)

What specific benefits, or value, are derived from your products/services that exceed those of your competitors?

Do we have any ideas to increase brand awareness via social networks like LinkedIn and Facebook, exhibiting at expos, producing webcasts marketed via email to buyer prospects, etc.

Should we test the use of in-house telemarketers to set appointments with new customer prospects?

Sales

What improvements in your sales and marketing methods, practices or personnel are needed?

What improvements are needed in your sales staff for an upgrade of sales personnel?

Does the organization need more and better training?

Does your sales department excel at selling organization products/services? (Do they, for instance, take part in discussions about individual and group quotas and routinely meet or exceed those quotas?)

What aspects of your sales team are least effective? (A "no" answer in any of these areas may indicate a major Organization Weakness: Is there a clear sales process? Does the person in charge of the sales team know what the process is? Do all members of the sales team know what the process is? Is there an ongoing training and reinforcement initiative? Is there a clear sense of how long it should typically take to close a particular kind of sale? Do members of the sales team know when to stop pursuing an inactive lead and move onto another prospect? Is there a daily prospecting performance metric? Are salespeople hitting that metric consistently?)

Is there potential to sell additional products/services or new products/services to current customers/clients? (This is a low cost/low risk opportunity that often goes unexploited. It is usually much more expensive to acquire a new customer than it is to "up-sell" to an existing one! Can you improve your sales process to generate more repeat purchases and/or more purchases of different but related products and services? How can you increase referrals from your current base of customers? (Have your team members been trained in this skill?)

Are your sales too dependent on one product, customer, industry or geographical market?

Internal Communications

Do you have passive-aggressive employees? An aggressive employee might use inappropriate language to your face about why a certain assignment is "stupid" or might flatly refuse to carry out clear and relevant instructions. These directly aggressive employees are actually quite rare. Much more common is the passive-aggressive employee who makes a habit of procrastinating or does subpar work whenever he does not like the assignment. Passive aggressive behaviors by employees can be a serious strategic weakness because, by their very nature, these behaviors interfere with effective results. These employees generally won't come out and say they don't support something. They just won't do it, or do it poorly. Passive aggressive employees are one of the greatest sources of change resistance, which inevitably causes inefficiency in making your Organization Plans happen. Whenever you have passive aggressive employees, you have two choices: move them out of your organization quickly, or get a clear commitment that their passive aggressive behavior will be relegated to the past. (If a passive-aggressive employee makes this commitment and fails to follow through on it, you must part organization with the employee.)

Do your organization departments work well together in a spirit of Alignment? Imagine being in a rowboat with a bunch of other rowers, and one person is rowing in the wrong direction (or at a different speed, or with different timing). The result: inefficient forward progress. This lack of Alignment is a common and significant weakness in many organizations. Julio, a KDM who owns a manufacturing organization, discussed with me how one of his managers went to a subordinate of another manager to get action on something—because the two department managers were not in Alignment on the Organization Plan. There is an old saying about a house divided: it falls! Many organizations don't succeed with their plans, because the top KDM thinks that the employees are all rowing in the same direction ... but they're not. This can be a very serious Organization Weakness indeed.

Is there a clear social media plan? (Do customers who use social media channels ever have problems hearing back from your organization?)

What new products or services have been developed as a result of (formal or informal) collaboration between your organization and its best customers?

Customer Service

What area of excellence or customer/client impact needs to be given a higher priority in your organization?

What is your organization's reputation for resolving customer problems and answering customer questions? How does this compare to the reputations of your competitors?

How likely is a current customer to recommend your products or services to someone else? How does this referral rate compare to the referral rates of your industry competitors? (Make intelligent estimates if you do not have hard numbers to evaluate.)

What shortcomings exist among your personnel in terms of skills, personality traits or competencies? Consider factors such as technological skills, inability to follow directions, requiring micromanaging, bossiness, or an uncooperative attitude

What are your customers' stated or likely future needs? (Do you have a formal customer council that meets regularly? Do you engage regularly with your best customers to learn about the kinds of products or services they are looking for?)

What processes, if any, does your organization currently provide to your customers, clients, or users that may be provided more effectively by outsourcing? (Again: what are your competitors—both domestic and international—doing in this area?)

Operations

What better use of capacity or efficiency is needed to reduce per unit cost?

What improvements in your distribution method or ordering system effectiveness are needed?

Are changes needed in the location of your headquarters or distribution plants?

Do we need newer high-tech equipment to obtain greater plant cost efficiency?

Is your organization certified by organizations widely accepted in your industry such as the International Organization for Standardization (ISO)?

Are there any areas in which management hinders organization success? Closely consider factors such as communication, diversity, decision-making, consensus building, reliance, and innovation.

How do your operating costs compare to those of your competition? Analyze these costs in broad categories (e.g., payroll, marketing, facilities, etc.) on both an absolute basis and as a percent of sales. (If no hard numbers are available for your competitors, what is the best available estimate? What is your personal sense on where your organization stands competitively in this area?)

What operational factors keep you from reaching the success you want? (Is any process the subject of regular unresolved complaints from external or internal customers?)

What situations for improved operations exist for your organization? (Example: the use of new technology to deliver your goods or services.)

What opportunities exist to help reduce your operation expenses or shorten your production cycle?

What opportunities exist to improve your distribution methods? (What are your competitors doing in this area?)

How do your plant's/factory's capabilities compare to your competitors? (For instance: are their facilities located domestically or overseas?)

What opportunities exist to improve your inbound or outbound logistics?

What opportunities exist to improve your manufacturing processes and procedures, machining, packaging, assembly, equipment maintenance, testing, printing, and facility operations?

What opportunities exist to improve your procurement procedures, qualification rules and information systems for dealing with vendors?

If your organization is a manufacturer, does your organization have a lower cost of manufacturing than others who manufacture the same product in the same industry?

If your organization distributes for retail or services, does your organization have a low-cost value chain? If so, what benefits are gained from it?

What are your organization's strongest and most effective outlets/distribution channels? List any miscellaneous factors you feel give your organization an outstanding edge. (Example: a retail location for your organization that offers you a significant competitive advantage in the marketplace.)

What organization characteristics are most responsible for product or service failure in reaching current sales projections? (Is customer service a problem?)

Is there a possibility of key suppliers beginning to compete directly with your organization? (Have other organizations in your industry experienced this?)

Could international events result in a critical shortage of raw materials that are needed by your organization? (Which raw materials? Who are the suppliers? Are substitutes available for either?)

Are you overly dependent on a single supplier of critical raw materials, components, or sub-assemblies?

Information Technology

What improved technology or know-how is needed?

Does your organization have up-to-date and efficient information systems?

What new technology is available, or will soon be available, that may be able to lower organization costs? (Example: new software for client management.)

What newly available—or soon to be available—technology may create a need for a new product or service? (What communication technologies, for instance, are on the horizon? Closely consider the powerful current trends toward mobile computing and on-line purchasing, and think of how they may impact buyer behavior.)

What products or services can your organization produce, offer, or improve as a derivative of currently popular technology? (For example: could you create an application for the iPad or iPhone that makes strategic sense for your organization?)

What technological capabilities within your organization currently exist, or are in development, that may affect design, production or delivery of your products/services? (Which technologies are most likely to affect the customer experience for the better and drive repeat purchases?)

Are there technological changes on the horizon that your organization needs to keep up with? (Example: What percentage of your customer base would prefer to be able to make purchase decisions online?)

Corporate Finances

What prevailing economic and financial factors could give your organization a substantial, sustainable advantage over competitors? (Example: having no outstanding debt.)

What patents or other intellectual property and/or services owned by your organization have the potential for additional benefits to the organization beyond their current usage?

Does your organization have a financial risk-taking philosophy that could be viewed as a Competitive Strength in your industry? (In other words, are you more or less likely than competitors to be able to make intelligent investments—bets—with organization capital, based on new conditions in the market?)

What existing financial factors are a Weakness of your organization? Are there problems with poor cash flow? Inability to increase a required line of credit? Failure to meet payroll?

What current financial or economic conditions exist that could potentially benefit your organization? (These might include refinancing real estate at lower interest rates.)

Should capital expenditures be re-allocated for uses that bring about greater positive financial impact?

What are the worst/best-case budget scenarios for taking advantage of this opportunity?

Would dramatically higher or lower interest rates or availability of credit greatly impact your organization?

Does your organization have significant exposure for product liability, service deficiencies or the actions of your directors, managers, employees, agents, or contractors? (What liability issues do your competitors, or comparable firms in other industries, face?)

Human Resources Procedures

Is there the potential to upgrade personnel in your organization? Should your organization take advantage of this opportunity to "upgrade the gene pool" of personnel?

What would be the impact on your organization if a key manager quits, becomes incapacitated, or dies? (Who are the critical "key people"? Are there contingency plans in place?)

Is there a potential shortage of key non-management employees? (If so, what kind of employee shortage would be most damaging to your organization?)

CULTURE

Does your organization have a shared belief-system/organization culture that is positive and supports the Organization Vision?

Does the shared belief-system/organization culture currently have you on the path to becoming a more effective, competitive organization?

Is your organization innovative when it comes to new products and/or services? What are some examples of this innovation?

APPENDIX C

Glossary

Action Plans (also called Project Plans)— Action Plans (also called Project Plans)are usually assigned to the DR responsible for the functional area most needed for the success of the Action Plan. (Ch 5)

Alignment— The harmonious organization relationship that makes great results a daily reality for both Key Decision Makers and Direct Reports. (Ch1)

Alignment Bucket—Ten different factors of Alignment, each of which contribute to Alignment e.g. Commitment on Alignment. (Ch 12)

Alignment Roadblocks—The challenges faced by your organization, which hinder achieving Alignment. (Ch 12)

Annual Team Meeting—A once-a-year series of strategically focused meetings of the Strategic Leadership Team. This meeting occurs at a venue outside the normal office environment. (Ch 11).

Aptitude—Something you do better than most other people. (Ch 3)

Big-Picture Potential—Any activities that bring the organization closer to achieving the KDM's Vision for the organization. (Ch 3)

Charter—A document (generally one paragraph) that lays out expectations of behavior and gives suggestions for ensuring an effective Strategic Leadership Team Meeting. It is used to guide and focus team members during such meetings. (Ch 11)

The Organization's Culture— the Organization's Culture should be the practice of clearly articulating the organization's values (for instance, timeliness, honesty, and commitment to finish the job). (Ch 5)

The Organization's Culture Statement—An outline for the organization employees that states organization ethics and expectations, or 'the way we do things around here', compiled and written collectively by the KDM his/her DRs. (Ch 3)

Organization Opportunity—Potential opportunities which exist and can be utilized to help the KDM achieve his/her vision for the organization. The Organization Opportunity is one of the four items that makes up organization Critical Success Factors. (Ch 5)

Organization Strategic Direction—The Goal and its Strategies relating to a specific CSF together make up an Organization Strategic Direction Initiative. (Ch 5)

Organization Strategic Plan—A plan that gives direction on how to achieve the stated, essential, organization-wide Goal. It has a clear focus on the associated Strategies that will drive the plan. (Ch 11)

Organization Strategic Plan Statements— Short, concise, and easy-to-follow statements. They create a clear path of where the organization needs to go and what needs to be done to get there. (Ch 11)

Organization Strength—Organization Strengths are what your organization finds easiest to leverage successfully when seeking to gain additional business, results, or market share. They are your organization's "strong suits". (Ch 10)

Organization Threat—A threat to your organization is something that can have a significant negative impact on your organization and is outside your control. (Ch 10)

Competitive Edge Strengths—An individual skill or ability for which you have a strong Passion and aptitude for, which supports the "big picture" Vision for where you want to go next in your life and is something you can do while maintaining an Empathetic Personality. (Ch 3)

Core Values—Values that determine the organization's culture. Stated values every member of the organization should always follow. (Ch 7)

Critical Success Factor (CSF)— Objectives so essential to your enterprise's success that your organization will not succeed without attaining them. (Ch 1)

Cultural Moment of Truth— A situation where you must decide whether or not you are willing to fix the organization's unaligned culture (a mismatch between the stated, desired culture and the actual culture) or not. (Ch 3).

Direct Report (DR)—The managers in the organization who report directly to the Key Decision Maker. (Ch 1).

Driving Critical Success Factor (DCSF)— The organization Critical Success Factor (CSF) that is most critical to the success of your organization. (Ch 11)

Execution Commitment—The ability to produce a tangible result and not get caught up in abstractions. (Ch 7)

Evergreen Alignment—Deep, enduring Alignment created when the KDM and all the DRs work continuously on all the factors of Alignment you have read about in this book. (Ch 12)

High-Impact Direct Reports—Direct Reports who, by practicing Evergreen Alignment, are a valuable asset to the organization and help the KDM achieve his/her vision for the organization. (Ch 3)

Key Decision Maker (KDM)— The person in your organization who makes the final decisions on organization goals, strategies and distribution of resources (typically the owner or founder of the organization). (Ch 1)

Key Performance Indicators—Measurable achievements that indicate how the organization is performing in relation to Organization Goals. (Ch 4)

Passion—When you love doing something you have a driving Passion for it. This creates great focus and ensures you end up with results that simply cannot happen without that level of focus. (Ch 3)

Personal Organization Strengths—The things in your organization that you have a Passion and Aptitude for, that leads you to your 'big picture' Vision of your life and you can achieve while being Empathetic to your personality. (Ch 3).

Plan and Priority Review—As a DR you should meet with your KDM and review your plans and priorities so they are in line with the KDM's Vision for the organization while making the most of your Personal Organization Strengths. (Ch 4)

Pocket Vision— privileged subjects the KDM wants to see as part of the future of the organization that are not included in the organization's written Vision Statement. These are situations where the KDM elects to keep certain facts, plans, and personal conclusions "in his or her pocket." (Ch 8)

Priority 'to-do' List—Your Priority To-Do List identifies what, specifically, you will be doing next. (Ch 4)

Project Plans (also called Action Plans)— Project Plans (also called Action Plans) are usually assigned to the DR responsible for the functional area most needed for the success of the Project Plan. (Ch 11)

Project Plan Template—A template utilized to keep track of the status and progress of Project Plans. (Ch 4)

Spotlight Update—Time allocated in each weekly Strategic Team Meeting in which a designated DR shares updates and major non-project activities with the other DRs and KDM. (Ch 11)

Strategic Leadership Team—A group limited to the KDM and the KDM's most important DRs. (chapter 1)

Strategic Leadership Team Meeting—Weekly meetings between the KDM and the KDM's most important DRs. (Ch 1)

SWOT—An in-depth analysis to determine your strengths, weaknesses, opportunities, and threats. (Ch 3)

Tactics—The commitments you and your subordinates follow to bring about a successful Project Plan. Tactics are both specific and measurable. (Ch 4 p. 12)

www.ingramcontent.com/pod-product-compliance
Lightning Source LLC
Chambersburg PA
CBHW052012230326
41598CB00078B/2808